Boys Will See Boys

CULTURES OF CHILDHOOD

Susan Honeyman, Series Editor

Boys Will See Boys

Folklore, Friendships, and Emotions in Boyhood Snapshots

Jay Mechling

University Press of Mississippi / Jackson

The University Press of Mississippi is the scholarly publishing agency of
the Mississippi Institutions of Higher Learning: Alcorn State University,
Delta State University, Jackson State University, Mississippi State University,
Mississippi University for Women, Mississippi Valley State University,
University of Mississippi, and University of Southern Mississippi.

www.upress.state.ms.us

The University Press of Mississippi is a member
of the Association of University Presses.

Publisher: University Press of Mississippi, Jackson, USA
Authorised GPSR Safety Representative: Easy Access System Europe –
Mustamäe tee 50, 10621 Tallinn, Estonia, *gpsr.requests@easproject.com*

Library of Congress Cataloging-in-Publication Data

Names: Mechling, Jay, 1945– author
Title: Boys will see boys : folklore, friendships, and emotions in boyhood snapshots / Jay Mechling.
Description: Jackson : University Press of Mississippi, 2026. |
Series: Cultures of childhood | Includes bibliographical references and index.
Identifiers: LCCN 2025035804 (print) | LCCN 2025035805 (ebook) |
ISBN 9781496861894 hardback | ISBN 9781496861900 trade paperback | ISBN 9781496861917 epub |
ISBN 9781496861924 epub | ISBN 9781496861931 pdf | ISBN 9781496861948 pdf
Subjects: LCSH: Boys—United States—Pictorial works | Boys—United States—Psychology |
Boys—United States—Social life and customs | Male friendship—United States |
Masculinity—Social aspects—United States | Photography of youth—United States
Classification: LCC HQ781.5 .M43 2026 (print) | LCC HQ781.5 (ebook)
LC record available at https://lccn.loc.gov/2025035804
LC ebook record available at https://lccn.loc.gov/2025035805

British Library Cataloging-in-Publication Data available

FOR HEATHER
Our daughter, who knows a thing or two about raising boys

Contents

Boys Will See Boys

Introduction

Figure 0.1

The idea driving this inquiry is that children construct a secret world away from the surveillance by adults and that the snapshots children take of each other might provide information about the autonomous lives of children, information not easily discerned in the more public behavior of the children and youth. In particular, as much of my work is about the lives of boys and men in American culture, the focus here is on the body of snapshots we have good reason to believe are of boys taken by boys.

There are few other sources of evidence about the secret lives of boys. Some historians have attempted to pierce the veil of boy secrecy by using diaries or letters written by boys. Therapeutic encounters sometimes yield this hidden world, but (of course) the written accounts of those interviews (e.g., Coles 1977; Pollack 1998) are by the adults, who can never be sure the boys are not telling them what the boys think the adults want to hear. Even snapshots by adults of boys tend to construct an understanding of boys' lives through the ideas the adults hold about the boys. The snapshots I offer here for interpretation may provide another way to enter the guarded world of boys when they are relaxed and in their friendship group, their male folk group.

Take, for example, the snapshot at the head of this introduction. For many years I have used this snapshot as the wallpaper on my two computer screens, which means that I see it every day. I bought the snapshot years ago in an eBay auction. I was attracted to the image for several reasons. These boys are playing and having fun. They are using a high-quality camera, possibly belonging to a parent, so there might be a forbidden aspect to this event. The boys are "goofing," playing, and bonding in their side-by-side play. The folklorist in me sees in this snapshot two boys treating the mirror as a "magic portal" to a looking-glass world, much as girls do when they play "Bloody Mary" in the mirror at slumber parties (Dundes 1998). The hand gestures of the boys and their facial expressions also suggest a magical conjuring.

Mirrors have fascinated humans for centuries, playing roles in science, art, and social history (Melchior-Bonnet 2000). The mirror distorts reality—and not just funhouse mirrors. In one of the fictional dialogues (he calls them "metalogues") Gregory Bateson constructs with his daughter, Mary Catherine Bateson (a distinguished anthropologist like her father and mother, Margaret Mead), Gregory discusses with the daughter the puzzle that our reflections in mirrors reverse left and right but not top and bottom. Another magical, paradoxical feature of mirrors.

And, of course, a mirror makes possible a photographic self-portrait, as does the photobooth, which I shall explore later. Art historians understand the puzzles and attractions of self-portraits (Cumming 20009; Hall 2016), and social historians have used painted self-portraits to speculate on a culture's ideas about the self. From the Puritan portraits in New England in the seventeenth century through the self-portraits by artists in the Enlightenment (eighteenth century) and into the nineteenth and twentieth centuries, painted self-portraits are filled not just with the human subject but also with objects and settings meant to convey the artist's sense of his (usually his) subject's public self and, occasionally, a glimpse of his private self. The invention of photography around 1839 expanded the genre of self-portraits, but the genre is still a sideshow in the scholarship on the history of art.

The teenage boys in the snapshot above surely discovered the pleasures of mirrors when they were younger. Any adult observing children cannot help noticing they are fascinated with mirrors, as are chimpanzees, though the nonhuman primates soon lose interest in their own image in a mirror, whereas the fascination in children lasts. The developmental psychologists, from Piaget (1954) to Winnicott (1971), have observed this behavior in children as young as eighteen months, and by age two the child fully recognizes that the image in the mirror reflects the self, as others see us. While not all developmental psychologists would agree with Lacan's (2006 [1949]) formulation of the "mirror stage" of identity formation, all pretty much agree that gazing at ourselves in a mirror helps establish our unique identity. So the two boys in the snapshot above are "performing" aspects of their selves, their identities, as much for their own selves as for each other.

Experiencing our performing versions of ourselves in mirrors (e.g., dressing up, practicing facial expressions, playing with our faces) helps us understand that the "public face" of our identity is a performance and might not actually reflect our "authentic" selves. Goffman (1959) argues that all social reality resembles theatrical drama (roles, scripts, props, front stage, back stage), and a fundamental idea in feminist approaches to gender is that gender is a performance, not an essence (Butler 1990). And (as I explore in a later chapter) males dressing as females are playing with and disturbing the usual visual clues in our performances of gender.

Parts and Wholes

Reading a snapshot like the one opening this introduction assumes that any individual part, no matter how seemingly insignificant or trivial, can lead to an understanding of the whole culture. That is a big claim but one fundamental to my approach to culture. The approach assumes that culture is systematic and, like most systems, parts are connected in a pattern, what Gregory Bateson calls "the pattern which connects" (Bateson 1979). Whatever "truths" we think we discover when studying American culture, for example, lie in the pattern connecting parts into wholes.

Since I already have used the word "culture" several times not far into this introduction, and since I will use it many times in this book, I probably owe the reader a definition of the term. I'll not review all the definitions of culture that social scientists and humanists have trotted out over the centuries. Instead, I'll make this simple. And that reminds me of a story.

Bateson tells the story of a computer programmer who wonders if his computer will ever think like a human being. He poses that question to his computer, which works on it a while, and then the computer prints out an answer. Rushing over to the printer, the programmer reads the brief message: "That reminds me of a story."

There it is. To think like a person is to think in terms of stories, so we could do a lot worse than simply thinking of culture as the stories we tell each other and ourselves in order to make sense of our individual and collective lives. The stories (the culture) bring order to the disorder of everyday experience.

This view of culture is simple but not simplistic. For example, we must think of stories broadly. Bateson writes, provocatively, that all systems think in terms of stories, from individual minds to redwood forests (Bateson 1979; Mechling 1983). They are all systems, parts connected in patterns to make a whole. To imagine the "story" a redwood forest tells demands that we see the story in every system. Scholars who write about culture, therefore, write about "texts" and mean a whole range of things beyond what literary critics call texts. In this book the snapshots are the "texts." I seek to "read" these visual texts, to understand those snapshots as part of a larger pattern, understanding that not every snapshot is as revealing of the culture as another.

The "pattern which connects" is a public pattern, which means that culture is a public, not a private, phenomenon.

My narrative interpretation of the snapshot of two boys playing with their own images in a mirror suggests the several disciplines that come together in the act of interpreting a snapshot in all its contexts (historical, social, cultural, and intertextual, that is, how one image becomes a "text" shadowing another), disciplines ranging from history and art history to folklore, anthropology, sociology, developmental psychology, evolutionary psychology, visual studies, gender studies, and even ethology (the chimps in mirrors). My training in American studies has always been thoroughly interdisciplinary, so I am comfortable posing an interesting question about a cultural event or text or object and drawing upon whatever disciplines seem to me to offer ideas toward making "best sense" of the cultural text, in this case a snapshot. As Henry Nash Smith wrote long ago, the "method" of American studies is "principled opportunism" (Smith 1957), which is not a bad description of my method.

Gender Studies and Visual Studies

This book lies at the confluence of two streams of my scholarship within interdisciplinary American studies.

One stream is the study of the social construction, maintenance, and repair (when necessary) of masculinity in American culture. I was a Boy Scout, and I am an Eagle Scout ("Once an Eagle, always an Eagle" goes the saying). Scouting was an extremely important part of my upbringing. In graduate school in American civilization at the University of Pennsylvania in Philadelphia (1967–71), I initiated my scholarship in masculinity studies with a graduate seminar paper using the records of the Philadelphia Boy Scout Council, founded in 1912, just two years after the founding of the Boy Scouts of America (the BSA), to create a statistical portrait of the men who became Scoutmasters in those early years. That seminar paper was a test run on a dissertation idea, but I turned out to write my dissertation on advice literature for parents across American history (Mechling 1975). Then, as a newly minted PhD and assistant professor of American studies at the University of California, Davis, I returned to writing about the Boy Scouts, starting with a draft article about the popular novels for boys, which had a history before the founding of the Boy Scouts of America (the BSA) in 1910 and which branched out into novels with Boy Scouts as the central characters.

As I talked with a student about my study of the Boy Scout novels in the mid-1970s, he suggested that I visit his troop at their annual summer encampment high in the Sierra Nevada. I did go up to that troop's camp the summer of 1976 (they created their own camp, rather than go to the BSA Council Camp), and I was so impressed by what I saw on a weeklong visit that I knew my study of the Scouting *experience* beyond the printed material and my own memory culture would have to include descriptions and analysis of that troop's culture, just as an anthropologist would immerse herself in a culture. In the late 1970s, American studies scholars (e.g., Caughey 1982) and some anthropologists (e.g., Messerschmidt 1981) were beginning to see their ethnographic work as "anthropology at home," and it was in that vein that I understood my need to add to my research on the actual experience of Scouting ethnographic fieldwork with a living troop of Boy Scouts.

I visited that troop ("Troop 49," not their real number) every second or third summer from 1976 through 1999 and wrote several scholarly articles about it during those years. When I came to write the book, I wrote it in a way that preserved the scholarly observations but set aside (or explained) any scholarly jargon, in order to make the book readable for the general audience, especially for men (like me) for whom Scouting was an important institution.

In the first few years of my Scouting research and writing, masculinity studies was just emerging as a variant of gender studies. The women's movements and the academic field and institutions they spawned reached a stage of maturity such that female and male scholars were ready to turn the ideas and approaches from women's studies back upon men, the famously "unmarked" gender. I found myself, from 1976 on, increasingly reading and writing in the emergent field of masculinity studies. I shall not recount that history and literature here, except to say that I found most useful in my own work the ideas of feminist scholars who worked generally with depth psychology (about which I have more to say later in this book) and who formulated ideas about the construction of masculinity in men's individual lives and in their groups, a long line of feminist scholars from Melanie Klein (1952) and Karen Horney (1937) to Nancy Chodorow (1978), Dorothy Dinnerstein (1976), and Juliet Mitchell (1974), among others. Those theories also served me and my Marine Corps veteran coauthor very well when we sought to understand the ways the everyday, folk practices in the male friendship group in the military provides short-term psychological first aid for the stress experienced by warriors in the combat zone (Wallis and Mechling 2019a).

The second stream of my scholarship that joins my masculinity studies in this book is my work in visual studies. My own interdisciplinary training in American studies included lots of experience interpreting visual culture, from art to film and television. When in the 1970s I began to appreciate the value of fieldwork-based, ethnographic studies of people's cultures within American studies, I began to see the immense value of documentary photography as a companion to the written ethnography. I think my reading of *Let Us Now Praise Famous Men* (Agee and Evans 1960 [1941]), a collaboration between writer James Agee and photographer Walker Evans, triggered my interest. It is impossible to read that now-classic work of American studies without understanding how the words and the images work together to create both understanding and an *emotional response* to the lives of the people portrayed. At about the same time, I think, I was teaching a comparative ethnicities course, and in preparing for that course I came across the book *Through Navajo Eyes* (1972) by Sol Worth and John Adair, in which they taught selected Navajo informants how to use an 8-mm movie camera and film editing equipment to create their own films, which the anthropologists then interpreted in terms of their understanding of Navajo culture. Worth collaborated with other anthropologists, notably Jay Ruby, in creating the new field of visual anthropology, embodied in a new scholarly organization, the Society of the Anthropology of Visual Communication, and a journal, *Studies in the Anthropology of Visual Communication*.

My University of California, Davis, colleague Jon Wagner introduced me to the International Visual Sociology Association and its journal, *Visual Sociology*, which has published some of my work (Mechling 1999; Grady and Mechling 2003; see also Wagner 1999). Eventually I published scholarly articles using amateur photography, snapshots, to study the world of hunters (Mechling 2004), children's folklore (Mechling 2005b), and soldiers (Mechling 2012, 2021). I have also used snapshots to complement the analysis in scholarly essays on play with guns (Mechling 2008b, 2024), play with sand (Mechling

2016b), the game of tug-of-war (Mechling 2023), and scholastic wrestling (Delfino and Mechling 2017). In all these cases, the photographs were more than mere illustrations; I treated them as independent texts that might reveal meanings not obvious from other sources of evidence, written and oral.

I took a great many photographs at Troop 49's summer camp (the troop's real number and hometown never revealed in my writing). Those photographs became an important source of taking notes, and when I sat down to write the book, I had before me both my written field journal and the photographs (Mechling 2001). I could not use those photographs in the book; I had to preserve the anonymity of the boys and men and the troop. So I looked instead to the public realm of snapshots for sale on eBay (founded in 1995) and in vintage photography shows I began attending. Eventually my collection of snapshots grew to thousands, and some of those appear in this book when I am convinced that the snapshot likely was taken by one of the boys and not by an adult.

Visual Autoethnography

Looking at the photographs boys take of other boys brings together two research methods used by folklorists, anthropologists, and sociologists when they study the everyday lives of children and youth in their "natural" settings. The first of these is autoethnography, and the second is visual ethnography. The resulting hybrid method, visual autoethnography, deserves some explanation in this introduction.

Folklorists, anthropologists, and sociologists often rely upon fieldwork observations for their description and then interpretation of cultures. The research activity is ethnography—writing about people, as the Greek roots of the word (ethno+graphy) suggest. The researcher visits the group being studied, ideally for months or even years, and returns home to write the ethnographic report on the culture(s) of the people being studied (see Van Maanen 1988; Agar 1996).

Anthropology, a field born in the late nineteenth century in the wake of Darwinism, aimed to be scientific, first engaging in what was called "salvage ethnography," capturing the cultures of "primitive" people thought to be facing extinction in the face of modernity, and later simply striving to document the diversity of human cultures. Sociology, another discipline born out of Darwinism, also embraced ethnography as a method, finding rural and urban America in the early twentieth century as the sites for the field research. For many years the American anthropologists and sociologists respected a division of labor; it was understood that anthropologists did their ethnographic work away from the United States, while the sociologists stayed home for their ethnographic work. There were always anthropologists drawn to studying American cultures, though.

Relevant for my purposes, of course, is the use of the ethnographic method to study the cultures of children and adolescents. The field of folklore studies is as old as the other two disciplines using ethnography, and the history of the ethnographic study of children's play and games begins with Newell's *Games and Songs of American Children* (1883) and continues to the present. Folklorists, sociologists, and anthropologists have done fieldwork on playgrounds (e.g., Thorne 1993; Beresin 2010), city streets (e.g., Goodwin 1991, 2006), group homes (Horan 1988), schools (e.g., Foley 1990; Pascoe 2011; Kahn 2012), sports teams (e.g., Fine 1987), and summer camps (e.g., Mechling 2001). Sadly, the moral panic over the abuse of children has made it almost impossible to get institutional permission to study boys in their natural settings, so ethnographic studies of children get scarcer each year.

In my own study of American masculinities, I have always trusted field-work-based, ethnographic studies of boys' small group cultures in natural settings more than the interview and experimental studies conducted in the therapist's office or the psychology laboratory. Those formal settings of office and lab can yield some insights into the lives of boys (e.g., Pollack 1998, certainly, and Way's 2011 intensive interviews with boys, first as a high school counselor and then as a researcher in developmental psychology). Adult interviews of youth, though, pose some difficulties in knowing just how frank the young person is being with the interviewer, an authority figure. A good ethnographer can become almost invisible doing fieldwork, thereby observing boys' folk cultures somewhat away from adult supervision and with minimum concern that the behavior (oral and customary) of the youth is inauthentic, "performed" for the adult.

The concept of "autoethnography" arose in the 1980s when anthropologists and other ethnographers challenged the goal or even the possibility of a scientific understanding of others' cultures. The intellectual move toward postmodernism involved abandoning the Enlightenment ideal of objective knowledge and made ethnographers hyperaware of how involved their own cultures and their own social locations (gender, social class, ethnicity, sexual orientation, etc.) were in the ways they could observe and understand the cultures of others. The possibility and impossibility of writing about other cultures created something of a revolution in ideas about ethnography (e.g., Clifford and Marcus 1986; Behar and Gordon, eds. 1995).

As those writing ethnographies became increasingly aware of their own life histories and social positions in attempting to tell the story of others' cultures, the concept of autoethnography was born (Denzin 2014). Initially understood by sociologist Norman Denzin and others more narrowly as "interpretive biography," the genre soon evolved into what came to be called "autoethnography"; the author of the ethnography reflexively wrote "the self into and through the ethnographic text" (Denzin 2014, 22). The concept assumes that the self is a performed cultural construction, both the self of the subject of the writing and the self of the writer.

It was also in the 1980s that ethnographers in the three disciplines formulating the notion of autoethnography—folklore, anthropology, and sociology—began to get serious about visual images (still photography and film) as important evidence in writing about cultures. "Visual sociology" (Harper 2012) and "visual anthropology" (Collier and Collier 1967) emerged as specialties within those disciplines, eventually coalescing into a field called "visual studies." Much of the thinking in these fields was about the uses of photography (still and film) by the ethnographer to supplement the writing, but scholars also turned attention to photographs and films as cultural evidence.

These too-brief discussions of autoethnography and visual ethnography led me to think about how the snapshots of boys by boys in my large collection of amateur photography of children and youth *might be viewed as visual autoethnography of the everyday lives of boys.* The boys take snapshots of their everyday lives without the expectation that adults will ever see or be able to censor the snapshots.

Before I explain how I "read" a snapshot for its many layers of meaning, I should make it clear who are the "boys" taking these snapshots and in the photographs. With a focus on photography and, especially, photography with film cameras, the lower end of the age span for "boy" probably is around ten years—just a guess because some younger boys might have had access to cameras using film. The advent of digital photography with smartphones that also serve as cameras no doubt has lowered the age of boys taking snapshots, since some very young children have smartphones. I do not include digital photographs in my collection, but it is important to realize that digital photography has exploded the number of potential vernacular photographs of boys by boys. I restrict my collection and analysis here to snapshots taken with conventional film cameras.

As for the upper age limit of what counts as a boy in my study, I would say age twenty-four or so, roughly the age limit of most traditional college and university students. Those of us who study the folklore of children and adolescents recognize that the folk practices we find in younger males show

Figure 0.2

up in the friendship groups of men in colleges and universities (Bronner 2012). A college fraternity is much like a Boy Scout troop, and both are much like a platoon in the military (Wallis and Mechling 2019a). Science adds an additional reason for seeing young men ages eighteen to twenty-four as still "boys," namely, the fact that the boy's brain does not fully develop until the mid-twenties (Aamodt and Yang 2012; Steinberg 2014; Sapolsky 2017, 154–73).

Inexpensive Cameras for Boys

Although there were precursors, such as the camera obscura, photography as we know it was invented in 1839. It took sixty more years for the invention of an inexpensive, lightweight camera using film rather than heavy, bulky wet plates for cameras to find its way into the hands of children, leading to

Figure 0.3

the true snapshot. The Kodak Brownie camera was introduced in 1910 and sold for one dollar. Eastman Kodak sold more than one hundred thousand Brownie cameras the first year, and ten million by five years after its introduction (Olivier 2007). The name George Eastman gave to the camera reflected his intention to market the camera heavily to children and youth, as a series of "brownie" books about those elfin creatures in British folklore were popular at the time. Magazine advertising for the Brownie camera clearly expected children to be able to use the camera, and Kodak encouraged youth under age fifteen to join the Brownie Camera Club. The Photography merit badge was one of the first badges a boy could earn in the Boy Scouts (Boy Scouts of America 1926). The first *Handbook for Boys* (1911) pictured the badge and the requirements to earn it, and in the advertising section of the *Handbook* one finds a full-page ad for the Brownie camera, along with a photograph of two Boy Scouts taken with a Brownie. Kodak's advertising of its cameras

in the BSA handbooks and in the organization's magazine *Boys' Life*, signals
that the company thought that those boys were an identifiable group of likely
consumers. The inexpensive handheld Kodak cameras evolved over the years,
and the camera I bought and took to Boy Scout camp as a teenager in the
late 1950s was the Kodak Brownie Starflash, which was introduced in 1957
and featured a built-in flash unit that took small bulbs. One advertisement
for the Brownie Starflash aimed at Boy Scouts urged the boy to "win your
photography merit badge with a Brownie Starflash Camera" and offered
Scoutmasters and merit badge counselors an address at Kodak headquarters
in Rochester, New York, where they could get "teaching aids, course outlines,
and other materials" for coaching the boy through the requirements for the
Photography merit badge. The Girl Scouts of America (GSA), founded in
1912, two years after the BSA, created a Photography merit badge for the
girls by 1916. In the 1920s the GSA officially named their younger members
"Brownies," following the lead of Lord Baden Powell, who named the Scouting organization for younger girls "Brownies," also with the British folk
stories in mind. Clearly those two organizations, the Boy Scouts and the Girl
Scouts, with millions of members, collaborated with Kodak in promoting
photography by children and adolescents. In part the youth groups encouraged photography, especially nature photography, as a way to teach young
people how to carefully examine the world around them.

Some schools also began teaching photography, seeing its educational
value. This movement began early in the twentieth century in American
colleges and art schools (Francisco 2007). The high school yearbook was
born around 1880, with the advent of inexpensive printing of photographs.
Of interest here are not the posed portraits of individual students and even
group photographs representing student classes, clubs, and teams, but the
candid photographs taken by yearbook student photographers. Those snapshots published in the junior high school and high school yearbooks are
of little use for my purposes, since what gets published had to get by the
censoring eye of the adult yearbook adviser. The treasure trove of snapshots
taken by students of other students, snapshots that never were published, are
lost to history, which breaks the heart of the historian trying to use amateur
photography to write the history of young people in the US.

The Snapshots of Boys by Boys

The attribution of a snapshot of a boy by a boy is never surefire. The scholar has to make guesses about the photos, guesses based on clues in the snapshot. For example, children and youth are generally subject to a great deal of surveillance by adults, so if a snapshot shows boy behavior that adults would disapprove of, it is likely that the photo is by a boy. As we shall see in chapter 2, photobooth photos with just a boy or boys in the booth present a pretty good view into the life of boys "behind the curtain," as it were—the curtain of the photobooth (Goranin 2008). Boys, though, can find areas under little or no adult supervision, as in play fights in corners of a schoolyard or in the boys' bathroom at school. Or in a boy's bedroom behind closed doors. Or in the woods behind the homes, the perfect place to play soldier and other physical games.

The snapshot presents elements that are likely to persuade the person examining the photograph that the image is "true." The viewer understands that the snapshot captures a split second in time, often a "candid" moment, one not planned or expected. Snapshots often have flaws, also signaling their capturing an "authentic" moment. Amateur photographers sometimes misjudge light and shadows, blur an image, accidentally create a double exposure by failing to advance the film from one frame to the next in the camera, and make other "errors" that brand the photograph as an amateur snapshot (G. King 1964, 49–57), Paradoxically, the more errors there are in the photograph, the more I believe the image captures an "authentic" split second in the lives of boys.

Doubtless there are many millions of snapshots around, and probably many millions more lost or destroyed. I began collecting vintage snapshots decades ago, first collecting snapshots of Boy Scouts but then expanding the search for ones of boys. Within my large collection of the latter (several thousand) is the much smaller body of snapshots I judge to be taken of boys by boys. Thus, I have a "sample" of snapshots of boys by boys (roughly from the 1930s into the 1980s), but it is in no way a scientific sample. At the same time, I have seen enough snapshots of boys to recognize patterns in the images and in the vernacular practices captured in the images.

Dealing with "surviving orphan snapshots" reminds us that the snapshot we are looking at has undergone multiple stages of "editing." The photographer edits the image through the lens. The adult developing the negative and printing the snapshot might disapprove of the subject matter and censor the image. The candid photographs taken by students of students for school yearbooks have to receive the approval of the teacher who is the yearbook advisor. The printed snapshot is then edited again—perhaps put in a safe place to save, perhaps put into an album to document lives. A family member or other agent decides whether to throw away the snapshot(s); if the snapshot survives and made available to others, the collector and dealer of vintage photographs edits yet again in deciding which snapshots are "interesting," both to the collector or dealer and to his or her customers. At times I did not acquire an interesting snapshot because I was outbid during an online auction.

The reader will notice, no doubt, that most of the snapshots in my collection and in this book are of white boys, a product of what I found (and won) in auctions and at vintage photography shows. Vintage snapshots of boys of color are relatively rare in the venues I searched, and while I do have a few of African American boys I believe were taken by boys, I wish I had more. In some cases boys from low-income families, no matter what race or ethnicity, simply could afford neither cameras nor the expense of developing the film. So my sample is also skewed toward middle-class as well as white boys.

My own ethnographic work and the work I know by most folklorists and other ethnographers examine the everyday lives of white boys in their friendship groups in natural settings away from classrooms, psychology laboratories, and therapy sessions, and it is against the ethnographic work that we can evaluate the added information the snapshots give us. Scholars have written ethnographic accounts of boys of color, though many studies purporting to be ethnographies really are just structured interviews away from any natural setting in which boys interact. In reading many of those studies (notably Way 2011), I have seen little to persuade me that the dynamics of friendship in those groups of boys of color differ significantly from what I have observed in the boys I lived with and studied at summer camps for over forty years.

I would account for the similarity in the ways boys use play and other folk genres to manage their performances of self and the dynamics of their friendships by pointing to what the brain scientists, neuroscientists, and evolutionary psychologists tell us about the biological basis of male pubescent and adolescent behavior (Sapolsky 2017). I summarize in chapter 1 on "boys' nature," the scientists' view, and boys' "second nature," the view of historians and ethnographers. They remind us that boys' behavior is not just based in biology but also in the social environment, still recognizing the power of the changes in the boy's body in that stage of the life cycle.

I do wish I had a more diverse collection of snapshots of boys by boys. The sorts of databases I wish I had simply do not exist; at least I have not found them. I have often wished that we could retrieve somehow the troves of candid photographs taken by high school student yearbook staff photographers;

alas, most of those probably end up discarded. The only effort I have discovered to use high school yearbooks' text and photographs to say something about American youth is a little-known book, *School Spirit* (2003), a collaboration between the French artist Pierre Huyghe and the famous Canadian writer Douglas Coupland.

I have to work with what I have, of course. In some ways every boy is unique. In other ways, established in the science of the body, every boy is the same. That sameness helps us account for the fact that, for example, male puberty rites can be found across time and across diverse cultures. Many of the rites share a formula structure (Bettelheim 1954; van Gennep 1960), all responding to a biological fact, but cultures also invent different ways to test and initiate boys. We see some of those tests in these snapshots.

How Shall We "Read" a Snapshot?

Many scholars who have used photographs, including snapshots, as evidence of the everyday lives of Americans, one way or another address the question of method. What does it mean to "read" a snapshot for information? Ibson (2002), for example, offers a methodological "epilogue" to his study of the photography of men from the late nineteenth century to the mid-twentieth century, and his shorter study of the amateur photography of boys (Ibson 2007) appears to use the same approach as his book. Ibson is a historian, so for him the "contexts" for the "texts" (the snapshots) are changes across time in the ideas and institutional pressures around masculinity, and especially ideas about masculinity and friendship. Anthropologists approaching snapshots see broader cultural contexts for them (e.g., Chalfen 1987), and sociologists bring from their discipline a set of ideas for understanding structures of meaning in everyday lives, as evidenced by snapshots (e.g., Becker 1995; Levin 1998; Harper 2012).

The best I can do here is explain briefly my own interdisciplinary approach. I seek what the anthropologist Clifford Geertz (1973b) calls a "thick description" of culture, a phrase he borrows from philosopher Gilbert Ryle. A thick description of an event (e.g., the behavior captured by a snapshot) sees the event within a larger pattern of signification, of making meaning through verbal, gestural, and material symbols. In the case of the snapshots I present here, the contexts are the everyday folk cultures of boys, which we know thanks to ethnographers. The ethnographic record of American boys' folk cultures is spotty, episodic, incomplete. But we can see patterns across time and space within the United States. I read these ethnographies, but my own fieldwork with boys across four decades also informs my understanding of the patterns of culture in the male friendship group.

I believe that my interpretations of snapshots are not mere idiosyncratic opinion. Geertz (1973b, 26) argues that interpretive anthropology is scientific in the same sense that the medical inductive method of "clinical inference" is scientific. The physician gathers information and formulates a diagnostic hypothesis about what makes "best sense" of the known data. The physician treats the patient based upon that hypothesis, and the patient gets better or not. If not, the physician gathers more data and tries a new treatment based on a new diagnostic hypothesis. The anthropologist or folklorist also uses inference, using evidence to formulate a hypothesis that makes "best sense" of the data. Thus, in what follows you will observe my making claims about the meanings of the behavior being captured by a snapshot of a boy by a boy. "Hypothesis" seems too formal a word for what really are guesses and hunches based on my reading of ethnographies of boys' lives and my decades of experience studying boys in natural settings. If the reader is not persuaded by my hunch (in my experience the resistance comes most strongly in response to my use of depth psychology to understand a snapshot), my rejoinder is this. A boy chose to take this snapshot of another boy and chose to save the snapshot because he, the photographer, thought the event being captured by the snapshot was significant in the lives of the boys. If you have another hunch or hypothesis that you think makes "best sense" of the snapshot, then let us compare the interpretations. Not all interpretations are equal; some account for more data in the image, some account better for something strange in the image, and so on. The scholar always tries to make "best sense" of the evidence, looking for patterns within an image and across images.

Some scholars who use amateur photographic evidence (snapshots) in their writing social and cultural history insist that we must have large samples of snapshots in order to see a pattern across time and space. Sample size and the "representativeness" of a single photograph concern Ibson (2002); and some others who have contributed important work in using photographs as historical evidence are skeptical about reliance on a single photograph to make any useful generalizations. Ibson explicitly criticizes the sort of idiosyncratic, subjective interpretations offered by Roland Barthes (1980).

My interpretations of the meanings of the many snapshots I analyze in this book might seem too subjective, but interpretations of a photograph can be compared and evaluated as they propose to make "best sense" of it. Thomas Kuhn (1970) argues that in the long history of science, one paradigm replaces another as much through persuasion as through irrefutable evidence. In many cases the more persuasive argument in science involves matters such as the amount of data the new paradigm explains, solving puzzles unexplained by the old paradigm, and sometimes the new paradigm wins the argument by appearing simpler and meeting the aesthetic arguments scientists sometimes offer, as in an "elegant" or "beautiful" mathematic proof or solution to a scientific puzzle. I believe that we can compare interpretations of snapshots with similar criteria—comprehensiveness and elegance, recognizing that the second class of features of an argument is highly speculative.

Folklorists and other scholars who study culture like to talk about the "contexts" for a "text," understanding that a "cultural text" is a broad category that includes oral, customary, and material practices. In the case of these snapshots, there are historical, social, cultural, generic, and intertextual contexts, the "webs of significance" Weber (Keyes 2002) wrote about. I draw upon historical contexts in an interpretation of a snapshot when I think the era of that snapshot (not always easy to determine) might tell me something about the practices captured by the image. The social context for a snapshot's image has to do with what we know about the social structure, norms, and practices within the young man's friendship group. I am not including psychology in this list of contexts, though as a folklorist I am alert to the ways folk practices sometimes address social anxieties and sometimes address psychological anxieties, which (in my view) demands reaching into depth psychology for understanding unconscious motives. The cultural context for these snapshots consists of ideas about childhood, youth, and masculinity in American culture, which ideas are not fixed in time (back to historical contexts). The generic context reminds us that vernacular photography is a genre. Genres of visual culture have as many conventions as do genres in literature and other art forms. Knowing the conventions of the genre sometimes helps us understand the choices made by the photographer. Finally, "intertextual context" simply means that some texts provide contexts for new texts. Brummett (1991, 2004) calls these "shadow texts." In my examination of snapshots, I know that the boy taking the photograph has been exposed to a world of images and that sometimes previous images help determine the choices he makes when he frames and takes a photograph.

I have referred a few times already in this introduction to the fact that a photographer makes choices that result in the snapshot we hold in our hands. One of the ideas underlying my interpretations of American cultural texts is Kenneth Burke's "pentad," a central notion in his "dramatistic" model of social action. In his study of any rhetorical act, Burke looks at the act, the scene, the agent, the agency, and the purpose (Burke 1969 [1945], xv). In my folklore studies, I always ask and attempt to answer the following complex question: "Who performed what traditional practice, when, where, how, for what audience, why, and what was the outcome?" The "why" in that question refers to what Burke calls "motive." Note that we can observe all the elements in that question except motive. Identifying a motive for the performance involves speculation, again a "best guess," and that speculation in turn rests on depth psychology, because the motive the performer of the practice might offer the observer is a "thin description," whereas making a good guess at the unconscious motive for the choices made provides a "thick description" (Geertz 1973b).

The depth psychology I draw upon for interpreting snapshots is psycho-analytic theory, sometimes Freud but more often the feminist revisions of psychoanalytic theory, revisions useful in understanding the performance of masculinity (Chodorow 1978; Frosh 1994). The subset of those of us who use psychoanalytic concepts to study the everyday lives of children run into considerable resistance. Alan Dundes, probably the most famous folklorist consistently using psychoanalytic theory, regularly ran into resistance, and the resistance intensifies when writing about the meanings of children's everyday folk traditions, not least because of Freud's ideas about sexual-ity in the psyches of children. Bronner (1988) makes use of psychoanalytic concepts in his study of children's folklore, and I have in my work on mas-culinity (Mechling 2001, 2021). The reader of this book certainly can skip over my discussions of psychoanalytic concepts when I interpret a snap-shot, but doing so misses what might be some important insights into the unconscious motives and meanings captured in it. Given what I have said above about interpretive anthropology and clinical inference, I believe that a psychoanalytic interpretation of a snapshot can and should be subjected to a comparison with alternative interpretations, so long as the alternative interpretations also address the matter of motive.

The advent of digital photography and the technological advance of smartphones that take snapshots complicate the terrain of everyday, ama-teur photography even more. Boys taking snapshots with their phones edit through the lens and then can decide immediately whether to keep or delete the picture just taken. A boy can put a digital snapshot on what-ever social media site he uses (not Facebook so much anymore now but more likely TikTok, SnapChat, or Instagram). Digital snapshots do not go through the hands of adults who might censor them, so in some ways they are more authentic evidence of young people's everyday lives than are analogic snapshots. Boys using a smartphone can record and save images involving "bad behavior," from actual crimes to snapshots of one's penis to send to others (for "sexting" with girls or other boys, for example). I have no digital images here.

I draw here upon the body of scholarship on the small group (folk) cultures of boys (e.g., Mechling 1986; Bronner 1988; Sutton-Smith, Mechling, Johnson, and McMahon, eds. 1995; Mechling 2005a). The interpretation of these snapshots also rests on the substantial body of scholarship in masculinity studies. In most cases the generalizations historians and social scientists (including psychologists) make about boys work well using what has been called "the boy code" (Pollack 1998; Kimmel 2008). What complicates our understanding of boys— aside from the problem of generalizing in ways that don't violate individual differences in age, social class, sexual orientation, and gender identity—is generational change.

Generalizing about wholes from parts is risky business. One historian (Metzger 1963) puts the dilemma this way. From one point of view, every human being is the same. From another point of view, every human being (even an identical twin) is different. The problem of generalization is finding a "true" statement that does not do much violence to either truth. I will make generalizations here as carefully as I can, recognizing that every boy is different, that gender and sexual identity vary considerably, that boys are socialized in different families with their own particularities (social class, ethnicity, religion, and so on), and that the forces that shape the socialization of boys change over time.

At the same time, some things seem to remain constant in American boys. In 1970 or thereabouts, I read Berger and Luckmann's book *The Social Construction of Reality* (1966), and I taught that "treatise in the sociology of knowledge" for many years. Epistemology, theories about how we know what we think we know, fascinated me from high school reading in philosophy and science, so the Berger and Luckmann book seemed the perfect touchstone for understanding one of my central topics, the socialization of children. Privileging the social construction of gender over the biological forces made sense in the 1970s, especially at a time when it was important to reject the "biological essentialism" that justified social and cultural arrangements keeping women trapped in a narrow range of social roles.

I embarked on the study of the Boy Scouts a thorough social constructionist. The fieldwork extended over more than two decades. As I observed, described, and interpreted a number of changes in the boys' practices from 1976 to 1998, I gradually came to realize that some things did not change with the age cohorts. One explanation is that the troop had a strong, distinctive culture, strong "traditions," shaping the boys' practices, a constant structure persisting across time when other things changed. An additional explanation, one to layer on top of the social constructionist one, is that the biological foundation for boys' practices in their friendship groups is a lot stronger than

I suspected or allowed. Chapter 1 explores both boys' "nature" (the biology and evolutionary psychology) and boys' "second nature" (their socialization).

About the Writing

By now you have figured out that I steer away from the usual academic style of writing in order to make this book as readable as possible. I avoid jargon, and when I must use a word perhaps not familiar to all readers, I do define the term. There are no footnotes in this book, though I do write the occasional "excursus" here as a sort of long footnote in the body of the text. Peter Berger and his colleagues introduced me to the use of the excursus in their book *The Homeless Mind: Modernization and Consciousness* (Berger, Berger, and Kellner 1973), and I used the narrative device in my book *Soldier Snapshots: Masculinity, Play, and Friendship in the Everyday Photographs of Men in the American Military* (2021).

In many ways my intellectual heroes are scholars who write for the general audience and explain some of the most complex ideas in ways those readers can understand. William James, one of the fathers of American scientific psychology and a key figure in formulating the American philosophical tradition of pragmatism, had a knack for explaining radically new ideas to audiences of teachers and other adults in ways easily understood. The same can be said for a long line of scientists who write for a general audience, whether it is Carl Sagan and Neil deGrasse Tyson on astrophysics, Stephen Jay Gould on evolution and other mysteries of natural history, or Oliver Sacks, Robert Sapolsky, and a number of neuroscientists I have been reading in order to understand the role of biology in the behavior of boys and men.

Plan of the Book

The chapters in part one introduce some basic things we know about male adolescents. Chapter 1 tackles the issue lurking behind every examination of the social performance of gender; namely, how does the interaction of biology, evolutionary psychology, and the culture of small groups determine the social practices surrounding the construction, maintenance, and repair (if necessary) of normative masculinity in American culture? An excursus follows chapter 1, bringing into the conversation the psychoanalytic ideas proposed by Erik Erikson and Nancy Chodorow on male adolescence and identity, revising the old school of thought about "culture and personality," updated by Chodorow and aimed by her to understand the dialectical relationship between the individual's private, inner reality and the public, everyday reality of the social world we take for granted. Chapter 2 looks at male friendship and comradeship.

Part 2 presents the snapshots by theme. Chapter 3 looks at boys' "stuff," the objects and other material culture that show up in their snapshots and provide some clues to how boys make meaning in their lives through objects. Chapter 4 examines three categories of objects—forts, clubhouses, and rafts—because, as material objects built by boys, their use tells us some important things about American ideas. Chapter 5 considers customary behavior by boys as they use their bodies to both perform their masculinity and to bond with other boys. Chapter 6 documents the ways boys prove their masculinity by passing "tests." Chapter 7 borrows Clifford Geertz's notion of "deep play" to examine snapshots that reveal a darker side of boys' play.

A long excursus on "play and fantasy" anchors the discussion in chapters 3 through 7 about the snapshots, identifying patterns across the snapshots and adding to the discussion the crucial role of play and, especially, fantasy in creating the practices captured by the snapshots. Popular-culture fantasies turn out to be the "mythologies" shared and enacted by the "tribe" of boys.

Finally, chapter 8 makes a small foray into comparative visual autoethnography by examining a sample of the snapshots in my collection featuring the Hitlerjugend (H-J; Hitler Youth) of the 1930s, a comparison that has always nibbled at the edge of my study of the Boy Scouts by dint of the fact that some people see little difference between American boys in uniforms and the young men in brown uniforms in Nazi Germany. I can claim no special expertise in German culture, but the existing scholarship on the Hitler Youth movement, including a fascinating commentary by no less a figure than Gregory Bateson interpreting a famous Nazi propaganda film, provides useful context for understanding the German snapshots of boys by boys.

The coda is less a summary than a closing judgment about why the boys take the snapshots, share them, and save them, and this coda echoes the theme of grief at the loss of male friendship I wrote about in the coda to *Soldier Snapshots* (2021).

This introduction now out of the way, let me show you some snapshots of boys by boys, and let me explore some hunches I have about what the snapshots reveal about the individual and collective experiences of boys when the adults are not looking.

Part One

Theory

Chapter One

Boys' Nature and American Boys' Second Nature

Every American adult, male and female, thinks they understand boys. Men think they understand boys because they once were boys; most women think they understand boys because it is difficult to grow up female in the United States without an awareness of the generally privileged status of boys among children, even now, despite decades of efforts to level the playing field in raising daughters. Parents often debate with friends whether it is harder to raise a son or a daughter, and when I once posed to a seminar of first-year students on gender, "Who is harder to understand, men or women?" the female students insisted "men," while the male students answered "women." Each side thought young people in their gender group were "easy" to understand. Young women think they understand women; young men think they understand men.

The main players in this book are the boys, though most boys lead their lives among females, from mothers and female teachers to sisters and female friends, so writing about boys always must take into account the girls, even if they are not the focus. Boys' self-awareness develops in large part in reaction to what women and girls think of boys and how they treat boys. Near the end of my book on a troop of California Boy Scouts at their annual summer encampment high in the Sierra Nevada, I discuss the puzzlement I felt when, at the end-of-year "After Campfire Campfire," when all the younger boys and their families left the campfire, I observed the older boys and alumni of the group tell very sexual and "gross" jokes and stories in front of their girlfriends and wives (Mechling 2001, 271–74). The Scoutmaster, who was also a high school teacher and had a pretty good grasp of the psychology of boys, told me later, when I expressed my puzzlement, that he thought that boys acted "gross" in the presence of girls because they knew that girls think boys are "gross," so the boys simply upped their level of gross behavior for the female audience. Boys do perform "gross" for each other in their male friendship group, and the genre of children's folklore called "Grosser than Gross" jokes is primarily found among boys (Bronner 1988, 131–33). When they perform "gross" for girls, it is a sort of protest against the judgment by girls. Bateson (1972) called this phenomenon "schismogenesis," when the behavior of one actor is in response to the behavior of another actor in the frame, a system of action and reaction.

My focus here is on the amateur photographic capture of how boys behave in the presence of other boys, in their friendship groups, away from surveillance by adults but also largely away from surveillance by girls their ages. Boys can hide from the adults, but they cannot "hide" from the ideas held by adults about the "nature" of boys, ideas that the boys sometimes accept as true, sometimes reject, sometimes resist, but can never escape.

The popular and scholarly literature on boys is vast, even more so when one includes the images of boys and boyhood we see in films and other mass media. I attempt in this chapter to provide a brief, useful survey of ideas about boys as a context for understanding the snapshots of boys by boys, useful for my goals here.

I deal separately with "folk ideas" about boys and what I call "scientific" ideas about boys, which includes both natural sciences and social sciences. I also distinguish between boys' "nature" (what the biologists and evolutionary psychologists tell us about the roots of boys' behavior in their male bodies) and boys' "second nature," a term used by many, both professionals and lay adults, to describe socialization.

The earliest study of boys' nature and second nature emerged from what historians call a "moral panic" about what was happening to American masculinity in the closing decades of the nineteenth century, a crisis felt largely by white, middle-class men who perceived a loss of status and warned about the dangerous feminization of the American boy by mothers and female schoolteachers. That panic led to corrective measures, such as the "muscular Christianity" movement and the founding at the turn of the century of youth movements meant to restore and ensure the rugged masculinity of American boys. The publication of G. Stanley's Hall's two-volume study in 1904, *Adolescence*, provided youth workers with the scientific ideas for understanding that newly discovered stage of human development. Hall draws on science to write about both boys and girls, but it is clear that boys are the most important topic for Hall. The Boy Scouts of America (BSA) was founded in 1910, a watershed year in the modernization of consciousness (Cochran 1964), and the adult founders and leaders of the BSA rested their ideas about youth work with boys on the scientific ideas provided by Hall and others. The BSA began publishing a *Handbook for Scoutmasters* in 1914, and across the years one can see in subsequent editions of that *Handbook* the reliance of Boy Scout authors on the growing literature on boys' nature and second nature.

Henry William Gibson, a leader in the Young Men's Christian Association (YMCA), invented the term "boyology" in his book by that title (1922 [1916]). I was taken by that neologism when I began writing about the Boy Scouts in the 1970s, and Kidd (2004) revived the word in his examination of the "feral boy," the wild boy, in American popular culture. By 2007 it seemed to several scholars that there was enough interest in boys among researchers from several disciplines that it was time to create a new journal, originally titled *Thymos: Journal of Boyhood Studies*, and then just *Boyhood Studies*. So as of this writing, there is a considerable body of scholarship and advice literature about boys. The following discussion draws upon that scholarship to make "best sense" of the snapshots I examine here.

Folk Boyology

I cannot offer here an exhaustive list of the "folk ideas" (Dundes 1971; Mechling 2019a) adult Americans hold about boys, often condensed into the proverb "Boys will be boys," but here is a partial, suggestive list. Boys are competitive, are rambunctious (great word!), take risks, often make poor choices, will bully other boys, are wild rather than tame. "Wild boys" is a long-standing motif in American thought. It shows up in American literature as early as the nineteenth century. Although *Lord of the Flies*, by the British Nobel Prize–winning author William Golding, is not an American fantasy, the novel (1954) is still required reading in a great many English classes in schools, and the film versions (1963, dir. Peter Brook; 1990, dir. Harry Hook) are popular enough that the story of civilized boys turned savage when returned to the wild must touch something in us, in our ideas about the nature of boys.

Alongside the folk ideas that boys are aggressive, violent, and wild, we can also find a set of folk ideas less discussed. Adolescent boys can be very sensitive, emotional, insecure. Often I have heard the mothers of boys say something like this: when he was little he was such a sweet boy, but when the hormones kicked in he changed. Boys probably are as complicated and difficult to figure out as the women in my class opined.

Commercial and professional photography of boys provides a visual set of folk ideas about boys to complement (and sometimes contradict) the verbal expressions of such folk ideas. Photography of children has a long history, from studio portraits in the late nineteenth century to the snapshot in the twentieth (Mechling 2005b). By the mid-twentieth century, most books featuring photography of children were simply photobooks (Ballen 1979; Parr and Badger 2004, 2006) with little or no commentary, much less interpretive analysis of the photos. Photobooks such as Barbara Morgan's of the "life cycle" of children at a summer camp (1951), Lauren Greenfield's two books (1997 and 2002) of photography documenting the lives of young people in Los Angeles, and Adrienne Salinger's (1995) photobook of teens in their bedrooms tease us with provocative photographs but offer little or no scholarly commentary.

The photobooks of boys tend to be of two sorts, neither sort especially useful for scholarly understanding of the everyday lives of boys in America. On the one hand are photobooks of boys in some natural setting, street corners or play spaces, photos begging for some analysis. A good many of those photobooks of boys promote the theme of childhood innocence. Others go the other direction, showing us the dark side of male adolescence, including drug use and adolescent sexuality (e.g., L. Clark 1971, 1987, 1993). The problem with most of these books is that adults took the photographs, which means that we are looking at children's lives through the eyes of adults; the photographs make the children "subjects" without agency (Holland 2004).

It is tempting to view the studies using the method of "photo elicitation" with children as something closer to their own view of their everyday lives (C. D. Clark 1999, 2011, 158–74). That method has been used in many ways, but for our purposes we would want to consider the studies where the scholar gives cameras to young people, tells them to go out and photograph things important in their lives and return to show the photographs to the scholar and talk about the images (e.g., Ewald et al. 2000; Walker 2004). The problem I see with this method is that the researcher never can be sure if the young person is making choices (what to photograph and what to say about the photographs) that the young person thinks the researcher wants to see and hear. This is precisely what bothered child psychiatrist Robert Coles (1977) when he interviewed affluent teenagers for his *Children of Crisis* series of books.

It seems that the "folk ideas" about boys, both in words and images, are ideas held by adults. We still yearn to discern a set of folk ideas about boyhood held by boys. Boys rarely use words to express folk ideas about boys. They don't *tell* us, they *show* us. That's where ethnographies of boys in their natural settings and snapshots taken by boys of boys in those natural settings come to our rescue in attempting to move beyond adult accounts of what it means to be an American boy.

Scientific Boyology

For this discussion I distinguish "boys' nature," the biological and evolutionary foundations of boy behavior, from American "boys' second nature," by which I mean the socialization of boys into taken-for-granted ideas and behavior, socialization that is strong and not easily extinguished, seemingly as determinative as boys' biology. We expect "boys' nature" to be fairly stable across time and space, as the boy's biology and the evolutionary history of his physiology and psychology remains fairly constant. Boys' "second nature," on the other hand, is cultural. Adults attempt to "socialize" the boy into being able to perform competently as a member of the culture. Put differently, the adults attempt to "tame" the "wild" boy, help him learn acceptable behavior.

Of course, this distinction between the force of biology and the force of culture on boys' practices leads us astray; as many of the scientists, especially primatologists, who write about male behavior insist, the behavior of boys is not simply driven by biology and evolution or purely socially constructed. In the nature/nurture debate, says Sapolsky, a primatologist and evolutionary psychologist, it's not just biology or just environment but "the interaction between the two" (Sapolsky 1997, 156). Keeping that warning in mind, let me begin with the biological and evolutionary foundations of boy behavior.

Boys' Nature

The biology of childhood, puberty and then adolescence has always been present in the boys' bodies, but it was not until G. Stanley Hall, one of the "fathers of American psychology," published his two-volume work, *Adolescence* (1904), that scientists, teachers, parents, and other adults working with youth had a concept to describe what they knew already; namely, that the stage of life roughly between ages ten and twenty-four has distinct qualities in the life cycle (Steinberg 2014, 5).

Rejecting the common stereotypes that boys are wholly innocent creatures or wholly violent savages, Hall describes boys' nature with a series of binary oppositions. Hall argues that the sexual energy experienced by adolescent boys (what Freud calls libidinal energy) is the heart of their emotional character, and the emotional character of boys is an important element in interpreting photographs, as we shall see.

"Youth loves intense states of mind," Hall writes, "and is passionately fond of excitement" (1904, 2:73). In Hall's view the instability of adolescent boys' inner emotions surfaces in the "overenergetic action" and "oscillation between pleasure and pain" in young men. Boys experience "a vacillation between knowing and doing," between selfishness and altruism, good and bad conduct, kindness and cruelty, conservative and radical instincts, and wisdom and folly (2:75–88).

Neuroscientists today have sophisticated tools for mapping the links between areas and activities in the adolescent brain, on the one hand, and the behavior of adolescents, on the other, tools Hall did not have in 1904. It turns out, though, that Hall had it right. One of the key observations notes the "neuroplasticity" of the brain, a term first used by William James in *The Principles of Psychology* (1890). The brain, especially the adolescent brain, modifies itself when confronted with new situations (Galván 2017, 85–115). In fact, the hormonal changes in puberty lead the adolescent to seek out new experiences. The "remodeling" of the adolescent brain "occurs primarily in two regions—the prefrontal cortex and the limbic system," the former responsible for "self-regulation," and the latter responsible for "generating emotions" (Steinberg 2014, 70). Here, though, is the catch. The emotional limbic system remodels earlier than the reasoning prefrontal cortex. Accordingly, starting in puberty "teenagers become more emotional (experiencing and displaying higher 'highs' and lower 'lows'), more sensitive to the opinions and evaluations of others (especially peers), and more determined to have exciting and intense experiences" (70). It is not until age sixteen or even later that the prefrontal cortex begins catching up with the limbic system and becomes better at regulating adolescent impulses, "thinking about the long-term consequences of their decisions and resisting peer pressure" (71). So, again, Hall had it right when he argued that adolescence extends to age twenty-four.

Those who study the behavior of adolescent boys observe the consequences of an unregulated limbic system of emotions and impulses in early-to-middle adolescence, including irrational risk-taking. Moreover, experiments show that "the most risky behavior occurs in the presence of friends" (Galván 2017, 172). We shall see abundant evidence of this when we consider many of the snapshots of boys by boys.

The neuroscientists of adolescence also see a positive, adaptive aspect to this risk-taking with peers—namely, the adolescent brain adapts well in the transition from dependence upon older caregivers to independence, resulting often in the "creativity, rebellion, and progressive thinking that characterizes this period," early-to-middle adolescence (Gaván 2017, 175). We shall find in some of the snapshots evidence of the strong adolescent male drive toward independence.

In adolescence boys acquire the ability to read the body language of peers, a necessary goal for the creation of prosocial group solidarity. What neuroscientists call "face processing" begins early in life, but it is during adolescence that the skills sharpen. The adolescent limbic system, especially the amygdala, "helps organisms process emotions in the self and read the emotions of others," including direct threats (Gaván 2017, 189). One positive outcome of this amygdala-driven skill is the empathy needed in the adolescent male friendship group, a skill aided by "mirror neurons" in the brain (see Iacoboni 2009).

Another valuable feature of the ability to read emotions in faces and bodies concerns the "fight or flight" response to threat (Gaván 2017, 189). Neuroscientists and others who write about male adolescence always address the issue of anger and aggression. "Both sex and aggression activate the sympathetic nervous system," writes Sapolsky (2017, 43). In *The Trouble with Testosterone* (1997), Sapolsky taps his expertise in both neuroscience and primatology to lay out the basic psychophysiology of the male, though he is careful not to claim that biology explains all male behavior. His chapter "The Trouble with Testosterone: Will Boys Just Be Boys?," begins with the well-documented proposition that men tend to be violent, that most of the aggression in the world is committed by men. Testosterone is an easy hormone to blame for this male aggressiveness. Testosterone "seeps into the brain," he writes, "where it binds to those same 'androgen' receptors and influences behavior in a way highly relevant to understanding aggression" (150). Sapolsky reviews the research in favor of a causal link between testosterone and aggression (including the "subtraction experiment," where aggression disappears with castration and reappears with injections of testosterone).

Then Sapolsky complicates the psychophysiological picture. Individual differences and then culture mean that there is no neat causal link between testosterone and aggression and violence. "Study after study has shown," notes Sapolsky (1997, 151–52), "that when you examine testosterone levels when males are first placed together in the social group, testosterone levels predict nothing about who is going to be aggressive. The subsequent behavioral differences drive the hormonal changes, rather than the other way around." In the nature/nurture debate, he says, it's not just biology or just environment but "the interaction between the two" (156).

Thus, while acknowledging a psychophysiological substrate for understanding male aggression and violence, Sapolsky opens up the conversation for the examination of the role of culture—and in our case the role of the small group culture of the male friendship group. He describes an experiment with a group of male monkeys (say, numbers 1 through 5) and observes that such a group soon creates a dominance hierarchy. "This is the hierarchical sort of system," he writes, "where number 3, for example, can pass his day throwing around his weight with numbers 4 and 5, ripping off their monkey chow, forcing them to relinquish the best spots to sit in, but, at the same time, remembering to deal with numbers 1 and 2 with shit-eating obsequiousness" (1997, 154). If you shoot a massive dose of testosterone into monkey number 3, he still recognizes the hierarchy, "kowtowing to numbers 1 and 2." All the added testosterone does is make him "a total bastard to numbers 4 and 5" (155)—which supports his conclusion that "testosterone isn't *causing* aggression, it's *exaggerating* the aggression that's already there" (emphasis in original, 155). Adolescent boys usually have acquired the ability to understand the hierarchy of power in the male friendship group and know their places in the hierarchy.

Adolescent boys' mastery of reading and responding to their own emotions and to the emotions of others in the friendship group makes it possible for boys to regulate the emotions of their peers. Sutton-Smith (2017, 70–89) argues that play and games trigger secondary emotions (pride, empathy, envy, shame, guilt, and embarrassment) that help control the primary emotions (shock, anger, fear, distrust, sadness, and happiness), and I have extended that point to make the claim that all folk traditions serve the purpose of making our emotions visible to us and to others (Mechling 2019b). This concept of the regulatory and control functions of folk traditions in the male friendship group will come up several times in the later chapters of this book.

It is difficult to talk about the boy's biology, his "nature," without sliding into talk about socialization, or the boy's "second nature." So let me leave the biology talk here and turn to the socialization of American boys.

American Boys' Second Nature

True, "boys will be boys," but boys are boys mainly in groups. The male friendship group, from an early age, shapes the performance of normative masculinity in the boy and then young man.

What follows applies mainly to American culture, though much of it is true of other Western cultures as well. I necessarily generalize here, recognizing that there is wide variety in the ways boys create and perform their individual sexual and gender identities. In gender studies we recognize that within-group (same-sex) variations may be greater than between-group variations; men tend to have greater upper-body strength than do women, but there are plenty of women who have greater upper-body strength than do many men (a fact relevant as more and more women engage in scholastic sports like wrestling and enter professions like firefighting and the military). In masculinity studies, we find that the ways of performing masculinity are varied, to say the least.

Keeping in mind these limitations, I plunge now into trying to describe clearly and succinctly the culture of the male friendship group.

A common starting point in masculinity studies is the somewhat surprising proposition that masculinity is a fragile social construction in American culture, surprising because many young men "perform" a rather bold, confident, macho style that seems anything but fragile. Behind this performance lies male anxiety, which can be traced to the fragility of the performance. I summarize in my chapter in Bronner's *Manly Traditions* the chain of reasoning that leads scholars to see masculinity as a fragile construction in constant need of maintenance and repair (Mechling 2005a; Kimmel also summarizes the theory, 2005, 31–33). Briefly, feminist psychoanalytic theory sees masculinity as a negative, as "not female." The infant's first attachment usually is to the mother. For the female infant and then child, the mother is the culturally proper role model for identification. Eventually separating the female self from the mother has its own drama, but for the male infant and male child, the separation has to be complete. The default position is that male is "not female," which accounts for much of the homophobia and misogyny in the folk cultures of male friendship groups.

The problem for prepubescent and adolescent boys and men is that the construction and maintenance of the male performance is never complete. As Beneke (1997) and others note, every day young men face "tests of manhood"; manhood must be proven over and over again. And the tests come from many quarters, sometimes beginning with the father, but the most salient for male children and adolescent men are the tests within the male friendship group. The 1986 theatrical film *Stand by Me* (dir. Rob Reiner) and the Stephen King novella the film is based upon, *The Body* (1982), nicely illustrate the dynamics of the pubescent male friendship group, including the dares the boys test each other with, beginning with the dare that drives the action: the boys take off on a search for the dead body of a boy they heard was killed by a train. Each of the four boys comes from a dysfunctional family and has something to prove to his friends; namely, that he is tough and a survivor.

Play

I need to pause here to introduce an important concept for my analysis of the male friendship group. In the mid-1950s anthropologist Gregory Bateson observed otters and monkeys at play at the zoo in San Francisco (he was at the nearby Palo Alto Veterans Administration Hospital at the time, working with a group of psychiatrists on a double-bind theory of schizophrenia), and watching animals led him to speculate on how it is that mammals can play. In his essay "A Theory of Play and Fantasy" (1972 [1955]), Bateson lays out his theory of frames, using as his prime example the play frame and, in particular, play fighting.

Play has puzzled scientists for many decades. Play seems to make no evolutionary sense, as it consumes calories, distracts attention from surveillance for predators, and risks injury. Yet mammals play. Sociobiologists posit explanations for the evolutionary survival of play behavior, such as practicing skills in youth for later use by adults, but I like Sutton-Smith's (2017) answer that we play because it is fun. Play does not have to be functional; play does not have to serve evolutionary fitness. Play can be expressive and consummatory, rewarding the player with pleasure, which is a sort of evolutionary fitness (the subtitle of his last book, *Play for Life*, published posthumously [2017], is *Play Theory and Play as Emotional Survival*).

It is therefore in the interest of mammals to play, and Bateson explains how it is that two or more mammals can enter the play frame. The participants must exchange what Bateson calls a "metamessage," a message about messages. In this case the metamessage is "this is play," and the mammals can signal this metamessage through nonverbal behavior (body language—like the canine play bow), through paralinguistic behavior (e.g., tone of voice), or through language ("let's play"). Humans have all three channels of communication to use in the invitation to play, and if the other mammal accepts the invitation, then they have agreed to a play frame and have agreed that messages exchanged within that frame do not mean what they would mean outside of the frame. In the play fight, for example, nonverbal and verbal messages do not stand for real aggression but, rather, for a stylized aggression.

Two important points follow. First, entering the play frame already assumes a level of familiarity and trust between the players. It is very hard to enter a play frame with a stranger, and it is very easy to enter a play frame with a close friend or partner. Second, play frames (and their cousin, ritual frames) are fragile, easily broken. In a play fight the too-hard hit or the wrong words can break the play frame and even devolve into a real fight. If the players value their relationship, they will then work to repair and restore the play frame.

One shortcoming of Bateson's theory of the play frame is that he assumes that the participants are there voluntarily, can choose to come and go as the frame serves their needs and satisfaction. When the sociologist Erving Goffman (1974) adopted the idea of the play frame to argue that all social reality is, in essence, a confidence game, he opened our eyes to Bateson's error. Clearly, some people create a play frame as a way to control others, from simple, benign deception to criminal deception. Sutton-Smith and

Kelly-Byrne (1984) note that people will use play to "mask" other motives; the sibling pleads to the mother that "we were just playing" when he pinches his sibling too hard, or the person who tells a sexual joke in the workplace pleads that it's "just a joke," not sexual harassment. Goffman and Sutton-Smith and Kelly-Byrne alert us, then, to the fact overlooked by Bateson; namely, that not everyone in a play frame is there voluntarily, that some would pay a price for breaking the play frame, that there are power differentials among the players, and that the play frame can mask other motives.

Boys Will Be Boys Redux

Turning our attention back to charting the folk culture of the pubescent and adolescent male friendship group, we should keep in mind that the friendship group is what folklorists would call a "high context" group, a group with lots of familiar history, the context for all of their communication, spoken and unspoken. They can communicate a lot with a little.

In the boys' folk group they learn the "rules" of being a male. Both Pollack (1998, 23–24) and Kimmel (2005, 30–31) turn to Brannon and David's (1976) summary of the Boy Code:

1. "No Sissy Stuff!" One may never do anything that even remotely suggests femininity. Masculinity is the relentless repudiation of the feminine.
2. "Be a Big Wheel." Masculinity is measured by power, success, wealth, and status. As the current saying goes, "He who has the most toys when he dies wins."
3. "Be a Sturdy Oak." Masculinity depends on remaining calm and reliable in a crisis, holding emotions in check. In fact, proving you are a man depends on never showing your emotions at all. Boys don't cry.
4. "Give 'Em Hell." Exude an aura of manly daring and aggression. Go for it. Take Risks.

The boys and men in the friendship group enforce this code, and the boy often internalizes the code so that after time he enforces the code for himself. Moreover, as we said, the group tests the boy and man, meaning that he has to "prove" his manhood over and over again.

The group enforces "no sissy stuff" with the misogyny and homophobia embedded in their joking and teasing. "Be a Big Wheel" recognizes that boys and men in groups figure out very quickly the hierarchy and their place in it. Recall Sapolsky's example of the band of monkeys and the fact that the hierarchy remains in place even when one of the monkeys gets massive injections of testosterone. The third point of the "Boy Code" recognizes that boys are not permitted most emotions, certainly not the emotions we associate with the female. But boys are permitted anger (Stearns and Stearns 1986), which can be a source of trouble.

The fourth point of the Boy Code encourages aggression and risk-taking. Males are capable of real aggression, which would damage the relationships in the male friendship group. So most boys learn early how to perform "stylized aggression" in the play frame. Sometimes the stylized aggression is verbal, as in trading insults, and sometimes it is physical, as in rough-and-tumble (R&T) play fighting (see Wallis and Mechling 2015; Delfino and Mechling 2017). Although the play frame is fragile and easily broken in episodes of stylized aggression, the ability to sustain the play frame while trading insults or actually participating in R&T play fighting paradoxically signals to the players their strong bond of trust. As Oring (1984) says in writing about dyadic folklore, if a member of the group stopped engaging in everyday stylized aggression with others in the group, that would signal a problem.

I just noted that the primary emotion boys may express openly is anger, but, as Kimmel says, if "masculinity is a homosocial enactment, its overriding emotion is fear" (2005, 34), fear of violating the boy code, fear of a failed performance of masculinity, fear of appearing or acting feminine. The fear is a hidden emotion. "What we call masculinity is often a hedge against being revealed as a fraud. . . . This, then, is the great secret of American manhood. *We are afraid of other men*" (35).

Susan Bordo adds yet another fear as she discusses the fragility of masculinity. Men tend to identify their masculinity with their penises, and the problem is that the penis is not a wholly reliable organ. While the cultural phallus is a symbol of power and authority, "the penis haunts the phallus," as she puts it so well (Bordo 1999, 95). The penis can test the man and fail him. Always being tested to prove his manhood.

The most recent collection of interviews we have on the Boy Code and the Guy Code (Orenstein 2020) confirms the continued presence of the codes and the ways a boy's friendship group enforces the codes. Peggy Orenstein interviewed more than one hundred boys over two years, boys aged sixteen to twenty-two, and the boys' description of "the ideal man" sounds a lot like the codes described by Pollack and Kimmel (Orenstein 2020, 11), especially the rule that a boy should not show emotions, other than anger. Time and again the boys Orenstein interviewed used the metaphor of the "wall" the boy had to erect to separate his public performance from his private feelings (15). Boys often pointed to their fathers as the "primary source of restrictive messages about masculinity" (12). Boys long for what Orenstein calls "emodiversity" (16).

What Orenstein has to say about "boys and sex" in her aptly titled book *Boys & Sex* (2020) largely describes the "jock culture" and "bro culture" that leads not only to the suppression of emotions, misogyny, and homophobia but also to the tendency of adolescent boys to brag about their sexual "conquests" with girls. Those observations are less useful for my analysis of boys' snapshots of boys, but boys' sexuality does deserve my attention as an ever-present reality in the lives of pubescent and adolescent boys, a biological reality that gets shaped by cultural norms but never goes away. From a scientific point of view, these boys ages ten to twenty-four are at the height of their sexual drives, and it would be very strange if the snapshots did not address these drives, albeit in a displaced way. So I turn now to a brief description of adolescent male sexuality, privileging the individual's experience, emotions, and accompanying feelings, and paying less attention to the actual behavior, which will not show up in snapshots in any case.

Boys' Sexuality

Arbitrarily taking age ten as the beginning of boyhood for my inquiry into the visual autoethnography by boys finds the youngest just entering puberty. Even the books designed to explain the changes in puberty adopt titles reflecting the puzzlement and anxiety felt by boys, from the physical changes in their bodies to the new feelings that sweep over them. The boys and girls in Figure 1.1 are teens, and the snapshot nicely captures both the typical separation of boys from girls in gatherings during puberty and early adolescence but also captures the gaze of the boys at the bodies of the girls.

Hall devotes considerable attention to the biological changes in the boy's body in *Adolescence* (1904). The first volume describes in detail all the anatomical, physiological, and endocrinological developments as a boy enters puberty. Those details provide a context for his interest in the emotional lives of boys, both the positive elements (e.g., religious feelings) and the antisocial ones (e.g., juvenile delinquency).

The title of chapter 6 in the first volume, "Sexual Development: Its Dangers and Hygiene in Boys," reflects the general nervousness felt by American adults about adolescent males at the turn of the century. I write some about this "moral panic" in *On My Honor* (2001), about the "boy problem" and anxiety about urban, unsocialized, often lower-class and immigrant boys

Figure 1.1

"prowling" the streets of American cities like packs of wild animals (Forbush 1902; Gibson 1922). The men who created organizations to deal with "the boy problem"—notably the Boy Scouts of America, founded in 1910—knew of Hall's work and attempted to use its ideas to steer the adolescent boy toward socially constructive behavior and away from delinquency and crime.

For a scientist, Hall held a very romantic view of male sexuality. I could quote many passages from this chapter, but this much will do: "The *vita sexualis* is normally a magnificent symphony, the rich and varied orchestration of which brings the individual into the closest *rapport* with the larger life of the great Biologos, and without which his life would be a mere film and shadow" (Hall 1904, 1:413). The word "normally" in that sentence tips off Hall's worry, for he understands that boys experience spontaneous ejaculation early in adolescence and that the pleasant feelings associated with the orgasm often lead the boy to the "dangerous" habit of masturbation, of "self-abuse."

Hall writes about masturbation at a time when the religious reasons for condemning the habit were slowly giving way to a less moralistic, more scientific view, but still one cautioning boys to avoid the habit (Laqueur 2003; van Driel 2012). Mixing his scientific and religious understanding of adolescence, Hall writes, "One of the saddest of all the aspects of human weakness and sin is onanism" (Hall 1904, 1:432). He calls the habit of masturbation "evil" and a "perversion." He acknowledges that even children masturbate and that it is most common in early puberty, from ages twelve to fourteen (Hall 1904, 1:435). Hall proceeds to describe the habit and possible medical and nonmedical ways to discourage it. In short, Hall recognizes that the spontaneous emissions of semen cannot be easily controlled but that adults should take every measure possible to discourage masturbation, conveying to the boy that the "proper" use of the penis and its discharge is in sexual relations in marriage, sex aimed at producing children.

"Enlightened" adults who worked with boys in those first decades of the twentieth century did not shy from explicit talk about "self-abuse." Even the early handbooks for Boy Scouts and Scoutmasters address the issue (Mechling 2001, 189–92). Once the adolescent boy was "discovered" in 1904 and a nascent field of "boyology" developed (Gibson 1922; Kidd 2004), it seems that youth workers well understood the strong sexual instincts boys experience and worked on ways to create programs to sublimate that libidinal energy. In some ways the adults working with boys still see the boy's sexual impulses as a "problem." The Scoutmaster of the troop I studied (1976–1995) did not want to facilitate joint activities with a troop of Girl Scouts camping by the same lake, because he considered girls a distraction for the boys (Mechling 2001, 93–94). Since then, the Boy Scouts finally (February 2019) welcomed female youth into the movement, renaming the organization Scouts BSA (and, more recently, Scouting America). Whether the Scoutmaster of the troop I studied was right that the mixing of adolescent boys and girls in the same youth movement is a bad idea is something many are waiting to see.

The onset of male puberty, the bodily changes described by Hall and by subsequent experts, varies in timing; some boys start later than others, but in general the changes begin around age twelve, so most of the boys in these snapshots and most of the boys taking the snapshots have been experiencing the biological changes and the emotional changes that accompany the flood of hormones. Adolescent boys think often about sex and often experience unwanted erections.

Boys think about these changes even if they do not talk about them with others, even with peers, though boys often will talk with their peers about their sexual desire for girls and might even describe real or fantasy experiences of intercourse with girls. Since in most cases girls enter puberty earlier than boys, boys at age twelve often show interest in the developing girls. In my fieldwork with the Boy Scout troop in the 1980s, I heard boys talking at night after lights-out about girls they knew in their schools, talk that also signaled some curiosity about menstruation (Mechling 2001, 25).

Boys who experience sexual feelings toward other boys usually do not talk about those feelings with their male peers, given the strong cultural norms favoring heterosexuality, norms that are changing, but norms certainly strong during the years most of these snapshots were taken.

Curiosity about sex often leads boys to seek out images of naked people and of sexual behavior, and the curiosity often leads to experimentation, including masturbation and even sexual play with girls and boys. Folklorists who study the play of adolescents, for example, find games that either have explicit sexual content and goals or mask sexual content and goals. A mixed-sex party among teens often provides a play frame for kissing, hugging, and "making out." Spin the bottle is the tamest version of such games, while seven minutes in heaven sends a boy and a girl into a dark closet for seven minutes to do whatever they want out of view from their peers. Sutton-Smith (1959) and Tucker (2008) examine adolescent kissing games, and find that older adolescents, even college students, play games like strip poker and truth or dare, games meant to either get the players naked or get the players to reveal secrets about their sex lives.

Boys experience the biological and emotional changes with puberty before they are cognitively and emotionally prepared to make wise decisions about their sex drives. They understand norms of behavior voiced by adults, including (in some families) religious injunctions against nudity, masturbation, and sexual intercourse. All those injunctions aim to dampen the behavior stemming from the hormonal storm occurring in the adolescent male body, but they have little chance of extinguishing the emotions and feelings.

The reader might wonder why I have recounted these experiences in puberty and adolescence, feelings and experiences the audience for this book can recount from their own youth. Boys do not capture in snapshots internal sexual desire or even sexual behavior, though the advent of digital photography and video with smartphones probably has changed that lack of a visual record of sexual behavior. Neither do the snapshots capture sex talk among peers. At best, as in the snapshot placed at the head of this section on boys' sexuality, the photographs can give us a glimpse of the "male gaze" at females.

I have reminded us of the stormy, sexual experiences of male puberty and adolescence because that is the ever-present reality that helps drive and energize the patterns of behavior in the adolescent male friendship group, the boy's folk group. The snapshots examined here capture the customary behavior boys actively construct in order to enact and, if necessary, repair their friendship. Male friendship, which I discuss at length in chapter 2, has erotic dimensions when the bonds are strong. Boys experience strong emotional attachments to friends, especially to "best friends," and in order to abide by cultural norms of heterosexual masculinity, boys must come to understand their strong, emotional feelings of attachment to a male friend as friendship and not sexual desire. Some boys actually understand their attachments to other boys as sexual, but in any case what we see in the snapshots are the ways boys use their customs and play in order to enjoy the nonsexual, erotic attachment to friends under the mask of play.

I describe this pattern in male snapshots in my book *Soldier Snapshots* (Mechling 2021), snapshots that picture males the age of or not much older than the boys in the snapshots I analyze here. There are plenty of snapshots of soldiers (and marines, and sailors, and aviators) embracing each other as physical gestures of friendship, but I came to realize that the snapshots that best reveal the emotions and feelings of close friendships the warriors experienced were of the soldiers at play. I bring to this study of boys' picturing boys that same insight.

Finally, the foregoing discussion of male sexual drives and desires in puberty and adolescence sets up my use of depth psychology, notably psychoanalytic theory, especially as feminist scholars of gender have modified and elaborated classic psychoanalytic theory. Freud's "theory of infantile sexuality" is a crucial starting point for understanding male adolescence (Erikson 1963 [1950], 43–102), and in the "excursus" between this chapter and the next, I rely heavily on Erikson's writing.

What Fieldwork with Boys Tells Us

Pollack discusses the Boy Code from his perspective as a therapist, Kimmel lays out the Guy Code from his experience as a sociologist who has interviewed many young men, and Orenstein adds to the testimony with her interviews with adolescent boys. Orenstein muses a bit on whether the boys are editing their comments because she is a woman, but the continuity between the findings of Pollack, Kimmel, and Orenstein gives us some confidence that the boys are telling Orenstein pretty much what they told the two male interviewers.

I mentioned earlier that the evidence of the everyday lives of boys I trust most is based on ethnographic fieldwork among boys in their natural settings. I consult other ethnographies of boys, but I also rely heavily on my own firsthand experience. That fieldwork experience began in my youth, as a Cub Scout and then a Boy Scout. My scholarly fieldwork, which resulted in several publications, including my 2001 book, lasted from 1976 to 1997. Then, from

2007 to 2012, I was a volunteer leader for my grandson's California troop (not the troop I studied for the book), and I attended several campouts and five weeklong summer camps in Northern and Southern California. That gave me another five years of close observation of adolescent boys at Scout camp.

Based on my reading of ethnographies of the friendship groups of pubescent and adolescent boys and on my own experiences, I think the tenets of Pollack's Boy Code and Kimmel's elaboration of that code as practiced and policed by older adolescents and young men miss some nuances in the actual practices of pubescent and adolescent boys in the US. I am prepared to modify the elements of the code and to provide my own list of the elements of the second nature of boys, at least of American boys. A good deal of my thinking about these elements stems from my thinking about hazing and initiations in this age group (Mechling 2008c; Mechling 2009; Delfino and Mechling 2017), and I explicitly examine hazing among the tests of masculinity in chapter 6.

The more I examine the Boy Code and the Guy Code and consult the ethnographic record to compare the codes with the actual practices within the boys' friendship group, their folk group, the more I see discrepancies. True, the Boy Code identifies the very public forces ("imperatives," Pollack calls them) boys are exposed to in the public culture of words and images defining a normative performance of masculinity. The ethnographies seem to capture changes, even resistances, over time. The messages to boys turn out to be complex and often in conflict. Let me explain what I mean.

The first "imperative" of the Boy Code, in Pollack's view, is the "sturdy oak," the imperative that males be "stoic, stable and independent" (Pollack 1998, 23–24). "Taking it like a man" is the shorthand for this injunction, and there is no doubt that boys see and hear this message in a great deal of the popular culture they consume and in the comments by adults and even peers in organized sports (Messner 2002). On the other hand, fieldwork with boys in their folk groups often reveals the experience of some boys that the friendship group is a refuge from precisely that injunction.

Way's (2011) portrait of boys' friendships across ethnic groups is based on her two decades' experience as a high school counselor and then as a researcher in developmental psychology, and the portrait fits well my experience with fieldwork with boys aged twelve to eighteen. Way nicely summarizes the conclusion she draws from her close look at boys' friendships with reference to two well-known popular culture texts. The vast majority "of the hundreds of boys whom my research team and I have interviewed from early to late adolescence," she writes, "suggest that their closest friendships share the plot of *Love Story* more than the plot of *Lord of the Flies*" (2–3). Put differently, her research shows that "boys are both having and wanting intimate male friendships" (7). Moreover, some scholars in masculinity studies (Gray 1989; Cole 2003) distinguish male "friendship" from male "comradeship," the former term describing the intimate bond between two friends and the latter term describing the bonds between male members of the larger group, a distinction first made in the study of male friendships in the military and then extended to other male friendship groups (Mechling 2021).

The "sturdy oak" injunction aimed at the boy suggests that the boy's performance of masculinity varies considerably according to the audience. Outside the friendship group, the boy well might attempt to portray himself in a stoic, independent way, all the time also valuing the "softness" and dependence he enjoys in the male friendship, a respite from the demands of tough, aggressive masculinity.

The second "imperative" of the Boy Code elaborated by Pollack is "give 'em hell," an injunction to show "extreme daring, bravado, and attraction to violence" (Pollack 1998, 24). Fieldwork with boys provides plenty of evidence of these behaviors, and the snapshots I examine in chapter six illustrate the sort of bravado boys show in accepting "tests" of their masculinity. Boys' friendship groups might not expect the boy to pass the tests, though. Raphael (1988), surveying initiation male initiation practices across cultures, offers the surprising view that initiates almost never fail the test so often a part of the hazing and initiation. In the case of American male initiations, I think the low failure rate may be due to a paradox in the culture of the fratriarchy. Boys like to test each other to see who can "take it like a man," but the other driving force in the group is male friendship, and I think a boy can be as welcome in a group for having qualities other than "bravado" and a propensity for violence.

The third imperative of the Boy Code Pollack turns to, "the big wheel," is the injunction for boys to seek and value "status, dominance, and power" (Pollack 1998, 24), also an imperative that does not quite capture the realities within the boys' friendship group. The problem I have with this injunction is a generalization suggested by the Sapolsky lessons from primatology and evolutionary psychology—namely, that boys are most comfortable when they understand their niche in the friendship group, and those niches often have nothing to do with power and dominance. Boys bring several defining qualities of their identities to the friendship group. Boys know who is the strongest, who is the best athlete, but also who is the smartest (school), who is the funniest, who is the most clever, who is the kindest, who is the most generous, who has the most artistic talent, and so on. Again, what the ethnography shows us is that boys often see their friendships and comradeships as safe harbors from the stark imperatives of the Boy Code.

The last imperative of the Boy Code that Pollack addresses is "no sissy stuff," the injunction to avoid feelings that the society associates with females, feelings such as "dependence, warmth, empathy" (Pollack 1998, 24). Way's research, as I have indicated already, distinguishes the public injunction from the private reality of close male friendships that are indistinguishable from the stereotypical female friendship.

The title of Way's book, *Deep Secrets* (2011), describes the male friendships she and her research colleagues find between boys in early and middle adolescence, starting with the onset of puberty and lasting until age fifteen or sixteen. Boys in that age group, across ethnic groups, told researchers that what they valued most in their relationships with their best friends was *trust*. They could tell those friends anything and everything, including secrets. Those friendships were a safe harbor from the larger group that might enforce the Boy Code. The boys reported that they could be emotionally vulnerable with those best friends, sharing feelings they might be embarrassed to display to the others in the group. The importance of trust means, also, that the boys carry a fear of betrayal (99).

Recall that an important necessary condition for the play frame to work is trust. Playfighting and verbal teasing, for example, make the player vulnerable. Entering a play frame implicitly signals to the participants that their relationship is one of trust.

Sadly, says Way, many boys lose those special male friendships in late adolescence. Within the Boy Scouts the joke among adult leaders is that at age sixteen, when the boy enters high school, he often drifts away from Scouting and those male friendships, succumbing to "the fumes," which means gasoline fumes and perfumes. For the boys interviewed in Way's study, there were various causes of the loss of those special friendships. Friends moved away, started having girlfriends, spent most of their time in sports, and so on. Boys experience a deeply felt loss when the close friend drifts away, and Way suggests that the problems faced by boys in late adolescence, including substance abuse, depression, declining success at school, and even suicide, can be traced back to the loss of a trusted friend (2011, 184–85). In defense of the emotional hurt, those older boys declare that they "don't care"; but, of course, they do (194).

In my own life I experienced precisely the pattern Way charts. From age eight I was actively involved with Scouting and loved it. Aside from school, much of my time in early and middle adolescence was consumed by Scouting and the friends I made there. I was a camper and then counselor at the South Florida Boy Scout Camp in Sebring, making many friends in that role. I earned the rank of Eagle Scout in December of 1959, at age fourteen, and at age sixteen I expected to continue my engagement with Scouts. At the suggestion of a high school friend, I signed up to take a debate class my junior year (age sixteen), and debate seduced me away from Scouting. It was also that year that I had my first serious girlfriend (also in debate), so in retrospect my late adolescence followed precisely the pattern Way describes, including the grief I felt (but could not articulate) at the loss of my life in Scouts and those close friendships. Way's discovery of the intense "feelings" many boys discover in their close friendships primes us to be alert to the ways the snapshots boys take in their friendship groups reveal a world often very different from the one we would expect from the public injunctions of the Boy Code and the Guy Code.

The Resistance

Clearly, the Boy Code and then the Guy Code do not tell the whole story about how boys experience the construction, performance, and repair of masculinity in their friendship groups. The ethnographic evidence of boys' lives in their friendship groups both describes the codes and shows how the boys resist the codes, seeing their friendship group as a haven from the rigors of the code. As I show in the following chapters, the snapshots give us a glimpse of both the presence of the codes and the boys' resistance.

Sadly, moral panic about adult sexual exploitation of minors, a panic not without good cause, has made it increasingly difficult for folklorists, sociologists, and anthropologists to study children and adolescents in their "natural" settings, not in psychology labs, not in therapy sessions, and not in counseling sessions. Some intrepid ethnographers go through the elaborate procedures of getting permission to study children and adolescents in their natural settings, and many folklorists have resorted to studying their own children. This trend makes all the more valuable the use of autoethnography by children and youth, including visual autoethnography.

Male Adolescence and Identity

Nancy J. Chodorow's *The Reproduction of Mothering: Psychoanalysis and the Sociology of Gender* (1978) is an important book in masculinity studies, and her most recent book, *The Psychoanalytic Ear and the Sociological Eye* (2020), skillfully brings together the two fields—psychoanalysis and sociology—in which she is trained. Recall that in my introduction I described my version of Burke's pentad and noted that the only element that cannot be directly observed and described is motive for the practice. That is why we must turn to depth psychology for help in inferring motive. Chodorow's thoughtful bringing together the insights from depth psychology and the insights from symbolic anthropology and sociology helps revive the tradition of culture-and-personality studies that began in the 1930s and 1940s, when psychoanalytic theory permeated anthropology.

Reading her newest book (Chodorow 2020, 2), I was struck by her comment that she was "swept away in [her] earliest college years by *Childhood and Society* (Erikson 1963 [1950]) and *Patterns of Culture* (Benedict 1934)." Taking a course, "American National Character," in my junior year (1965–1966) I also encountered Erikson's *Childhood and Society* and several of the anthropological works in culture-and-personality, including Benedict's famous book cited by Chodorow. From that point on, one way or the other, I was always studying the lives of children and puzzling through the ways children internalize culture, but also how children project their unique psychic experiences into the shared world of social relations and cultural patterns of behavior. Chodorow values Erikson's work because he works incessantly trying to understand how the individual child's experience moves from internalization to externalization and back into internalization, a dialectic Berger and Luckmann (1967) chart in their sociology of knowledge.

Chodorow names the blending of ego psychology and the interpersonal, cultural school of psychoanalytic theory "intersubjective ego psychology" and considers this approach a distinctive "strand in American thinking" (Chodorow 2020, 3), which appeals to my American studies mind and comports with my view that the line of social theorists working in "the Pragmatic attitude" from William James to the present all share an orientation that puts the individual's experience at the center of the analysis of social interaction and cultural customs.

Following Chodorow's claim that Erikson's intersubjective ego psychology provides a solution to the puzzle of internal and external realities, I shall provide here a sketch of Erikson's approach and of how I see his ideas as helpful in forging a thick description of the snapshots in this book. Lest the reader think that Erikson is no longer applicable to understanding male adolescent lives, I note that there is a revived interest in Erikson in the study of self and society (Schachter and Galliher 2018).

Childhood and Society (1950)

While Erikson writes about both male and female children and adolescents, often (like Freud) describing at length a therapeutic case from his own practice, much of what he has to say is especially relevant to our understanding of boys and young men. Erikson belongs to the school of psychoanalytic thinking called "ego psychology," the ego being "a concept denoting man's capacity to unify his experience and his action in an adaptive manner" (1963 [1950], 13). Those familiar with Freud's map of the psyche recognize that the ego mediates between the instinct-driven id and the strong social norms of the superego. While the superego enforces strict control of the libidinal id, the ego also relies upon society but not the punitive elements we find in the superego. This sketch grossly simplifies the id-ego-superego dynamic, but for our purposes it is important to realize that the ego serves the individual, not the society, but it serves the individual in ways meant to make the individual a mentally healthy, autonomous actor who can interact in society in ways making the individual happy. The road to a healthy, happy, autonomous individual often faces conflicts, among them the conflicting demands of the id and the superego. The goal of the psychoanalyst in therapy is to help the individual strengthen the ego, but from the viewpoint of the anthropologist or the sociologist or the folklorist, the individual's close social group

invents traditional practices (customs) that can also have therapeutic value
for the ego, apart from formal therapeutic treatment. That principle governs
the approach Wallis and I take in *PTSD and Folk Therapy* (2019), where we
show how folk practices in the military male friendship group in the combat
zone offer the individual early, informal therapy for the symptoms of trauma
related to combat.

Erikson introduces in *Childhood and Society* (1963 [1950]) one of the ideas
he is most famous for, the idea that the individual's life cycle can be understood as a succession of eight stages (239–65). Before discussing those eight
stages, with special attention to the fifth stage, "puberty and adolescence"
for the purposes of the study of boys' snapshots of boys, I should explain the
"theory of infantile sexuality" that underlies the scheme.

Famously (or infamously), Freud introduced to the world the idea that
even infants have sexual forces at work in their lives and psyches, and when
anthropologists worked to fashion an approach to "culture and personality"
in the 1930s and 1940s, many were enough under the influence of psychoanalytic theory that they looked to the socialization of bodily systems—oral,
anal, genital—as the genesis of personality traits. When parents (especially
mothers) socialize, that is, control, those bodily zones, they are usually invok-
ing societal norms and methods, which vary considerably across time and
cultures. All infants are weaned, eventually, but there is enormous variation
in the customary ages and means by which children are weaned. So, too, the
socialization of the anal and genital zones varies by culture. There emerged
among the culture-and-personality crowd the idea that "patterns" of child-
rearing lead to patterns in the adult personalities in the society. The study of
"national character" in the 1930s and well into the 1960s (recall that I read
Childhood and Society in a course on American national character in 1965)
assumed that in the patterns of the socialization of children in a society lay
the formation of adult national character.

This theory of infantile sexuality permeates Erikson's scheme of the "eight
ages of man." He presents the scheme in *Childhood and Society* (chapter 7,
239–66) and then elaborates the scheme in his 1968 book *Identity: Youth and
Crisis*. In each stage the ego must struggle with a characteristic binary. In the
first stage, the "oral-sensory," the dominant issue to solve is "basic trust v.
mistrust." In the second stage, the "muscular-anal," the binary is "autonomy v.
shame and doubt." In the third stage, the "locomotor-genital" stage, the binary
is "initiative v. guilt." In the fourth stage, "latency," the issues are "industry
v. inferiority." In stage 5, "puberty and adolescence," the one most relevant
to my study, the binary is "identity v. role confusion." And on through the
remaining stages of life, from young adulthood to adulthood to maturity.

It is now time for a deep dive into "identity v. role confusion."

Between Hall's 1904 description of male puberty and adolescence and Erikson's analysis, both in *Childhood and Society* (1963 [1950]) and then in greater detail in *Identity: Youth and Crisis* (1968), those who write about male adolescence invariably describe that stage in a young man's life as full of "sturm und drang," storm and stress. The biological realities and the hormonal aspects of puberty and adolescence create a precarious period for the boy. "The adolescent mind," writes Erikson, "is essentially a mind of the moratorium, a psychosexual stage between childhood and adulthood" (1963 [1950], 254). In this liminal stage between childhood and adulthood, young men "are now primarily concerned with what they appear to be in the eyes of others as compared with what they feel they are" (253). The young man's sense of "ego identity, then, is the accrued confidence that the inner sameness and continuity of one's meaning for others" defines the self (253). When the construction of this ego identity fails, the result is "ego confusion," including confusion about sexual identity (253).

Like Hall before him, Erikson recognizes the important role of "falling in love," "which is by no means entirely, or even primarily, a sexual matter. . . . To a considerable extent adolescent love is an attempt to arrive at a definition of one's identity by projecting one's diffused ego-image on another and by seeing it thus reflected and gradually clarified. That is why so much of young love is conversation" (1963 [1950], 253–54).

If we take "conversation" in that passage to include not just oral communication but communication through action, especially play and ritual in the adolescent friendship group, then we should look for signs of nonsexual "adolescent love" in the snapshots. Erikson's crucial point is that adolescent male friendship involves a (usually) nonsexual "falling in love" with the male friend, that the young man projects his own ego-identity upon the friend, and the friend projects his own identity back upon the young man in a complex dialectic of projection and interpretation. This dynamic is why the young man relies upon his peer group and, especially, on his "best friends" for his management of his own ego identity. Calling the close male bonding in those friendships "love" correctly conveys the emotions and feelings experienced in the friendship. Contrary to the injunctions of the Boy Code and the Guy Code to avoid emotions usually associated with females, young men openly express love in their close friendships and, as Way (2011) notes, boys suffer considerable grief at the loss of the close friendships. I elaborate these ideas in my next chapter on male friendship, but it is important here to acknowledge how clearly Erikson sees the role of male adolescent love in the male friendship group. Once you look for it, you can find signs of that love in the snapshots boys take of boys and men take of men (Mechling 2021).

Identity: Youth and Crisis (1968)

In 1968 Erikson gathered and revised essays he had published in the previous twenty years in order to focus more closely than he had in 1950 on the identity crisis typical in adolescence. Chodorow can make her claim that Erikson works "in the pragmatic attitude" because Erikson places himself there. In the prologue to *Identity* (1968), Erikson sees Freud and James as the two "bearded and patriarchal founding fathers of the psychologies on which our thinking on identity is based" (19).

What was happening in youth cultures in the US in 1968 is noteworthy. Examples of the very public "youth revolution" of the sixties permeate Erikson's discussion of the conflicts facing American adolescents.

When Erikson writes that the psychoanalytic approach needs to consider the "environment" in the construction of identity, his examples suggest that he has in mind some large aspects of history and social structure, such as the onset of technologies and social structures, such as systemic heteronormativity and systemic racism. He also means the smaller social structures, such as the family we are born into, and the increasingly larger social structures as we experience a circle of friends.

It would take this book in a different direction if I attempted to account for the snapshots of any period with reference to the large social and economic forces that are the context for identities and identity crisis of adolescents. I have no doubt, for example, that American boys' snapshots from the 1930s (I choose that decade because that is the decade for the Hitler Youth snapshots I analyze in chapter 8) reflect the anxieties boys experience in their own families and in the larger cultural discourses about the Great Depression. What is less clear to me is how a snapshot might reflect the boys' anxieties, given the fact that the snapshots actually show boys' moments of *escape from* the anxieties of everyday life. If anything, the snapshots attest to the therapeutic value of experiences in the male friendship group.

Put differently, in my experience the attention to external realities of history, technology, and ideology that Erikson pursues in understanding the social contexts for the externalization of internal, individual realties is not necessary for analyzing the snapshots boys take of boys. Rather, our clearest understanding of what we see in the snapshots and our guess at the motivation of the boy taking the snapshot examines the "communal" contribution to the boy's ego identity by the boy's male friendship group, and the nature of the folk culture of those friendship groups seems not to have changed much over the eras of the snapshots. Erikson makes this clear in his prologue to *Identity: Youth in Crisis*: "In psychological terms, identity formation employs a process of simultaneous reflection and observation, a process taking place on all levels of mental functioning, by which the individual judges himself in the light of what he perceives to be the way in which others judge him in comparison to themselves and to a typology significant to them; while he judges their way of judging him in the light of how he perceives himself in comparison to them and to types that have become relevant to him" (22–23).

The boy and his male friends thus are engaged in an endless process of interpreting their own and their peers' behavior as that behavior provides clues to the identity of each boy. Those identities are both stable and malleable. Boys compare themselves with the other boys. The maturing process of moving from childhood through puberty to adolescence presents the boy with changes. His body changes, his confidence changes, his sense of his skills and his shortcomings changes, and more. Boys find their niche in the friendship group, though that can change too.

We should not miss the importance of the body, both the boy's body and the girl's body, in the formation of adolescent ego identities. The hormonal changes and physical changes in puberty and then into adolescence make it impossible for adolescents to ignore their bodies in relation to their identities. Chodorow notes how important the girl's body has become in feminist understandings of female adolescence (Chodorow 2020, 4), and we shall see in the snapshots in this book that the boy's body lies at the nexus between his personal experience of himself as "having a body" and his active use of his body as a dramatic prop in his performance of masculinity and friendship.

Boys observe the bodies of their friends, comparing their own bodies with the bodies of their peers. This is one aspect of the symmetrical "judging" of one another I quoted in the passage from Erikson, above, as boys judge their own bodies in comparison with ideal male body types (drawn from mass-mediated, popular culture) and in comparison with their male friends.

Using the psychoanalytic terms favored by Erikson and by Chodorow, the boy projects into the life of the male friendship group his own internal reality, his own identity, and he introjects the dynamics of the friendship group into his identity. As documents of the male friendship group and the "communal" external reality that groups create together, the snapshots provide a window into the transference Erikson and Chodorow find at the center of a communal ego psychology.

Feelings

Finally, I want to highlight a point Chodorow makes in her 1999 book *The Power of Feelings*, namely, that "we create unconscious personal meaning in the experiential immediacy of the present" (1), a sentence that easily could have been penned by William James a hundred years earlier. This is the "theory of meaning" Chodorow draws from Erikson and from the Pragmatic tradition he belongs to. The meaning of personal experiences "combines the individually idiosyncratic and the cultural" and is "situated and emergent in particular encounters and particular psychic moments for the individual" (2). Another sentence James could have written. This approach to understanding the meanings of an experience to the individual "tells us why we feel deeply about certain things, certain experiences, and certain people and why these powerful feelings are part of a meaningful life" (2). The power of feelings.

Moreover, "our emotions are not raw, psychological affects but *feelings with stories*—about our self, our body, the other and the other's body, about self with other, and so forth" (Chodorow 2020, 252). A snapshot captures a split second, but that moment is a piece of a story, and you will find that when I examine individual snapshots, I also speculate on the "story" that contextualizes that moment. If snapshots convey anything about the personal meanings of a boy's experience with his friends, they convey feelings. The chapters that follow rely on this hunch to "read" the snapshots for signs of the feelings that bond the boys in the friendship group.

Chapter Two

Chums

When I began reading the early popular novels written for boys with Boy Scouts as the central characters, novels published from 1910 (the founding year of the BSA) through the 1930s, I noticed that boys in the novels had friends, but their closest friends were their "chums." Later, young men used to call their best friends "buddies," a word that shows up in popular songs of the 1930s and 1940s and a word that seems apt to Ibson (2002) as he analyzes male friendship before, during, and after World War II. I often ran across use of "buddies" in my research on the vernacular photography by men in the military (Mechling 2021). Growing up in the 1950s, I think we males simply referred to our friends as "friends," even those male friends we considered our best friends. Much later, as African American vernacular language began to saturate the folk speech of young men across ethnic and class lines, young men called each other "bros" (brothers) and "homeys," close friends from the neighborhood. I like the old term "chums," especially because (as we shall see) I want to include animal friends in this chapter about male friends. A dog can be a boy's best friend, his "buddy," his "chum."

A great deal of my reading and writing about masculinity requires clear thinking about male friendship, a topic that has received lots of attention since the Greek philosophers (Denworth 2020). I shall sketch here a general understanding of the nature of male friendship between the ages of ten and twenty-six, the cohort who take the snapshots I analyze here. Male friendship pervades these snapshots, and my expectation is that the snapshots will confirm some things we think we know about boys' friendships and sometimes will surprise us.

Boys' Friendships

Niobe Way's 2011 book *Deep Secrets: Boys' Friendships and the Crisis of Connection*, and Jacqueline Mroz's 2018 book *Girl Talk: What Science Can Tell Us about Female Friendship*, together give us enough of an interdisciplinary understanding of male friendship to "read" the snapshots. Across about thirty years as a high school counselor and then as a teacher and researcher of applied psychology and developmental psychology at New York University, Way has interviewed a great many adolescent boys across social class and ethnic lines, and her book forces us to revise the usual view of boys and their friendships.

Boys are subject to a great many narratives about boys' nature and second nature, narratives they hear from adults in their lives and in the popular, mass-mediated culture they consume. Boys are not passive consumers of the stereotypes about boys, though. "They also actively participate, resist, and challenge those cultures," she writes (Way 2011, 10). "While boys may accommodate, for example, the conventions of emotional stoicism and autonomy in their peer relations," the Boy Code and Guy Code we encountered in chapter 1, "they may also resist these conventions by having emotionally intimate male friendships" (Way 2011, 10).

That last point radically revises the older generalizations about boys' friendships. Boys, especially boys in early and middle adolescence, "have or want emotionally intimate friendships that entail shared secrets and feelings" (Way 2011, 11). In many cases, though, when a boy enters late adolescence at age sixteen or so, he begins to lose those close friends, who drift away for many reasons. Those boys, says Way, experience loss and grief when they lose those "deep" friendships, and the boy may grow to distrust close male friendships, sending them into feelings of loneliness and depression (12). I found Way's thesis helpful in understanding the nature of male friendship I "read" in the snapshots taken by soldiers, Marines, sailors, and aviators (Mechling 2021). I realized that many of the soldiers in the snapshots were, in many ways, still in late adolescence, and the strong male bonding evident in the snapshots testifies to those men's attempts to recapture their deep friendships in earlier adolescence, friendships lost and grieved. In the coda I wrote for *Soldier Snapshots*, I confessed that I finally realized that Way's thesis applied to my own experience, as I drifted away from Scouting at age sixteen and felt some pain in the loss of close male friendships there.

Reading Way's book was a great help to me in understanding the emotions (the biological state) and the feelings (the experienced state) involved with

Figure 2.1

deep male friendships and their loss, but actually the boys' snapshots of each other already put on display the emotional depth of their friendships. Boys take snapshots of friends, sometimes best friends, and the snapshot is a "souvenir" of the friendship, a memory aid about the feelings experienced between friends.

Ibson (2002) and Deitcher (2001) use the photographs in their books to write one version of the history of American male friendship, but both books rely heavily on studio portraits and other more formal, posed photographs, often ones taken by adults. The snapshots of boy friendships by boys capture the affection of boys away from adult surveillance. The two Boy Scouts in Figure 2.1, which has "July 1959" written in pen in the top margin, with evidence of a summer camp in the background, shows the affectionate pose I mean.

The boys are not posing for a picture. Snapshots convince us of the truth of the feelings in the photograph precisely because it appears as a split second in time, like the "snapshot" in hunting, a shot taken quickly. I could have used any number of snapshots to illustrate this point, so frequent are snapshots of boys clinging to one another affectionately.

Figure 2.2

Figure 2.3

Figure 2.4

At one of the high school wrestling tournaments my wife and I attended to watch our older grandson wrestle, the boys on the team took the occasion of an intermission in the action to lie about on the wrestling mat, touching each other, rolling around, playfully grabbing each other in soft forms of wrestling holds. "Look at them," my wife said. "They are like a pile of puppies." She was exactly right, and some of the snapshots in my collection record such puppy piles.

On the back of Figure 2.3, in a boy's hand, is written "HELP!" When boys get older, they call these playful piles of male bodies "dog piles," a term Wallis and I use in our discussion of male warriors' rough-and-tumble play fighting in the combat zone (Wallis and Mechling 2015; Wallis and Mechling 2019a).

Note that a boy or young man engages in rough-and-tumble play fighting with a friend or friends. The play fight, the puppy pile, affirms for the participants their relationship as friends. The fundamental paradox of the play frame (Bateson 1972) is that the messages exchanged in the frame "this is play" (the metamessage, the message about messages), messages triggered by actions, are not "real," they do not signify what they would mean outside the frame and in another frame: "This is a fight."

The violence and aggression within the play fight is stylized, not real. Young males are capable of real aggression and violence against each other, which would do damage to the solidarity of the male friendship group. Accordingly, most boys learn from an early age stylized, "pretend" aggression and violence safely enacted once the play frame is invoked. Most boys understand the distinction between real and fantasy violence, and some analysts argue that the violence in the mass media consumed by boys actually helps them understand precisely this distinction (Jones 2002).

The rough-and-tumble grappling, though, also serves other motives and meanings. We can begin with the well-established fact that we humans need to touch each other. Observations of nonhuman primates show that they are constantly grooming each other, a physical affirmation of their relationships. Some male primates will even fondle another male's penis and testicles as a gesture when making up after a fight or otherwise to confirm alliance (Wrangham and Peterson 1996; Sapolsky 1997; Kelleher 1997). Touching also has neurological consequences beyond the social communication of attachment, relationship, and hierarchy. Grooming and nonsexual touching, such as hugging, "cause your brain to release oxytocin, known as 'the bonding hormone.' This stimulates the release of other feel-good hormones, such as dopamine and serotonin, while reducing stress hormones, such as cortisol and norepinephrine" (T. Holland 2018).

Infants and mothers "know" these effects, as both take pleasure in cuddling, hugging, and otherwise touching. Psychoanalytic theory reminds us that the mother's body is the first important "object" the infant attaches itself to, an observation at the core of attachment theory and object relations theory. Cultural customs and norms differ, though, on nonsexual touching after infancy. Children have to be taught not to touch others so easily.

Boys soon learn that they are supposed to touch each other only in certain culturally approved ways. They learn to use the play frame to mask other motives, often the desire to touch other boys. We encounter here in the snapshots some of these uses of the play frame to mask the need to touch, including play fighting and building human pyramids. The most casual snapshots taken away from adult view often reveal a very affectionate touching and smile that signal the pleasure of the touch and of the male bonding with a good friend. The two snapshots in Figure 2.5 picture a group of friends at the beach, relaxing in a puppy pile and creating a human totem.

Sometimes the touching is secondary to the "goofing" with a friend or friends.

Goofing

"Goofing" is a folk term boys often use to describe their pointless play together, where the goal is not to accomplish something but simply to enjoy each other's company, often while doing something adults would consider silly. It is a wonderful word for describing what boys are doing in many of the snapshots of boys by boys. Etymologists differ some on the origins of the

Figure 2.5

Figure 2.6

word. Both English and French have old words, "goff" and "goffe," respectively, meaning "fool," which suits my use here because boys interchangeably say they are "goofing around" or "fooling around." I cannot document it, but I am pretty certain girls do not use those phrases to describe their time together. Girls do not like to think themselves a fool; boys seem to wear "foolish clown" as a badge of honor and, indeed, among the niches in the boys' friendship group is the group clown, who can make everybody laugh.

I shall let Figure 2.6 stand for a great many I could show here. The boys are touching in that snapshot, but more important is their "goofing." The following two photos—Figure 2.7, a photo booth strip, and Figure 2.8, a single frame cut from such a strip—are especially valuable examples of "goofing," because the photobooth is a place to hide from adults.

The photobooth has a long history in the US and Europe (Goranin 2008). Often placed in places of entertainment where boys gather, like game arcades, the photobooth bypasses the professional film-developing stage and the possible censorship by adults. Once inside the photobooth with the curtain closed, the boy is faced with all sorts of possibilities.

Figure 2.7

Figure 2.8

Many photobooth individual snapshots (cut from a strip) and strips of snaps are simply self-portraits alone. The more interesting ones feature two or three boys who cram into the booth to take a series of snaps. The photobooth puts together two (sometime three) people in a very small space, so the boys must feel comfortable having their bodies pressed together. Ibson (2002 and 2007) finds in the cycles of intimate touching and distance in the snapshots of men and boys clues to the attitudes about male friendship and sexuality. The men in many of the snapshots Ibson analyzes have more space to spread out in studios and other spaces, which makes more meaningful for his analysis the close, intimate physical contact between the young men. The small photobooth forces intimacy in the poses, so those images are more ambiguous for our interpretations. Adolescent boys, some still unsure about their sexual orientation, understand that their maintenance of a normative heterosexual performance of masculinity permits certain sorts of touching of other boys carefully framed as play. The close touching in the photobooth, then, does not threaten the boy's performance of normative heterosexual masculinity, because the boys understand that the photobooth is a site of play.

In both the strip (Figure 2.7) and the single frame (Figure 2.8), the boys are doing things with their hands. To just pose in the photobooth—and one can find many of these— would not count as "goofing," but the funny expressions and the hand gestures are the "fooling around."

The obscene gesture in snapshots of boys by boys deserves a closer look. The gesture, always involving the middle finger (the symbolic penis) flanked by two knuckles (the testicles) is an ancient obscene gesture in Western cultures, meaning "fuck you" and its variants. The gesture was commonly used in classical Greece and Rome and came into American usage by the late nineteenth century (Nasaw 2012). I certainly found examples to include in my book on snapshots taken by men in the military in WWII (Mechling 2021). In the case of the young soldiers making the gesture for a buddy taking the snapshot, the gesture seems to be aimed at the circumstance of being caught in a war and in a military war machine. "Fuck the suck," is a common saying among warriors, especially marines, in response to the admonition to "embrace the suck"—that is, to show the discipline necessary to get through a tough situation.

What should interest us is that the gesture can also be a gesture of friendship and male bonding. I think I first fully realized this when our older grandson, first as a teenager and then well into his twenties, commonly made the gesture when being photographed by a friend. In fact, a group of male friends (e.g., his motorcycle club) often smile for the camera and flash the finger.

The two boys in Figure 2.11 are in the midst of rough-and-tumble play fighting, when one pauses long enough to gesture obscenely at a third friend taking the snapshot. The meanings of messages are very contextual. "Shooting the bird" at someone when angry or at some circumstance, such as a war, when frustrated is an aggressive gesture and might even become an invitation to a real fight. The boys' flipping each other off in the snapshots, however, is a nonaggressive, safe gesture, because the boys make the gesture in the play frame. They are smiling. Male bonding often includes obscene gestures and words, gestures and words that would mean something very different in another frame.

Folklorists long ago collected and analyzed the ritual verbal insult games among male adolescents, a tradition first found in African American friendship groups (Abrahams 1962) but then also found in white male adolescent folk cultures (Ayoub and Barnett 1965). Snapshots do not capture the oral,

Figure 2.9

Figure 2.10

Figure 2.11

verbal culture of trading insults in the male adolescent friendship group, of course, but the snapshots of boys "flipping the bird" at each other and at a boy taking the snapshot capture a gestural version of the oral tradition.

The key to understanding how boys experience pleasure participating in obscene oral insult sessions and in making an obscene gesture is trust. In most cases people enter a play frame—especially oral or rough-and-tumble play fighting—with people they trust. Even engaging in the obscene gestures and words signals a close relationship between sender and receiver of the message. Moreover, the message "tests" the masculinity of the receiver, who must "prove" that he can "take it like a man" and give as good as he gets.

Male Bonding Side by Side

Tannen (2007) and other observers of interpersonal communication note that men and women tend to have different styles of communication when we examine their use of the gaze. Women tend to prefer face-to-face communication, reading the face of the other for signs of feelings and honesty. Research shows that girls are more adept at reading emotions on the faces of others than are boys (Mroz 2018, 39). Men tend not to communicate face-to-face with friends. In primates the direct gaze can be an aggressive, threatening gesture in males, sometimes an invitation to fight. Whatever the reason, American males tend to communicate with friends by participating in an activity side by side rather than face-to-face, often without speaking a word (Mroz 2018, 85). A father and son working on a manual project together, two or more young men sitting on a sofa playing a video game, and two young men building a fort in snow or sand can experience strong, intimate male bonding in that side-by-side activity.

This gender difference might be waning as the socialization of young women becomes more like the socialization of young men (e.g., Title IX and team sports), but we certainly see in the snapshots boys take of boys a pattern of enjoyment in doing something side by side.

Animal Chums

I devote an entire chapter of my 2021 book on the snapshots taken by men in the military to the images of those men with animals of all sorts. I shall not devote an entire chapter to animal chums here, tempting as that is, but I want to make a few important points about what the boys' snapshots of boys with animals tell us about boys' friendships.

In one respect, I could treat a boy's pet dog or other pet animal as one of the "things" he owns, but the discussion of animal chums belongs in this chapter on friendship because a pet is so much more. "A boy and his dog" is an iconic American image in advertising, films, novels, and television shows, so it is little wonder that boys and their dogs show up in so many snapshots boys take of boys. I should focus on the boys and their dogs here, and I hope to examine the relationship for its emotional depth.

All animals, but especially those we domesticate and keep as pets, are reflections of ourselves, by which I mean that humans project human emotions and motives and qualities onto all sorts of animals, whether wild or tame (Gillespie and Mechling 1987). The elaborate customs around

Figure 2.12

pet-keeping in America (Grier 2006) suggest that at times we treat pet animals as if they were human members of the group.

Wallis and I have a chapter on animal chums in our 2019 book on PTSD and the short-term therapeutic value of male folk customs, and the key point we make there, based on veterans' testimony and on Wallis's own experiences as a marine with two tours of duty in Iraq, is that caring for a "found" dog in the combat zone provides the soldier with a relationship of pure trust, a commodity both valued and easily destroyed in the male friendship group.

If a boy bonds closely with a pet dog, I believe that bonding closely resembles the male friendships Way (2011) describes in the early and middle adolescent boys she studied. Way's main interest lies in the emotional life of the boy and the special, intimate relations with a best friend or a few best friends in whose presence the boy can express feelings he is socialized to repress outside of that special friendship, feelings of vulnerability, self-doubt, and dependence incompatible with the Boy Code and the Guy Code. Trust lies at the heart of those friendships, and a breach of trust can be one of the events that destroys such a friendship.

Boys can trust their dogs, and dogs trust their boys. Love is a feeling in the mix, and young men genuinely can love one another, even expressing that love with an understanding that it is not sexual, and the boy and his dog can love one another just as intensely. Research on the effects of pets, especially dogs, on the well-being of their human chums points to many benefits, which is what makes dogs such good comfort animals, including their inclusion in some therapies for post-traumatic stress disorder (PTSD; Wallis and Mechling 2019a, 55–66). The endocrinology of pet-keeping affirms the same flood of pleasure hormones in the brain the scientists find in human friendship and touching.

Arluke and Rolfe (2013) examine photographs of humans with their cats, and they detect what they call "sentimentality signs" in the humans' expressions. Such signs are a commonplace in snapshots of boys with their dogs. In the introduction to this book I declared that snapshots are nonverbal evidence of the lives of boys beyond what we can learn from verbal evidence, and Arluke and Rolfe's findings points us toward signs of sentimentality in the boys' snapshots.

Friends and Feelings

Already I have indicated how useful I find Way's (2011) analysis of boys' friendships, but Way relies on her conversations with boys, first as a teacher and counselor and then as a researcher in developmental psychology. So all her evidence is verbal. The question I pose here for myself is whether the boys' snapshots tell us anything more about their friendships.

In "Folklore and the Emotional Brain" (Mechling 2019b), I argue that a major function of the everyday practices we call "folklore" (oral, customary, and material) is making our feelings visible to ourselves and to others. Chodorow, in her book *The Power of Feelings* (1999), highlights feelings as the key to understanding an individual's "experienced meaning," the product of the interaction of "the individually idiosyncratic and the cultural" (2). "Emotion," writes Chodorow, "is always intertwined with cognition, language, interaction, and the experience of social, physical, and cultural reality" (27; see also Damasio 1999).

Most studies of the photography of same-sex male friendship rely on photographs of men touching and embracing with some intimacy. Certainly we can infer that the men in those photographs have strong feelings of affection for one another. We rely on the "sentimentality signs" (Arluke and Rolfe 2013), primarily smiling, as clues to the feelings experienced.

Most of those interpretations, relying on body language, touch, and smiles to signal the feelings of the boys and men in the snapshots, stop with those sentimentality signs. My interpretations of the snapshots in the chapters that follow rely on those signs but also on depth psychology and the neuroscience of emotions in order to understand the unconscious forces of emotions that result in the conscious feelings of pleasure the boys are experiencing. Thus, boys are feeling emotions of close bonding and feelings of male intimacy even when they are not touching, when they are engaging in activities side by side. The culture of their male friendship group, the folk practices they import from other scenes and sometimes invent themselves, work to make visible to themselves and to their "chums" the feelings they have for each other, feelings often suppressed by the Boy Code away from the activities and places documented in the snapshots. Their folk practices often serve as ego to control their id. Put simply, there are more sentimentality signs in the snapshots, beyond touching and smiling.

Part Two

The Snapshots

Chapter Three

My Stuff

The late stand-up comic George Carlin performed in the genre called "observational comedy," featuring routines based not on jokes but on humorous observations about the absurdities of our everyday lives. His ninth comedy album, *A Place for My Stuff* (1981), includes this fragment from one of his observations about "my stuff": "That's all I want, that's all you need in life, is a little place for your stuff, ya know? I can see it on your table, everybody's got a little place for their stuff. This is my stuff, that's your stuff, that'll be his stuff over there. That's all you need in life, a little place for your stuff."

The routines from talented observational comedians are full of insights worthy of a sociologist or anthropologist or psychologist. If a goal of anthropology is "to make the strange familiar and the familiar strange," then good observational comedy amounts to good ethnography, examining everyday, taken-for-granted reality and understanding how cultural is that so-called common sense. Carlin's routine "A Place for My Stuff" is prescient for my purposes here, as he draws attention to the centrality of "our stuff" in defining us to ourselves and to others.

Around 2001 I had a student, Jesse Gelwicks, who wanted to do his senior honors thesis in American studies on his experiences working in a group home for boys, one very much like the one Horan (1988) worked in and wrote about. In both cases, Horan's in New Jersey and Gelwicks's in Northern California, the group homes housed a relatively small number of boys "at risk" and served as an alternative to incarcerating the boys or to placing each alone in foster care. The counselors working with them tended to be college-age men with an interest in the sort of social work with boys that the homes represented.

Gelwicks had read Horan's work and other ethnographies of children, so much of the resulting senior thesis and a published paper (Gelwicks 2002) described and analyzed the culture of the group home, paying attention to the fact that there really were three cultures in the home—the folk culture the boys created for themselves, the staff culture, and the culture that emerged at the borders between the boy culture and the staff culture. Gelwicks wanted to add another ethnographic method Horan had not used—photoelicitation with snapshots taken by the boys (approved by the supervisor of the home). Gelwicks bought each of the seven boys a disposable camera. "I explained the project to the boys in short information sessions right before giving them the disposable cameras," he writes. "They were told to focus on 'stuff,' not people, but they could include people as they saw fit. I asked them to take photographs of the things they felt were important to them" (Gelwicks 2002, 78). He gave them no other instructions about what pictures to take, and when a boy finished the roll of film in the camera, he returned it to Gelwicks to have developed. Gelwicks had two sets of prints made from each roll; one set he put into a small album for the boy to keep, and the other set he kept himself. He would sit down with a boy and have the boy show him the snapshots and talk about them.

Gelwicks asked the boys to take snapshots of the "stuff" that was important to them. He believed that his constant observation (over eleven months) provided lots of evidence of how the boys managed their social relations with each other and with staff members. His (and my) hope was that a focus on the things, the objects important to each boy, would provide new insights into how each boy was negotiating a difficult social and psychological set of circumstances of everyday life.

Horan observed that boys in the home he studied used objects as props in their negotiating relationships. Having some objects (like cigarettes) and sharing or not sharing those objects with others turned out to be crucial gestures in negotiating the power relations within the boys' folk culture, a culture where potential violence between the boys was always a possibility. Gelwicks was eager to see how the boys in his group home used their few possessions to manage their social relationships, including their place in the power hierarchy. As we learned in chapter 1 from Sapolsky's discussion of the tendency of male primates in groups to establish power hierarchies, boys find it comfortable to know their individual places in the power hierarchy of the friendship group.

Gelwicks found a lot of diversity in the objects the boys chose to photograph, from a dead rat to toys and bicycles and posters on the walls of the boys' rooms. One particular case echoes Horan's findings. One boy,

Nicholas (not real names) in Gelwicks's study took a picture of another boy's, Jake's, Pokémon Gameboy. Gelwicks observes that Jake had taken Nicholas "under his wing" when Nicholas arrived at the home. "For Nicholas," writes Gelwicks, "the game may have had a double importance; it is fun to play, everyone likes playing it, and it also symbolizes his friendship or at least connection with Jake, the most powerful boy in the house" (Gelwicks 2002, 81). Other photographs by boys confirmed for Gelwicks that many boys used objects to cement their friendship with Jake, the "strongest and toughest" boy in the home. Some of the boys also took pictures of themselves or had another take the picture and would carry the self-portrait with them most of the time, proof that they "exist" (Gelwicks 2002, 83).

In those few examples lie some of the themes key in the functions of "stuff" in the snapshots boys take of boys. They took snapshots of objects meaningful to them but also of objects they saw as crucial in negotiating relationships, even friendships, within the group. Much of the folklore of boys in their friendship groups can be understood by looking at how they play with power (Mechling 1986). And we should not miss the point in both the Gelwicks and Horan ethnographies that using objects to exercise power helps avoid the use of force, violence, within the group.

Of course, the circumstances creating the snapshots I present and analyze here differ from the common uses of photoelicitation used by folklorists, anthropologists, sociologists, psychologists, social workers, and others who use the method to elicit testimony from children about their lives. Cindy Clark (1999) has used the method several times in her work with children and teens, and she adopts the term "autodriving" (used in marketing research) to describe her work. In fact, autodriving (letting the person who is being interviewed "drive" the interview) with photographs is a method commonly used in medical interviews, especially with children.

The snapshots in this book were not taken by boys at the direction of an adult with power, implicit or explicit, over the boys. Nor is it likely that the boy photographer showed the snapshots to a parent or other adult and discussed the snapshot with the adult. Without verbal testimony from the boys taking these snapshots and appearing in them about the motives and meanings, we are forced to construct those motives and meanings ourselves. Folklorists and other scholars interested in the everyday lives of children have turned to their "material culture" for evidence, so let us start there.

Boys' Things

Observational evidence, confirmed by the photographic record of the everyday lives of boys, suggests that we can lump boys' "things," the material objects in their world, into two categories: commercial toys and folk toys, the second category encompassing "playthings," by which I mean material objects we would not normally think of as toys, but boys play with them.

There is a considerable amount of scholarship on commercial toys (e.g., Sutton-Smith 1986; Kline 1993; Cross 1997), though most of the historians and social scientists who write about commercial toys use the toys as evidence of larger cultural practices and patterns, including topics ranging from gift-giving traditions to the reification of gender in the toys to the linkage between television programming for children and toys themed to the television stories. The history of advertising toys, for example, provides clues to historical changes in adult thinking about children, but evidence of adults' ideas about children (including the nature of boys) is not evidence of the behavior of boys or their inner states, any more than adult photographs of children are evidence of how children experience their worlds.

The solution to that problem of understanding what commercial toys mean to boys is to observe directly how boys play with toys or, as Sutton-Smith (1986) does, collect from children their *stories* about toys. I most trust ethnographic observations of play with toys in what social scientists would call their "natural settings": not settings created by and surveilled by adults (e.g., classrooms, social science laboratories, "lab schools") but settings where the boys escape the adult control of their world and experience agency in their play and social interactions. Such ethnographic studies are pretty rare, because the presence of an adult researcher simply brings us back to the classic "experimenter effect"—how do we know if the children are behaving a certain way in response to the presence of authority figures? As I argue in my introduction, visual autoethnography might be a solution to the problem.

Understanding how boys play with commercial toys in natural settings would test the truth of an idea widely held by adults; namely, that children were more imaginative and creative in their play in the past, especially with folk toys, and that the advent of machine-made, commercial toys has harmed young creativity and imagination.

Those of us who have studied boys in their natural settings know this fear of machine-age modernity's destroying childhood is simply another form of moral panic fueled by adult anxieties about the effects of modernity on their own prospects of living authentically. Boys understand that the commercial toys come with an adult-approved range of uses, but when adults are not present, boys often play with commercial toys in ways adults would not approve. For example, in my essay on play with guns (Mechling 2008b), I came across examples of boys' creative solutions to adults' banning play with toy guns. No toy guns at preschool? Fine, we'll make guns out of the Legos. Sometimes boys actually destroy toys while playing with them, as in playing war. I have heard stories about unauthorized use of toy chemistry sets, magnifying glasses (e.g., burning ants), and microscopes. In one *Calvin and Hobbes* comic strip, Calvin builds a city, "Tokyo," in the sandbox and then imagines he is Godzilla destroying Tokyo. (Bill Watterson's understanding of boys, as evidenced in his *Calvin and Hobbes* comic strip, rivals the understanding by scholars who study boys.)

There is plenty of anecdotal evidence of forbidden play by boys with commercial toys, evidence that boys can be as imaginative and creative with machine-made toys as with other things they play with. The problem for this study is that boys are not likely to record the forbidden play in snapshots. One exception is play with toy guns, real guns, and knives, which I discuss below.

My guess is that parents take most of the snapshots of boys with commercial toys. Christmas and birthdays are among the occasions for adults' taking snapshots of boys and their commercial toys. Adults often might photograph boys playing with their toys (riding a bike, playing with toy soldiers, and so on), but those snapshots are evidence of the memories the adults want of the boys' childhoods. When boys play with their toys, they usually are not stopping to take snapshots of the play.

Folklorists and others who study the everyday lives of children and youth often focus on objects found or made by boys, as opposed to commercially manufactured toys. Just as girls fashion toy dolls from found objects, so boys fashion toys that replicate objects in their lives, including commercial toys (e.g., found objects transformed into trucks or trains or boats). Bronner's important essay on the material folk culture of children (Bronner 1995) begins with a long passage from Mergen (1982, 121–22) about a piece of stiff wire Mergen found as a child; he named the wire, and it was a favorite plaything for years. Bronner discusses a wide range of "found" objects children can turn into playthings, including sand and rocks (see also Mechling 2008a and Mechling 2016b).

The sticks in the hands of four boys in Figure 3.1, which I discuss below for the presence of pocket knives in the snapshots, shows us how readily boys will turn sticks into playthings, including play swords and play guns (Mechling 2008b). Children and adolescents also play with food, including "gross" play and food fights out of the eyesight of disapproving adults (Mechling 2000).

Figure 3.1

Even a commercial toy can become material folk culture if we shift our attention from the object itself to how the young person uses it. And that brings us back to the original lesson from Gelwicks and Horan; namely, that boys use material objects both as props in their construction and performance of their identity and as useful tools in negotiating friendships and power relationships in the male hierarchy of the small group.

Playing with Rope

My thinking through the many ways boys play with sand and mud (Mechling 2016b) led me to thinking about boys' play with another everyday object— rope. Jump rope comes to mind as a plaything that is both a commercial toy and a folk toy, but playing jump rope is primarily a genre of the play of girls. Boys' play with rope tends to be more risky or combative, and we do have some snapshot evidence of these forms of rope play.

Boys like to play in ways that defy gravity. One genre of play in this mode is climbing things, as in Figure 3.2. Boys also climb up ropes (Figure 3.3) and climb things with the assistance of rope, as in rock-climbing. In chapter 5, on boys' bodies, we shall encounter the human pyramid, which also is a genre of play in which boys "defy" gravity by climbing, in this case climbing on each other.

Figure 3.2

Figure 3.3

Figure 3.4

Figure 3.5

One pleasure of climbing lies in the potential of falling. Risky play is exciting because it prompts the body to begin dumping into the blood the same hormones associated with the fight-freeze-or-flight instinct (principally adrenaline and noradrenaline). Another pleasure of climbing lies in the changed perspective from high places. From my own experience as a teen, I know that climbing onto your house's roof transforms a familiar landscape into an unfamiliar, "uncanny" one (Freud 2003 [1919]).

The boy in Figure 3.4 is hanging from a rope, which in turn is looped over a tree branch to hang a tire for swinging, a classic folk toy. Older boys often will tie a rope high on a tree on the bank of a river or lake and use the rope to swing out over the water to drop into it from a substantial height.

Swinging is one of those genres of play that the play theorist Roger Caillois names *ilinx*, "the Greek term for whirlpool, from which is also derived the Greek word for vertigo (*ilingis*)" (Caillois 2001 [1961], 24). Unlike his other three categories of games—*agon* (competitive, combative), *alea* (chance-based), and *mimicry*—play relying on *ilinx* can be played alone and derives its pleasure from the experience of dizziness, vertigo. Play and games in this category "consist of an attempt to momentarily destroy the stability of perceptions and inflict a kind of voluptuous panic upon an otherwise lucid mind. In all cases, it is a question of surrendering to a kind of spasm, seizure, or shock which destroys reality with sovereign brusqueness" (Caillois 2001 [1961], 23). Caillois's wonderful phrase "voluptuous panic" tells us why this sort of play is so seductive for young people.

Tug-of-war (TOW) is one of those folk games with rope that begins when the boys are young, which is why I chose Figure 3.5 to show here. Elsewhere (Mechling 2023) I have published an article devoted entirely to TOW, and the reader can see there many more snapshots, most taken by boys at summer camps or by boys participating in traditional college "scraps" and contests between classes, often played in mud. The game of TOW actually entered the modern Olympic games in 1900 but was eliminated in 1920, and the Tug of War International Federation (TWIF, founded in 1999) sponsors regular competitions and helps the effort to reinstate the game in the Olympics (Tug of War Association, n.d.). My interest here is in the folk versions of TOW as played by boys, sometimes in the view of adults and sometimes not.

I shall not reproduce here my analysis (Mechling 2023) of the meanings of the game and what I take to be the elements of pleasure experienced by playing TOW. While girls and women do play TOW, even as documented in snapshots, I will say that boys are especially drawn to play the game as a contest of strength, which is very important to young men (more on this in chapter 5). The physical exertion playing the game causes a flood of hormones in the body, including the hormones (e.g., endorphins, dopamine) that target the pleasure centers in the brain. An additional feature of the game, however, is that it permits young men in the friendship group to sort themselves. Recall the observation by Sapolsky (1997) and other primatologists that adolescent male primates come to know their rank in the group, which provides security and comfort. Human male adolescents sort themselves in their friendship groups on a number of criteria, which might include physical strength, height,

Figure 3.6

intelligence, humor, and wealth (as evidence by possessions, things again). Lining up along a rope for a game of TOW makes visible for each boy his place in the group, just as building human pyramids (again chapter 5) sorts the boys by size and strength (see also Mechling 2021).

I mentioned above that many of the games boys play and record in snapshots involve mud. I could reproduce here any number of such snapshots. Boys generally like to get dirty. It is notable that games of TOW so often involve pulling the opposing players into mud. My essay on sandplay (Mechling 2016b) explores some of the social and psychological meanings of play in mud, and my essay on TOW (Mechling 2023) speculates on the pleasure a team of male players might enjoy when they pull another male team into mud, thereby infantilizing the other males and, as gender is coded in American culture, feminizing them through the infantilization.

I include Figure 3.6 as one of the very few snapshots I have of the darker side of play with rope, in this case play with "the hangman's noose." This snapshot is more formally posed by American soldiers of WWI vintage, and I easily could have included it in the hazing chapter (chapter 6). I include it here because in my long experience with the Boy Scouts, I know that once boys are given rope and taught to tie useful knots, they start playing with the rope, most notably creating the hangman's noose and sometimes simply tying each other up. Doubtless they know the hangman's noose from popular culture images, and their fascination with the noose suggests an adolescent fascination with death.

The Theory of Things

George Carlin offers us something of a folk theory of "stuff," but scholars from several disciplines also have theorized about the meanings of "things" in our everyday lives. Those scholars offer some useful ideas as we consider the role of objects, things, "material culture" in the lives of boys and young men.

Developmental psychologists, such as Piaget, have formulated theories of the ways infants and young children relate to objects in their environment, but parents understand even without the theories that infants attach themselves to objects for comfort, including blankets and stuffed animals. The British pediatrician and child psychiatrist D. W. Winnicott formulated his idea of the "transitional object" in a 1951 paper and later elaborated the idea (Winnicott 1971), the core of which is the notion that between ages four and twelve months the infant will become emotionally attached to an object, which attachment accomplishes a few things, including a transition from the mother as the primary object of attachment to other objects not the mother. Winnicott called the "transitional object" the "first not-me possession," which points us to an understanding of the role of objects in the creation and performance of "self" as the child matures.

Perhaps because they work out of the same school of philosophy as I do—American pragmatism—I am partial to the 1981 book *The Meaning of Things: Domestic Symbols and the Self*, by Mihaly Csikszentmihalyi and Eugene Rochberg-Halton. An added strength in their approach is that they interviewed over three hundred children and adults in eighty-two families in their homes about the "meanings" of the domestic objects with which they surround themselves (x). American pragmatism (especially the versions elaborated by George Herbert Mead and John Dewey, building on Charles Peirce and William James) provides the theoretical approach to how people "make meaning" in the world, and the ethnographic material, the interviews, provides the evidence for a nuanced understanding of the meaning of specific material objects to people in their homes.

I recommend the book to anyone interested in material culture, but I can summarize here their most important ideas with a series of bullet points:

- meaning is created through a process of "cultivation," an "active process of interpretation oriented toward goals" (xi); this is a fundamental premise of pragmatism, introduced by William James;
- meaning rests on intentions or motives (5);
- socialization focuses the individual's attention to some experiences over others (7);

- as symbols, things have the power to evoke emotions and feelings, an important element in the emergence of self-consciousness (21), and objects can also play a role in the young person's "control of impulses and emotions" (117);
- things can be "carriers of repressed desires," which suggests the need for an understanding of psychic processes (22);
- objects are symbols of power, including "magical" power (26)
- objects can be symbols of status (29);
- objects can be symbols of what Durkheim calls "sociability," social integration beyond the individual (33);
- in early childhood objects are important means for establishing a sense of self and agency (object relations theory), but as the child matures into adolescence, objects take on additional importance in "shifting the center of the self from one's own actions to one's position in a network of enduring relationships," an evolution mapped by Erik Erikson (1963 [1950]; 1968) in his models of stages of life (101);
- experiences with objects always have an aesthetic component, which is most obvious with artistic objects but also inherent in experiences with familiar, everyday objects (176–77); the pleasure of the aesthetic experience with an object often is due to its intrinsic qualities, not just the fact that it represents something else (177);
- while one's understanding of the meaning of an object might be formed somewhat by what Dewey calls "recognition," our ability to understand an experience in terms of previous experiences, sometimes we take an "active, critical" approach to understanding the meanings of an object to the extent that the intrinsic qualities of the object "may modify previously formed habits or interpretive associations," a process Dewey calls "perception" (179–81);
- intense, focused, "attentive" interaction with an object can induce a state of psychic "flow," which amounts to a state of consciousness apart from everyday reality (186–87).

This set of bullet points does not do justice to the details of the ideas and examples of Csikszentmihalyi and Rochberg-Halton, but I think these points alert us to the nature of the boy's experience with things he considers meaningful in his world, things meaningful enough that he and his buddies photographed the things and kept the snapshots.

We are ready now to examine a set of snapshots of boys and their "stuff."

Boys' Bedrooms

Based on his archaeological work in colonial American sites, Deetz (1977) argues that from the design of interior space in homes we can see material evidence of the emergence of the notion of privacy, when parents began sleeping apart from the children and some children began to have private bedrooms. Reid's (2017) historical analysis of the emergence of the notion of a separate bedroom for adolescents sees 1900 as a "turning point" in American thought about teen bedrooms, as psychologists began to give advice to parents about how to respond to the desire of adolescents to have control over their own space. That date also corresponds to the growing disposable income teens could use as consumers decorating their bedrooms. Reid notes that the nineteenth-century notion about gender and youth was that girls were in the bedroom while boys were outside. The notion that boys would spend a lot of time in their bedrooms was a new one in the twentieth century, as was the scientific notion that boys had emotional lives not wholly dissimilar from girls (Hall 1904). Adults came to realize that boys needed the privacy of their bedrooms as a refuge from "serious personal and emotional turmoil" (Reid 2017, 61).

In a chapter titled "The Home as Symbolic Environment," Csikszentmihalyi and Rochberg-Halton report from their interviews with families that children "tended to feel most at home in their own bedrooms," a not-so-surprising observation (1981, 135). "Children's special objects are most often found in their bedrooms" (137), but the importance to children of the bedroom as an "inner sanctum" in the home lies beyond the fact that their most-treasured, most-meaningful "special objects" are there. "For children, it [their bedroom] is a private area that gives a greater feeling of control over the activities and objects than other rooms and thus is a place where autonomy itself can be cultivated by 'dialogues' with the self, mediated by cherished possessions" (137).

I have not come across many snapshots of boys in their bedrooms at home. Salinger's (1995) photographic look at teens in their bedrooms offers no analysis of the variety of bedrooms, though the brief snippets of teen testimony quoted by Salinger do reinforce the point that American teens tend to see their bedrooms as refuges from adult surveillance and control. Twitchell's (2006) very interesting book on "where men hide," with photographs by Ken Ross, reminds us that the boy's desire for a refuge away from girls does not end in adulthood for many men, but both the Twitchell book and the Salinger book feature photographs taken by adults.

Figure 3.7

Figure 3.7 is one of the few snapshots I have of a boy in his bedroom, though many of the snapshots of boys with their toys are set in the bedroom, most likely taken by adults. I feel fairly confident that Figure 3.7 was not taken by a parent, as that would be intolerable for the boy, so I think it is likely that this snapshot was taken by a sibling or friend. We see only a bit of the way the boy chose to decorate his room.

Camp Tents and Cabins

An exception to the observation that I have seen few snapshots of boys by boys in their bedrooms is the body of snapshots taken in bedrooms away from home, either in a tent on a camping trip (most of the snapshots I have in that genre are of Boy Scouts) or in a cabin at a commercial summer camp, where traditionally there are separate cabins for the girls and boys. Tents and cabins are not the private spaces boys enjoy in their bedrooms at home, and many of the snapshots of those camp spaces do not reveal much about the boys. The professional photographer Barbara Morgan (1951) has a nice photo essay on boys at summer camp, but what of snapshots from camp by boys

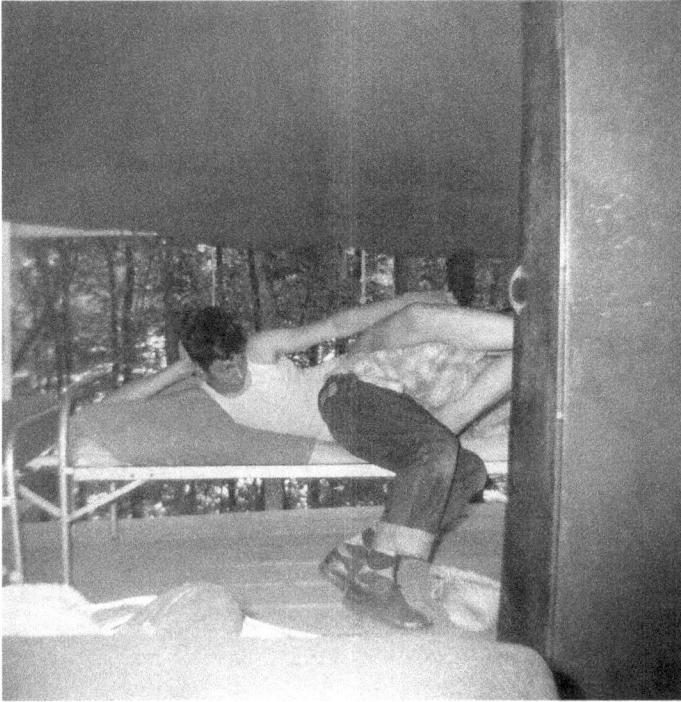

Figure 3.8

of boys? Two books that feature snapshots of boys taken by boys at summer camp are Andy Sweet's (2020), mostly his photos with little commentary, and *Camp Camp* (2008) by Bennett and Shell. For a folklorist's purposes, the Bennett and Shell book has a great deal of commentary to accompany the snapshots provided by former campers. Bennett and Shell (2008, 51–71) devote a chapter, "Bad Boys," focusing on the "boys' bunk," and that chapter has many examples of the pranks and play folklorists find in the adolescent friendship group, both snapshots and testimony. Mirroring a central idea I use here, the authors devote three pages (52–54) to a list and description of "20 Acts of Violence That Say 'I love you,'" the many aggressive ways boys torture each other in the boys' cabin when adults are not present.

What snapshots I do have of boys enjoying some camp time away from adult surveillance are interesting because of the playful wrestling in some, like Figures 3.8 and 3.9. I take a long, analytical look at playfighting in chapter 5, and these two snapshots certainly could go in that chapter, but I include them here to make the point that even in a total institution (Goffman 1961; Mechling 2019c) that seeks to monitor and control the lives of the campers, boys find space away from adult surveillance to "goof off" and otherwise enjoy each other's company.

Figure 3.9

Bicycles and Cars

One of the boys studied by Gelwicks proudly showed my student the photograph of his bicycle, and that object is a favorite for boys' snapshots of their stuff.

Figure 3.10 attracted my attention for a few reasons. At the outset I was drawn to the visual composition of the photograph, which I think likely has been taken by another boy. This amateur photograph has a modernist aesthetic, probably quite by accident, though some young photographers have talented eyes. The lines, the angles of the composition resemble famous modernist art and documentary photographs. I also like the fact that two objects important to boys—a bicycle and a car—are at the center of the snapshot. The snapshot captures a particular moment as the boy negotiates getting through a gate.

Figure 3.11 is of interest because in that snapshot the boy and his bicycle are the center of attention, but the pet dog shares the stage with the bicycle as an object worth our notice. It might seem strange to call a pet dog an "object" or a "thing," and I made the case in chapter 2 for a boy's dog as his "chum." Attachment to "things," including bikes and pets, can trigger even love. Let us consider the meanings of the bicycles in so many of the boys' snapshots.

Following Dewey (1934), we certainly should begin with the recognition that riding a bike is fun, that a boy might consider a bicycle a thing of

Figure 3.10

Figure 3.11

beauty, especially when brand-new and discovered beside the Christmas tree. Its intrinsic quality taps an aesthetic response. It is in riding the bicycle, however, that the boy experiences the pleasure of the object. Understanding that point requires us to characterize the phenomenology of the experience of riding a bike.

To begin with, we have to learn how to ride a bike, Younger children might have their first experience with the more stable tricycle, and a significant moment in a child's life is graduating from a tricycle to a bicycle, even if that transition is eased by the temporary presence of "training wheels" to make the bike more stable and easy to ride. In short, the first bike signals a transition from one stage of childhood to another, from an immature stage to a mature one. And the pleasure of finally mastering the balance necessary for successful bike riding is precisely that—the pleasure in mastery.

What makes riding a bike "a consummatory experience" (in Dewey's language) is the phenomenological experience of riding. This begins at the neurological and physiological level. Like other forms of vigorous exercise, cycling releases a set of hormones, "a pleasurable cocktail of norepinephrine, dopamine, endorphins, anandamide, and serotonin," most of which flood the pleasure center of the brain (Hunt 2018). Cycling stimulates blood flow, "increasing the brain's capacity to grow, function, and repair itself" (Hunt 2018). This is not surprising, as cycling is not just physical exercise but requires complex coordination between the body and the mind, including balance. Scientists have also discovered the benefits of cycling for emotional health: "Cycling floods our bodies with powerful neurotransmitters, the very same chemical compounds targeted by anti-anxiety and anti-depression medications" (Hunt 2018).

The phenomenological "fun" of cycling goes beyond the neurophysiology and endocrinology. Recall that the play theorist Roger Caillois (2001 [1961]) divides play and game into four basic sorts, one of which he calls *ilinx*, Greek for "whirlpool," which describes well the pleasure of vertigo we find in many forms of play and games. We shall have reason to return to the notion of *ilinx* in later chapters here, but for now we can recognize that cycling and the ever-changing sense of balance riding a bike resembles *ilinx*. Moreover, just as Paul Bouissac (1976), in his cultural study of the circus, notes that some acts "defy" gravity, holding off through skill the possibility of falling, riding a bike presents the same uncertain defiance of gravity.

That covers the biological, emotional, and mental pleasure of riding a bike, but there is more. A bike represents mobility, and escape from home, and that escape from adult authority and surveillance is attractive to some adolescents. I have a personal story to illustrate this point. When I was an

Figure 3.12

early adolescent, my Boy Scout troop met on Friday nights at a clubhouse about three miles from my home (Miami Beach). My parents trusted me to be able to ride my bike safely through the suburban neighborhood at night, both going and coming home a few hours later. This was in the late 1950s, admittedly before parents and other adults worked up a moral panic over "stranger danger" (e.g., child abductions), but I had no fear, only the exhilaration of riding my bike at night and taking control of my life. Over the years, when men learned of my scholarly work on the Boy Scouts, they often said that one of the attractions of the organization was that a Scout meeting was the first occasion for having a legitimate reason to be away from home during the night. The mobility of a bicycle (and I do not doubt many of those boys rode their bikes to troop meetings) represented freedom and autonomy, even briefly, from adult supervision, control, and surveillance.

But there is still more. A child can use a bike to help manage social relations and friendships. Kids give each other rides on their bikes (Figure 3.12); kids sometimes lend their bikes to others, a sign of trust; and sometimes kids refuse to share a bike ride or use of their bike, a power move with social and emotional implications.

Figure 3.13

Little wonder, then, that boys consider their bicycles as extremely important "things" in their social world, things worth photographing.

Directing our attention back to Figure 3.10, let us shift our gaze from the
bicycle to the car in the photo. There is no way to know if the car in that
photo belongs to the boy with the bicycle, but there is little doubt in my mind
that the boys in Figures 3.13 and 3.14 are standing in front of cars that are
"theirs" in some way, even if owned by parents. Most interesting in those two
snapshots are the poses assumed by the boys for the photograph. Part of the
competent performance of masculinity in American culture is knowing how
to assume the proper male poses. Goffman's book *Gender Advertisements*
(1979), for example, illustrates many of those poses, most with women. The
boy in Figure 3.13 assumes a classic male pose, thumbs in jeans pockets and
hands flared, framing his genitals. The teen boy in Figure 3.14 also assumes
a classic male pose: his hand on the car, his loving gaze at the car, and his
body language strongly resemble the poses Goffman (1979) reads as male
ownership of the female. And I hardly need add here that young men often
talk about their cars as female, so it is not surprising that the young men
touch their cars in ways similar to the ways they might pose with a girlfriend.

Figure 3.14

Figure 3.15

Figure 3.16

Figure 3.15 attracts our attention because we see in this snapshot the affectionate touching between three young men of the sort Ibson (2002, 2007) writes about. The car is what brings them together.

Leaving the larger things in boys' lives—from bedrooms to bikes and cars—let me turn now to smaller objects often photographed by boys.

Toy Guns and Real Guns

Guns, both toy guns and real guns, appear in several snapshots of boys by boys and make a useful case study of boys' uses of objects to display power. Elsewhere (Mechling 2008b) I have written at length about play with guns, mostly boys' play with guns. Here, I shall make a few key points explaining why and how guns become boys' "special objects," things so special that boys keep snapshots of themselves with their guns. I have many snapshots of boys with toy guns and real guns (Mechling 2004), but Figure 3.16 is a rich enough example that I can make my points with that image before us.

I feel fairly certain that this snapshot was taken by a boy, as I cannot imagine most adults would approve of the gun play pictured here. American boys seem especially drawn to play with guns. If we begin with the observation from the evolutionary psychologists that pubescent and adolescent boys are attracted to the power of magical objects that have an effect at a distance (tapping the child's desire for omnipotence), then it is a small step to observe that in American history guns have been part of cultural mythologies that feature them as just such magical objects (e.g., Slotkin 1992).

Boys know that guns are both forbidden and permitted. Boys in hunting families are taught how to use guns safely and appropriately (Mechling 2004), and both the National Rifle Association and the Boy Scouts of America worked hard to domesticate rifle shooting as good, clean, family fun (Mechling 2014a). Parents' and other adults' taking snapshots of boys holding long guns—Christmas morning snapshots, hunting trip snapshots, snapshots at organized target shooting events, and so on—conveys to boys that they can "play" with guns under adult supervision. It is in snapshots like Figure 3.16 that boys capture "forbidden play" with guns, play that fuses the cultural approval of guns with the young man's pleasure in feeling the full power of the gun when not under adult supervision.

Those snapshots of forbidden gun play send us looking to ideas from depth psychology to understand what is so attractive in playing with guns in ways that adults would disapprove. For example, psychoanalysts have long noted adolescent boys' fascination with death (e.g., Winnicott 1971,

145). That young men should contemplate their own deaths and the deaths
of others seems paradoxical, given the parallel belief by young men that they
are immortal. Yet, from the psychoanalytic point of view, the adolescent boy's
hyperawareness of his changing body focuses his attention on the vulnerability of the body (Lyons 2004). The famous funeral scene in Mark Twain's
Tom Sawyer, in which Huck and Tom, hiding in the rafters, observe people
at their own funeral, captures this adolescent fascination with death, but so
do the numerous first-person shooter (FPS) games played on computers
and video game systems, games that feature not only death by guns but also
"resurrection," with multiple lives (see the discussion of FPS video game
playing by warriors in Wallis and Mechling 2019, 89–103).

Depth psychology also draws our attention to the similarity of shooting
guns to sexual discharge. As in many things, we can look to the everyday
folk speech of boys and men to confirm this symbolic equivalence between
the gun and the penis, and between shooting a gun and shooting semen.
Grossman and Christensen (2008) make this point directly, using the words
of soldiers to describe the sexual excitement of shooting long rifles, especially
automatic weapons, and the common use of the word "shooting" in folk
speech to describe ejaculation.

These meanings of playing with both real and toy guns lie in the unconscious of both the prepubescent and adolescent boy, though the adolescent
boy might be able to articulate the resemblance between discharging a long
rifle and ejaculating. After all, men as young as seventeen are in the military
and expressed such feelings to Grossman.

Knives and Other Sharp Objects

Every one of the five summers from 2007 through 2011 that I attended Boy
Scout camp with our younger grandson, at his urging I bought him a new
pocketknife at the camp "trading post." The two camps (one in the mountains
of Northern California, the other on Santa Catalina Island in Southern California) were savvy, knowing from experience that teen boys will buy knives.
Every boy at Scout camp must earn his "Totin' Chip," a card certifying that
he has passed a test of knowledge and techniques for the safe handling of
knives and axes. There are legitimate functional and artistic uses of knives in
camp; earning the Woodworking and Pioneering merit badges teaches boys
these uses. At the same time, my own observation at those camps showed
me that boys take an intrinsic pleasure in carrying and using a knife. A
common activity by boys is to work incessantly at sharpening a stick, not

Figure 3.17

for any practical or artistic use, but purely for the pleasure of slicing away curls of wood.

In his book *Chain Carvers* (1985), based on his fieldwork and interviews with men who carve elaborate wooden figures and toys for pleasure, folklorist Simon Bronner argues that the boy's first knife (and when this happens varies according to several factors, including rural/urban residence, social class, and ethnicity) is a signal of responsible adulthood. Parents and other adults "trust" a boy when they give him a knife and expect him to use it safely and responsibly. Bronner (1985) also captures the pleasure and pride these men enjoy in carving small objects with knives. Thinking about my own experience as a Scout and then as an adult volunteer with my grandson's Scout troop, I asked Bronner if his adult male informants had anything to say about their attraction to knives when they were boys. Most of his informants lived in rural areas, so even as boys they understood that a knife is a useful tool, perhaps something to be carried at all times in a sheath looped to a belt. The men added, though, that the boy's first knife had a symbolic value, attesting to the boy's maturity, certifying that he was a responsible person who could be trusted to use the knife safely. You can see the pride of ownership in Figure 3.17.

Figure 3.18

My experience being a boy who had knives and watching boys with knives brings to this discussion a few salient points as I examine snapshots of boys with knives.

First, while there are practical uses for knives while camping, most of the time I saw boys using knives, they were engaged in a simple task of slicing away pieces of wood from a stick to make a sharp point at one end. Figures 3.1 (from earlier in this chapter) and 3.18 catch small groups of boys milling around and playing with knives and sharpened sticks.

Knives play a prominent role in Figure 3.1. I think it is a reasonable guess that a fifth boy took this snapshot. The boy on our left wears an empty knife sheath on his belt, and he might have loaned his knife to one of the two boys in the middle, both of whom are whittling on sticks. The fourth boy, on our far right, is watching the whittlers, perhaps waiting his turn to work on his stick. For the folklorist, this snapshot is a perfect document of what interests Bronner (1986, 1995) so much in his story of children's material culture, namely, the ability of children to make their own "folk toys" out of found materials.

Everything I have said so far about boys and knives in these snapshots amounts to a thin description of how boys use knives—as tools, as toys, as symbols of power. Boys also play-fight with knives and other sharp objects, but I save that realm of play with knives for a later chapter on "deep play."

From experience I know that many readers, scholars, and others interested in the everyday lives of youth reject insights based on depth psychology, especially psychoanalytic theory. Those readers can skip the next few paragraphs, but I remain convinced that depth psychology adds insights to understanding the everyday lives of young people, in this case, boys.

In making a complete accounting of the pleasures boys take in handling knives, we should consider the abundant evidence that knives and their longer kin—bayonets and swords— are symbolic penises. The folklorist Alan Dundes, well known for his psychoanalytic interpretation of folklore, defends his interpretations by pointing out that it is not the psychiatrists or the historians and anthropologists who use depth psychology to see symbolic equivalences; it is the folk themselves, as revealed in their folk speech. In the case of the symbolic equivalence of knives and penises, folk speech makes the case. Condoms are called "sheaths," and in my examination of "pissing and masculinity" in another publication (Mechling 2014b), I do cite an ethnography that describes how male counselors at a summer camp would "duel" with their streams of urine putting out the campfire (Goyton 1998).

Puzzling out why boys seem to take such pleasure in whittling sticks to have sharp points, I conclude that whittling the stick is a form of masturbation. It turns out that, in fact, "whittling" has a few variations as slang for masturbation, including "whittle the stick" and "whittle the wood" (Sex-Lexis 2016). Moreover, the repetitive nature of the incessant sharpening of the stick also fits the psychoanalytic theory. Of course, pubescent and adolescent boys usually do not dwell on the symbolic equivalence of the penis and the knife; that is largely unconscious.

The Ways of the Hand

For these concluding thoughts on boys and their "stuff," I have poached the title of sociologist David Sudnow's book *Ways of the Hand: The Organization of Improvised Conduct* (1978), recognizing that the material culture of childhood (including the clubhouses, forts, and rafts of the next chapter) involve the boy's hands. That point seems trivial, but the scientists who study the brain and the mind draw attention to the coevolution of our brains and hands. Wilson's 1998 book *The Hand* details this idea—our hands teach the brain as much as the brain teaches the hand. And Bronner, in an unsurprising expression of his longtime study of material culture, lately has come back to asserting the primacy of the "handiness" of tradition (Bronner 2019, 36).

Chapter Four

Clubhouses, Forts, and Rafts

In chapter 3 I presented and interpreted both the thin and thick meanings of mainly smaller everyday objects, "my stuff," carrying enough importance to a boy or to a boy and his buddies that the boy and his possession showed up in a snapshot that was preserved as an aid to memory. A personal object, a boy's possession, itself carries meaning in the mere possession, "that's mine"; but, as we saw, the relations a boy has with the objects in his possession can also model his relationships with people (attachment theory) and become part of an experience triggering unconscious emotions and the conscious feelings linked to those emotions. A snapshot of a meaningful or treasured object possessed by a boy can elicit memories of those feelings, a good enough reason to want to take a snapshot and keep it long after the stuff is gone.

In chapter 3 we also saw that there really are two categories of "my stuff"—some of the objects are material folk objects, objects most often found or created by hand as props in play, while other are commercial toys, objects also serving as props in play and games.

In this chapter we shift our gaze from smaller objects to larger constructions—clubhouses, forts, and rafts—all built by two or more boys. We are interested here in the folk versions of these larger constructions, though American popular culture is involved in their meanings because each of these three objects has some degree of iconic status in American culture. While it is likely that some boys have been exposed to some of these images and stories in the popular culture they consume, and while they might have absorbed unconsciously some of the meanings of the images and stories, I very much doubt that popular culture drives the boys to build and play with those things. In order to arrive at a thick description of those snapshots, we must attempt to uncover both the conscious and unconscious motivations that make clubhouses, rafts, and forts so satisfying that boys feel obliged to capture their constructions on film. We seek to understand the phenomenological meanings of these objects to the boys.

We must begin with the process of building things, because children (like adults) find pleasure both in the process of construction and in using the product made.

Boys' Material Culture

Folklorists typically divide the traditional, everyday practices they study into three categories: oral culture, customary culture, and material culture. These categories show up in the scholarship on children's folklore, as folklorists collect and analyze children's songs and stories (oral lore), traditional play, games, and slumber parties (customary culture), and children's material culture, from folk toys to cootie-catchers (Sutton-Smith et al. 1995). Among folklorists who study children's material culture, Simon J. Bronner (1986, 1988, 1995) stands out as the one who relies most upon his own and others' reports of ethnographic fieldworks in the natural settings where children and youth gather. Without surveying all of Bronner's writing about the material culture of children, we can take away a few key insights to bring to an analysis of the forts and rafts.

First, it is wholly understandable that children constructed handmade, folk toys before the advent of machine-made toys and their presence in the market of commodities. Girls constructed play dolls from wood and straw and bits of cloth before dolls left the assembly line. Boys constructed handmade swords and guns before toy manufacturers provided plastic versions. The history of toys largely is the history of commodities created by adults and marketed to children and their parents, often around traditional events like birthdays and Christmas (Sutton-Smith 1986; Cross 1997).

Reflect, though, upon the common complaint among parents that while they spent a great deal of money on commercial toys for a birthday or Christmas, the child ends up playing more often with the box the toys came in. That tells us something.

The first lesson we take from Bronner's look at children's material culture is that children continue fashioning handmade toys and other material objects even in the age of machine-made goods. The children are not unlike the adults in the impulse to return to handmade goods in the machine age; that, after all, was the impulse behind the Arts and Crafts Movement, which arose in the United Kingdom in mid-nineteenth century in reaction to the

Industrial Revolution. The movement spread to the United States and other countries over the decades, lasting into the 1920s.

In his interviews with adult male woodcarvers and children, Bronner discovers the ongoing power of *handwork*, the pleasure of the handmade object, both the pleasure of the making and the pleasure of the finished object, whether an art object or a practical object. Bronner grasped the importance of the hand in material culture long before the neuroscientist, Frank R. Wilson, wrote a book, *The Hand*, for the general audience, a book making clear the coevolution of the hand and the brain; the hand teaches the brain as much as the brain teaches the hand (Wilson 1998).

If we shift our attention from the handmade toy to larger constructions, we actually see in childhood the urge to build structures. If there is any plaything a parent or teacher gives to very young children, it is some sort of building blocks. Usually those blocks are machine-made, but Bronner points to children's using natural materials—stone, mud, sticks, leaves—for play constructions. We shall encounter these materials when we look at forts and rafts, below.

A second major insight I bring away from Bronner's work is that children favor a particular aesthetic in their constructions (1995, 267). The aesthetic anthropologist Robert Plant Armstrong (1971) distinguishes between what he calls "synthetic" (thesis-antithesis-synthesis) patterns of verbal and material art, the dominant aesthetic in Western art, and the "syndetic," an aesthetic more common in non-Western and in Western folk art, an aesthetic that makes meaning through accretion and repetition. I certainly see in children's play in sand and mud the syndetic aesthetic at work, and we can see that same aesthetic in the larger constructions I describe and analyze in this chapter.

The larger folk constructions in the snapshots examined in this chapter take two or more boys to build, and doubtless the pleasure of construction lies partly in working side by side. Those of us who study masculinity encounter what some scholars of gender patterns of interpersonal communication note; namely, that while women tend to value eye contact in face-to-face communication, men tend to avoid eye-to-eye contact and, instead, experience bonding with other males by engaging in activities side by side (e.g., Tannen 2007). It might be that eye-to-eye contact signals aggression in males; ethological studies of primates and other mammals suggest that meaning. In any case, and as much as this puzzles many women, boys and men do experience feelings of close male bonding by doing things side by side, whether it is a father and son working on a project together in the garage or a group of men sitting together on a sofa, their attention focused on the screen of the video game they are playing. All of this suggests that boys who build large constructions together are enjoying strong male bonding.

The photographic record rarely captures the process of construction by the boys, and the snapshots I have seen of a construction project under way (e.g., Boy Scouts constructing a lashed tower or bridge) seem likely to have been taken by an adult leader. After all, the boys have their hands full doing the constructing. The photographic record of the large constructions represented here, therefore, usually documents finished projects. The three sorts of constructions I discuss are clubhouses (which include treehouses), forts, and rafts.

Clubhouses

Anyone familiar with the *Our Gang* (also known as *The Little Rascals*) comedy films, 1922–1942, likely knows from those films the iconic image of the boys' clubhouses and the "No Girls Allowed" sign above the door. Years later, Bill Watterson uses that same iconic image in his immensely popular comic strip *Calvin and Hobbes* (1985–95). While *The Little Rascals* featured a gang of both boys and girls, black and white, Watterson's strip centered on a boy and his imaginary world. The little scholarship there is on *Our Gang* appropriately focuses on the series' vision of race relations in the US (e.g., Lee 2015), and I have not found any scholarship addressing the intriguing question of the films as verbal and visual narratives about urban childhood in America in the decades 1922–1942. The scholarship on *Calvin and Hobbes* rightfully notes both the philosophical and religious narratives in the comic strip (John Calvin and Thomas Hobbes, of course) and Watterson's keen insight into the imaginative minds of boys (e.g., Cavna 2020).

I shall resist the temptation to launch here into a fulsome analysis of what the *Our Gang* comedies and *Calvin and Hobbes* strips contribute to our understanding of the history of childhood and youth in America, though that would be an instructive project. I mention these two popular culture texts merely to indicate the iconic status of the boys' clubhouse and oftentimes gender exclusion in American culture.

One version of the clubhouse is the treehouse, which can be as crude as the one in Figure 4.1 or more elaborate. The clubhouse on the ground, such as the one the boys in Figure 4.2 are building, is more common and takes less daring, though boys do like to climb trees.

Figure 4.1

Figure 4.2

Figure 4.3

The snapshots of boys and their treehouses and clubhouses tell us that these structures are important to the boys, but we can say more about the motives and pleasures for building these. Part of the pleasure lies in building things side by side, activity that signals close bonds between the boys. In his useful essay on the material folk culture of children, Bronner devotes an early paragraph to the treehouse and to the rustic "hut" as examples of boys' clubhouses built from found materials (Bronner 1995, 252–53). Bronner opens with these examples to make a point important in the study of the material culture of childhood; namely, that learning to manipulate materials in order to create something the boys value helps develop in them a folk aesthetic for design. What Bronner says here resembles the process Lévi-Strauss (1968 [1962]) calls "bricolage," the creation of something new out of the stray parts of the old. The *bricoleur* strives to make something beautiful as well as useful, and Bronner admires the creativity of children and youth as they salvage the materials of everyday life—cast-off lumber and other materials—to fashion something new, useful, and beautiful to them. Even casual observation of children and youth provides evidence of the incessant creativity by children and adolescents, and in many cases the aesthetic of their constructions features syndesis as often as synthesis (Armstrong 1971).

We can plunge even deeper into the motives and pleasures of creating clubhouses. The boys' writing on the outside walls of the clubhouse in Figure 4.3 (and someone wrote "BOYS CLUB" in pencil on the back of this snapshot) reminds us of the "no girls allowed" signs on the clubhouses of boys in popular culture, so one motive likely is exclusion of girls to guarantee male bonding in the young group. Moreover, we have plenty of evidence that the treehouse or the clubhouse, away from adult surveillance, often is the site for forbidden behavior, including smoking and looking at pornographic magazines or, now, at porn on smartphones. Girls in a certain age group, usually prepubescent girls (ages ten through twelve), have slumber parties as their time to bond with other girls away from boys (Mansfield 2018). The boys' clubhouse serves a similar function and also appears to appeal most to the prepubescent boy.

Boys ages ten to twelve are at a precarious stage in their relationships with each other and with girls. Up until age eleven or so, boys and girls seem to waver between same-gender play and mixed-gender play on the playground (e.g., Thorne 1993; Beresin 2010). On the brink of pubertal change in their bodies, though, many boys begin to change their minds about girls, who generally enter puberty earlier than do the boys. Whereas younger boys might say that "girls have cooties" (or whatever the equivalent is today), when boys' hormones start flooding their bodies they begin to have feelings new to them. They often are puzzled by the changes in the girls at school, and as I explain in my 2001 book, the boys are puzzled by menstruation. The Boy Scouts I studied, especially those between ages eleven and fourteen, both wanted to maintain the exclusivity of their male friendship group and felt an intense drive to be around the Girl Scouts across the pond (Mechling 2001, 93).

It is no wonder, then, that the boys take snapshots of each other with their treehouses and clubhouses. The structures represent not only their building skills but also the "boy caves," where they hide from adults and girls.

Author James Twitchell collaborated with photographer Ken Ross to create a book, *Where Men Hide* (2006), that might provide additional clues about the motives and experiences of the boys in my snapshots as the boys retreat into private spaces populated only by other boys. Twitchell notes that historians have traced this male proclivity to be alone in a real or figurative "man cave" from at least the Old Testament times. He tells us that the first evidence of a man building a hut in the woods is from 1753 (2006, 9).

Twitchell observes that when men hide from the world in the company of other men, they engage in the sort of bonding behavior I see in the boys, much of the activity in the play or ritual frames (2006, 13). He also explains that there has been a decline in all-male institutions, including schools and fraternal organizations (2006, 19–21). I would now add the Boy Scouts. Twitchell draws on Putnam's argument in *Bowling Alone* (2001) that Americans are losing their experiences in groups, but I would offer the same critique of Twitchell's point here that I would with Putnam. Putnam draws on macrosociological trends, and my ethnographic bias tells me we should look to the actual, everyday practices of young men to see if they still seem to bond as often and in the same ways as their fathers and grandfathers. I have not followed the "boys picturing boys" thread into the digital photography age, but I suspect boys have not changed much in their need for time bonding with friends away from the surveillance of adults and young women.

The rest of the book nicely combines the words of Twitchell and the photographs by Ross in "deer camps, cellars, garages, Masonic temples, barbershops, sporting venues, bedrooms, churches, offices, and strip clubs" (2006, 22). For the young men I am studying here, those venues are bedrooms, summer camp cabins, treehouses, clubhouses, folk forts, folk rafts, camping trips, and more. Younger men than those studied by Twitchell, these boys are driven by the same instinct to retreat from the outside world into a private, safe space to bond with other males.

Forts

Playing soldier is such a widely shared experience in boy culture that we cannot be surprised that boys build what they would call "forts." Sometimes the forts are of wood and other materials we find in the clubhouses; at other times, a fort might be fashioned with snow (for snowball fights) or sand. In my calculation, forts differ from clubhouses in that they are usually open, public, and available for surveillance by adults (as clubhouses are not). At the same time, forts signal a defensive position against imaginary assault.

The American flag the boys in Figure 4.4 plant in the fortification of the urban fort they dig in what appears to be an empty lot suggests the military model for boys' folk forts. Folklorists have long documented the warlike games boys play, from snowball fights to organized games like capture-the-flag (see Dundes 1997; Mechling 2001, 152–62).

Twitchell makes much of the hole Saddam Hussein hid in, in which he was discovered by American soldiers (2006, 11–12). He is reluctant to offer a psychological analysis of holes and other underground places where some men "hide," writing while "it may be tempting to consider this to be a womblike regression, I'm not convinced that it's sexual. It seems enough to say that these are liminal spaces, spaces betwixt and between, where certain rules are held in abeyance and other rigorously invoked" (Twitchell 2006, 13).

I am not as reluctant as is Twitchell to see a deep psychological motive for boys' tendency to dig holes as their play forts. In his chapter "The Theory of Infantile Sexuality," Erikson (1963 [1950], 91–102) explores the patterns of

Figure 4.4

"genital modes and spatial modalities" he sees in children's play, especially their play with blocks. Whereas the girls he observed tended to create circular enclosures with the blocks, boys tended to build (erect) towers. In my article "Sandwork" (Mechling 2016b), I use Erikson's theory to help explain why I have snapshots of girls building circular sand structures (see snapshot on 2016b, 29), and of boys building sandcastles with towers (see snapshot on 2016b, 27).

Boys' digging holes for their forts and building walls of dirt and sand and snow around them seems to contradict Erikson's theory about the genital modes as they show up in the children's manipulation of materials. There must be another deep psychological reason why boys dig holes to separate themselves from the everyday landscape as part of their play and games.

In *On My Honor* (2001) I describe and analyze one example of boys' play with holes in the ground. In that case the boys' traditional game of "poison pit" (75) featured at its center a pit dug in the sand and filled with water, watermelon flesh and rind, and sometimes the urine of the older boys, the "camp staff." My interpretation of that game and its symbolic details rests on the idea that the pit represents the feminine, and that the game works to address unconsciously the fascination and fear the boys have regarding the female body and, especially, the menstruation they knew the girls at school were just beginning to experience (84). In my view, it's not much of a stretch to see the pits in earth and sand and snow as representing the comfort of the womb.

Rafts

Perhaps the most famous raft in American history is the raft Huck and Jim use on the Mississippi River in Mark Twain's *The Adventures of Huckleberry Finn* (1885). The raft Huck Finn and Jim share in Twain's novel lies at the symbolic center of the story and its messages about mobility and freedom. Steven Mintz titled his sweeping history of American childhood *Huck's Raft* (2004), a signal about the importance of the move toward freedom and mobility of children and youth he found in that history. Movement, mobility, is a central theme in American history. A Yale historian (Pierson 1962) wrote an article, "The M-Factor in American History," modifying Frederick Jackson Turner's famous "frontier thesis" to argue that it is American mobility, not just on the frontier but all through American experience, that accounts for the unique character of American democratic culture.

Middle-class American children learn early the link between mobility, freedom, and autonomy (including agency). As we saw in chapter 3, the child's first bicycle changes the child's world, and as she or he grows older, the distance that the bike can carry the youngster from home increases. This is definitely a middle-class and mainly suburban phenomenon, and the comfort of parents with long bike trips from home has changed over the decades as adults ginned up a moral panic about "threatened children" (Best 1993).

Of course none of these cultural meanings of a raft are on boys' minds as they decide to gather the materials to build a raft to carry them onto some body of water, most often a stream or river or pond or lake. Consider the three snapshots in Figure 4.5 from a photo album. Two things come together for the boys. First is the pleasure of building something together, and a few of the snapshots in my collection capture the building. We should note that most of these rafts are made of wood, scrap lumber if a more suburban environment, or actual logs if in a more rural environment, like a campout in the woods.

The second element giving boys the idea to build a raft lies in their unconscious desire to experience "the uncanny," in this case the uncanny experience of being on water and having a view of the land out of the ordinary. Freud wrote an entire long essay, *The Uncanny* (2003 [1919]), drawing upon Jentsch's essay "On the Psychology of the Uncanny" (1906). "Uncanny" is the rough English translation of the German *unheimlich*, *heimlich* meaning "belonging to home," so an "uncanny experience is unfamiliar, uncomfortable, untame, and even frightening.

Freud and Jentsch both were interested in the uncanny in relation to experiences in dreams and folktales and literature or in places like wax museums or experiences with automatons. My application of the notion of an uncanny experience with regard to rafts draws upon the interdisciplinary

Figure 4.5

scholarship on "uncanny landscapes" (e.g., Mitchell and Petty 2020). Words do not describe well the feelings (based in physiological emotions) one has standing on a raft in a body of water, feelings partly brought on by the uncanny waterscape but also by the movement of the raft, a movement far more responsive to the water than are boats. My speculation, therefore, is that boys have an inkling of the strange pleasure of being on a raft on the water even before they have that experience.

Figure 4.5

Capturing a photograph of the construction of a raft on land is easy enough; snapshots of boys on rafts pose greater challenges, and truthfully I cannot be sure who is taking a particular photograph of boys on a raft out on the water; it could be an adult, it could be another boy on land or even on a second raft. It seems to me that the more rickety and dangerous the construction of the raft, the more likely it is another boy is taking the snapshot, assuming (perhaps erroneously) that a responsible adult would never let boys go out on a raft sure to come apart.

Where Boys Hide

The snapshots of boys' larger constructions of clubhouses, treehouses, forts, and rafts tell us that the phenomenon Twitchell and Ross studied and photographed—the places *Where Men Hide* (2006)—actually begins often in pubescent and adolescent boys. The need to separate from the domestic family and especially from mothers and other women seems to be a strong motive for establishing "male" as "not female." The natural desire to "escape" adult surveillance as a step toward autonomy and agency receives support in the public culture, especially popular culture. Moreover, boys "hide out" together, experiencing the play in clubhouses and forts and on rafts as strong male bonding with friends. Finally, we should not dismiss the deep, unconscious comfort of the hiding place.

Chapter Five

Boys Bonding
with Their Bodies

Social scientists from several disciplines ground their analysis of thought and culture in the human body. We saw in chapter 1 how strong is the pubescent and adolescent boy's body in his consciousness. In a significant sense, boys "think" with their bodies. Lakoff and Johnson (1980) show how much of our thought and language is grounded in our bodies. Murphy (2001) surveys the metaphors men use to describe their bodies, and this folk speech begins when boys are young. More than one analyst has observed that women generally experience themselves as *being* bodies (monthly menstruation reinforces this sense), whereas men generally experience themselves as *having* bodies.

Stepping back from the ways boys and men experience, think, and talk about their bodies, the male body also carries symbolic weight. Bordo (1999) explores the meanings of male bodies, including the important point that the phallus is not the penis. Jeffords (1993) examines popular culture visual narratives where individual "hard bodies" come to represent the society, and Jarvis (2010) examines the uses of male hard bodies in wartime propaganda leading up to and during World War II. Sontag (1978, 1986) shows how metaphors of illness in the individual body and metaphors of "illness" in society bleed into one another. And folklorists (e.g., Young 1995) describe and analyze the various ways the human body enters everyday, folk talk, customs, and material culture. I have found most useful in my own work (Mechling 1981; Wallis and Mechling 2019a, 2019b; Mechling 2021b) anthropologist Mary Douglas's (1966) formulation of the human body as a symbol of society.

Boys use their bodies to communicate in the male friendship group. I have already mentioned how boys can experience a strong friendship bond merely by engaging in an activity side-by-side, such as building a clubhouse or fort or raft, as we saw in chapter 4. As we shall see in this chapter, boys' bodies are at the center of many of the play frames and ritual frames that structure and give meaning to their shared activities.

A notable feature of boys' friendship groups outside of the school class-room is the range of ages in many groups. Children's folklorists note that when two children or youth first meet one of the questions they ask each other is "How old are you?" Schools are usually strictly age-graded, but the informal folk groups of children and sometimes even more formal orga-nizations, such as a Boy Scout troop, often mix ages. Pubescent boys can belong to a friendship group dominated by adolescent males, which gives the younger boys a sense of the stage and status they will grow into within the group. It seems silly to observe this, but boys know they will get older, that they will get taller, their muscles will develop, their voices will deepen, they will begin getting facial and body hair, and their sex organs will develop, all thanks to the hormones carrying them through puberty into adolescence. Being in the presence of older boys assures them that their awkward stage of puberty will eventually end and they will enter adolescence. That is not an insignificant understanding a boy has.

Muscles

Somehow boys learn the classic muscle pose. Baby boomers may have learned the pose from the Charles Atlas and other advertisements in comic books, but however they acquire the knowledge, boys seem to know how to pose their biceps, even from a very young age when their muscles are not developed (largely because the muscles will develop with the rush of hormones in puberty).

One thing boys learn early is that hard muscles signal manhood (Kasson 2001; Bronner 2014). In fact, just as young women develop anorexia as a fundamental psychological disorder about their perception of their bodies, boys sometimes develop muscle dysmorphia, believing that they never have enough muscle bulk. Even boys who do not suffer from muscle dysmorphia seem to believe the same equation of muscles and manhood.

The snapshot in Figure 5.2 combines both the muscle-flexing theme and the human-pyramid genre to be discussed next. In that snapshot the boy flexing at the top of the pyramid literally displays his superior strength over the other boys, who, in fact, must be strong to support the weight on their backs.

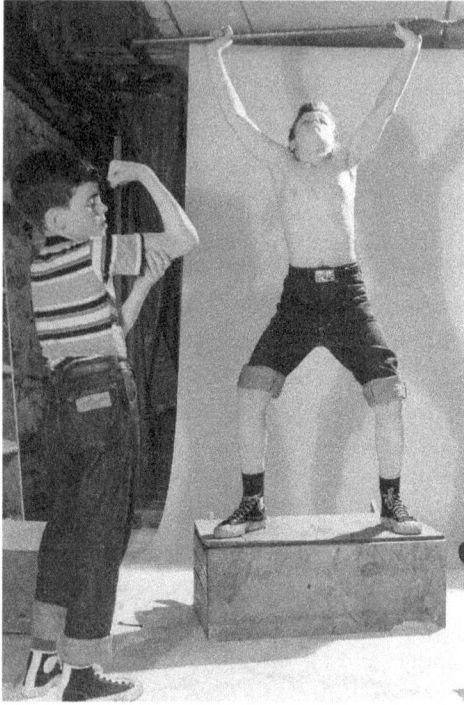

Figure 5.1

Figure 5.2

The snapshots of muscles, above, for example, display the bodies, but the muscles signal power and strength. What the muscles bring with them in the maturing, physically developing boy is the capacity for violent aggression. Sapolsky (1997) is quick to point out, based on his expertise in primatology, evolutionary psychology, and neuroscience, that although male hormones provide a biological push for male aggression, the socialization of the male in the family and in the male friendship group and in the society has a great deal more to do with the expression of physical aggression in any given male. Like other primates, boys establish hierarchies in the group and each boy knows his place. Some boys have the physical strength and potential to harm others to bolster their status in the group.

Violence in the male friendship group has the potential to disrupt the bonding in the group, so boys' friendship groups develop folk customs to substitute stylized aggression for real aggression. The two primary genres of stylized aggression boys engage in are verbal dueling and rough-and-tumble play fighting. Trading playful insults is hard to capture in a snapshot, but physical play fighting is not, as the many examples in my collection and elsewhere attest.

Play Fighting

Play fighting is common in mammals and in some other species. Wallis and I (2015, 2019) provide a concise summary of research on animal play fighting and play fighting in humans. The puzzle to scholars who examine play fighting in animals (e.g., Burghardt 2005) is that play fighting seems to work against competitive advantage in natural selection, as play fighting is a waste of precious calories, risks injury, and distracts the playing animals from attentiveness to the risk of predators. The ethologists find other benefits to the play fighting for animals, and when scholars turn to play fighting in children (e.g., Pellegrini 1988, 1993), they find many benefits for the social development of children, despite the risks.

Wallis and I (2015, 2019) launched our inquiry into the puzzle of rough-and-tumble (R&T) play fighting among soldiers in the combat zone as we contemplated the color photo by war photographer Tim Hetherington (2010) on the back of the dust jacket of the hardback edition of Sebastian Junger's *War* (2010). The marines in that photo are having an R&T play fight melee out in the open at their remote base camp in the mountains of Afghanistan, a highly dangerous outpost, a setting where an R&T melee seems somewhat crazy. And yet they were laughing as they tussled, mainly shirtless and smiling. Smiling. That's the key. If we examine photographs, including the

Figure 5.3

snapshots I examine here, to learn something about the experience of male bonding through contact play with bodies, then the smiles are the clue that the boys are feeling pleasure in the play and ritual.

The taboo against touching for American males who want to maintain a persuasive performance of normative heterosexuality, combined with the human need for touching, means that the play frame provides a "safe" space to touch other males. The paradox of male play fighting is that it functions as a bonding activity; play fighting requires trust, and the play frame signals a close relationship. Playfighting is stylized aggression meant to forestall the real aggression that can rise in the male group and threaten its cohesion.

Human Pyramids

Vintage snapshots often feature men, and sometimes women, creating human pyramids. I suspect that this folk form of play is older than the more formal, orderly, controlled forms of similar constructions of bodies one finds in gymnastics and, later, in cheerleading. The folk form of human pyramids is one of those events almost always created for an audience, often for an imagined audience for picture taking; young men and women rarely will create a pyramid without the thought that the accomplishment will be captured in a snapshot. I devote considerable attention in my book *Soldier Snapshots* (2021) to snapshots of male soldiers, marines, sailors, and aviators building human pyramids, at times even while naked.

Figure 5.4

Figure 5.5

Most snapshots of human pyramids in my collection are taken in public places, like beaches, playgrounds, summer camps, Scout campouts, and similar spaces. The snapshot in Figure 5.4 is typical of many others. The boys in Figure 5.4 are clothed (likely at a summer camp), but the boys in the pyramid in Figure 5.5 are in swimsuits in a pool. Many snapshots of pyramids of boys are taken on a beach (Mechling 2016b).

Young women also make human pyramids, judging from my sample of snapshots, but these are relatively rare, and the genre seems to be mainly one practiced by boys and young men. So why are boys so attracted to this form of play? The answer lies in the dynamics of boys' friendship groups, their male folk groups, and in the boys' management of touching each other's bodies.

A human pyramid requires strength in the bottom rows, and ideally the boys on the subsequent higher rows should be strong but increasingly lighter and smaller. The pyramid literally embodies the hierarchy of strength in the group.

The folk form of the human pyramid resembles R&T play fighting (see discussion, above) in that after the snapshot is taken, the pyramid usually comes apart by a physical collapse of the structure, boys tumbling over one another. Even when they can manage to deconstruct the pyramid slowly, reversing the order in which they built it, the salient fact remains—the pyramid is a folk custom permitting boys to touch one another, sometimes clothed and sometimes barely clothed.

The social history we have of attitudes and behavior regarding boys-touching-boys in American culture is pretty scant. Social histories of childhood, and even ethnographic observations of boys in natural settings (playgrounds, schools, camps, etc.) rarely discuss the comfort or discomfort American boys have in touching each other's bodies. Ibson's (2002) study of men in photographs, both snapshots and studio portraits, documents his thesis that men in the nineteenth and first half of the twentieth century appear quite comfortable touching each other in the photographs, and if anything that trend accelerated during WWII. The end of the war, argues Ibson, seemed to end the comfort of men posing for photographs with arms around each other or touching in other ways.

All of this is to say that since the mid-twentieth century American boys have experienced strong messages that they should not touch each other, except in special circumstances, such as sports. To protect normative heterosexuality, boys touching other boys is acceptable only if carefully framed so that the message within the frame does not mean what it would mean outside the play frame.

Some of the pleasure in building a human pyramid lies in the defiance of gravity. Bouissac (1976) notes that in some circus acts, like high-wire and trapeze performances, the pleasurable tension experienced by the audience is the defiance of gravity and the ever-present possibility of failure, of falling. Human climbing of any sort defies gravity and in many cases can cause the same pleasure in the tension between climbing and falling. Perhaps this combination of terror and delight lies deep in our evolutionary psychology as our ancestors moved from the trees to the grasslands. Certainly climbing things gives pleasure to the climbers, from children climbing all over playground equipment to adults climbing rock faces like Yosemite's El Capitan.

While pleasure lies in the tension provided by gravity and by acts defying gravity, paradoxically, falling also can be pleasurable. One of the four types of play named and analyzed by Caillois (1961) is *ilinx*, the feeling of vertigo provided by, for example, games involving spinning or falling. The collapse of the pyramid into a pile of bodies surely provides something like the *ilinx* Caillois describes, as well as the pleasure of touching other bodies during the fall and in the collapsing pile (Montagu 1986).

This full account of the pleasure of the human pyramid perhaps explains why so many snapshots capture such a pyramid and the smiles on the faces of the boys in the construction of bodies. Like only a few other moments of play and ritual in our everyday lives, informal human pyramids seem to exist only for the sake of taking a snapshot. Without snapshots, we might never know the long history of this form of play among boys. The smiles in the snapshots also help answer the question of what new information the snapshot adds as evidence, namely, the feelings and emotions of the participants (Mechling 2019b).

Skinny Dipping

Representations of the nude boy have a long history in art, including sculpture, painting, and photography. As Greer (2003) and other art historians document so well, the "beautiful boy" represents a Platonic ideal of innocence and beauty. Photography, emerging as a medium in the mid-nineteenth century, expanded the ways to picture boys nude, and for a while the fine art photography followed the fine-art Platonic view of boys' embodiment of beauty and innocence (Leddick 1998).

A common tableau in fine art picturing nude boys is of them swimming. The paintings of the English artist Henry Scott Tuke (1858–1929) began that tradition (Robinson, ed. 2021), and in the United States the famed artist Thomas Eakins (1844–1916) worked both in photography and in painting to create tableaux of nude men and women. Eakins's famous photograph (1884) and then painting *The Swimming Hole* (1884–85), of young men (his art students) swimming nude in the river reminds us that there is a long tradition of boys swimming together nude ("skinny dipping"). The term "skinny dipping" may have appeared first just after WWII, but the tradition of boys and men swimming together in the nude has a long history. In

Figure 5.6

Figure 5.7

popular culture, images of boys skinny dipping have appeared in commercial stereoviews, in postcards, and on the covers of the *Saturday Evening Post* (the August 19, 1911, edition, painting by Leyendecker, and the June 21, 1921, edition, painting by Norman Rockwell).

Many summer camps for boys in the first few decades of the twentieth century featured nude swimming in lakes and streams, as documented in photographs and in amateur films on YouTube. It was not uncommon for young men to swim nude in swimming pools at Boys' Clubs, at the YMCA, and at some high schools and colleges. Nude swimming in these institutions began disappearing in the 1970s. Skinny dipping is a folk tradition not easily extinguished, and anecdotal evidence suggests it persists.

Most snapshots of skinny dipping are set in ponds, lakes, and rivers in rural landscapes. Figure 5.6 is mounted in a large album from the 1930s documenting the hiking and camping expeditions by a group of young men in the Washington State wilderness, and in this case the young men have been skinny dipping in Lake Corral in the Cascade Mountains. The snapshot Figure 5.7 captures a group of Boy Scouts, some clothed and some nude, wading in a stream or river and pulling a boat loaded with their equipment. Clearly the nude boys felt comfortable in the presence of their clothed buddies.

Although some rural boys might swim naked alone, skinny dipping almost always is a group activity, so the social aspect of the tradition must be important to the meanings of the performance. In every snapshot of boys skinny dipping I have seen, the boys are pubescent or adolescent, judging from their stature. That may help explain the motive for boys' swimming nude with each other away from the surveillance by adults. Puberty and adolescence are stages of physical and sexual development in boys (the topic of this book, but true for girls too) that puts the boy's body at the center of his attention, including his anxieties. So, aside from the thrill of doing something possibly thought "naughty" by adults away from their surveillance, skinny dipping provides boys with knowledge about the development of their bodies as they mature.

Skinny dipping is a genre of play, and as Bateson (1972) puts it in his frame theory of play and fantasy, the essence of play is paradox—in the play frame messages do not mean what they would mean outside the play frame. The long-standing American tendency to see nudity as sexual and therefore harmful contributes to a boy's sense that skinny dipping is "naughty." At the same time, since in the play frame of skinny dipping nudity does not mean what it would mean outside the play frame, the boys can understand that their being nude in front of each other does not signal sexual desire. Thus, a paradox of nude play in the male friendship group is that it actually reinforces heterosexuality as the norm; boys can be nude in each other's presence because the nudity does not signal sexual desire (though that can be a motive for some boys).

In every snapshot I have seen of boys skinny-dipping, the boy taking the snapshot follows the convention familiar in fine art and in the popular culture images in stereoviews, postcards, and even magazines and photographic collections; namely, that the image of a nude boy is permissible if he is seen only from behind (Rubin 2018). The penis does not make its appearance in these snapshots, possibly because of fear of censorship in the developing and

Figure 5.8

printing of the snapshots, but more likely (I think) is that the boy photographer understands that the boy's buttocks are an acceptable public portrayal of boy nudity. Even in Figure 5.8, of three Boy Scouts photographed from behind as they urinate in line outdoors, the penis is assumed rather than shown (I discuss the relationship between urination and displays of masculinity in Mechling 2014b).

"Crossplay"

Boys have dressed as girls for centuries. The full history is better told elsewhere (e.g., Garber 1992; Senelick 2000), but I can narrow the focus here to boys dressing as girls in the United States. Males dressing as females creates a "category crisis" (Garber 1992, 16) in a Western world that favors binary thinking. The male dressing as a female is a "third" thing between normative categories, and that ambiguity creates discomfort, as do other things that occupy the liminal interstices between established and maintained cultural categories (Babcock-Abrahams 1975).

Settling on a term for the act of a boy dressing as a girl when, in fact, the boy identifies himself as male is fraught with controversy, as "cross-dressing"—a term I use in *Soldier Snapshots* (Mechling 2021, 130–50)—is viewed by some as outdated and even derogatory. The better term is "cross-play," a neologism. "Cosplay" (costume play) originated with males and females dressing as figures from popular culture but assuming the appearance of a character that matched the player's sexual identity. When a cosplayer dresses as the opposite sex in a play frame, "crossplay" better describes both the motive and the experience.

Since I have no access to the inner states of the boys who dress as girls, I am going to set aside those boys whose gender identity and sexual identity lead them to dress as girls. Rather, I am going to assume that the boys in these snapshots identify primarily as heterosexual males, though I know that at the younger range of "boyhood," gender identity and sexual identity are still in the making, exploratory, uncertain, fluid. I am interested here in the paradoxical phenomenon of boys dressing as girls as part of the boundary maintenance of normative heterosexuality.

Boys' crossplay is most public in the case of theatricals in all-male institutions, including fraternities, boarding schools, Boy Scout camps, all-male military settings, and colleges. Although boys played female parts in Renaissance theater, the modern practice of boys' dressing as girls in college theatricals began at Harvard in 1844 (borrowed from British schools) and spread to other Ivy League schools (Garber 1992, 60; Senelick 2000, 356–58). At the Boy Scout summer camp I studied for many years, the boys engaged in theatrical performances in two settings—campfire skits and a day of fun (Insane Day) themed around popular culture texts such as television's *Gilligan's Island* and the *Star Wars* and *Austin Powers* films (Mechling 2001, 84–85, 194–95)—and in all those theatrical performance of the older boys for the younger ones, there were teen boys who dressed as girls. Although boys' crossplay in theatricals and in a few other instances does not address crossplay in the informal snapshot, pausing here to consider the theatrical does help us begin to understand the pleasure of such play with gender away from the theatrical frame.

Theatrical occasions (formal theater, camp skits, and so on) for boys' crossplay are, for the most part, framed as play, which (as we saw earlier) means that the messages within the play frame do not mean what they would mean outside the play frame. Play is in the subjunctive mood, the "what if?" mood, imagining things as they are not (but could be). Festivals are in the play frame, and a common feature of festivals is that participants dress in roles they do not usually play. The essence of the pleasure of festival and carnival is nonsense, inversion (Stewart 1979). This is the paradox of play.

Figure 5.9

Consider Figure 5.9. We do not know for sure the context of this snapshot, or even whether the snapshot was taken by a boy or an adult. The boy second from the left appears to me to be wearing a Boy Scout belt and buckle, which suggests to me this probably is a group of Boy Scouts at camp or on a campout, and the snapshot reminds me of the crossplay I saw at the Scout camp I studied (Mechling 2001). They may have been swimming, as some are in swim trunks and others in cut-offs boys often wear for swimming. The boy who grabs our attention, however, is the boy wearing an improvised costume meant to suggest female clothing—a hat, a bra, and a skirt. Boys on either side of him are reaching over to squeeze his fake breasts.

We know nothing about the boy who dressed as a girl in this snapshot, so his private motives for volunteering to be "the girl" are unknown. Nor is it clear to me that the snapshot records some moment before or after a theatrical performance at a summer camp (as in Figure 5.10); again, the context is unknown.

The smiles on all the boys do tell us that they are in the play frame, certainly true of the boy dressed as a girl and the two boys grabbing his fake breasts. The play frame is safe for these boys, safe for the boy who dresses as a girl but is not a girl, and for the boys who can fix on the imagined female body without having an actual female body present.

Figure 5.10

The boys in this snapshot are not far past puberty, the stage when their bodies are changing and their surging hormones give them sexual urges new to them. Their own bodies are new to them, and they certainly are alert to the developing bodies of the girls they know. Most boys at this age feel a considerable amount of social and psychological anxiety about bodies, and crossplay actually condenses that anxiety and paradoxically resolves the anxiety and tension. Rather than hide and otherwise ignore the sexual and social feelings originating in the boys' bodies and minds, the crossplaying boy serves as a public condensed symbol, a play body that is both male and female. Enjoying the play body lessens the anxiety and replaces it with pleasure. The crossplaying boy actually bolsters the performance of normative heterosexual masculinity in the group. Such is the power of the paradox of play.

I have one more important point about crossplay by boys. Senelick (2000) notes that humans carry "a primordial belief that gender tokens are magical" (2000, 1). "Anthropological evidence," he continues, "provide any number of reasons why one identifies with the opposite sex by temporarily or permanently donning its clothing: the transfer of the experience of the other, the desire to deceive supernatural beings, sexual allure; but *in every case a magical symbol is involved*" (2000, 2; emphasis added). Later, in an excursus, I have more to say about boys' attraction to magic and the power magic seems to bring with it.

Chapter Six

Boys Proving
Their Masculinity

The fragile status of masculinity as described and analyzed in feminist depth psychology (e.g., Chodorow 1978, 1994), the status of masculinity being defined as a negative, as "not female," means that boys face peer pressure to prove their masculinity (Beneke 1997). Put differently, boys and sometimes girls pose "tests" that boys are expected to "pass" to prove they are "masculine enough."

Shorthand for this is the ability to "take it like a man." The "it" in that folk saying can be a verbal or physical test.

Verbal tests, of course, do not leave a photographic trace. Many ethnographies by folklorists and others who do fieldwork in the natural settings where boys' friendship groups gather record the ways boys challenge boys verbally. For example, one way to "take it like a man" is to respond correctly to a tease or taunt. Taking offense or being "butt hurt" (a phrase I learned from my marine coauthor, John Paul Wallis [Wallis and Mechling 2019a]) in response to a tease or taunt fails the test. The verbal male insult routines ("the dozens") first found by folklorists among African American young men is an oral tradition now commonly found among young men of various ethnic groups. Though they are physical, practical jokes share with verbal joking the necessity of the target's understanding that the prank played on him does not stem from true animus but is, paradoxically, a signal of friendship and trust, the paradox central to the play frame. Sometimes a member of a friendship group might use the play frame to mask another motive in playing the prank, the practical joke (Sutton-Smith and Kelly-Byrne 1984), but when the prank is captured by a snapshot, the smiles on the faces of both perpetrators and target of the prank suggest that it is all in fun.

The bulk of the snapshot evidence of "tests" of masculinity I examine in this chapter captures instances of risk-taking, which is a surefire way for a boy to prove his masculinity to his peers. In what follows I discuss first the general phenomenon of risk-taking by young men, and then I examine snapshots boys have taken of risky behavior. Three are more informal genres of play—involving climbing, swinging, and sliding. The fourth genre of testing is more formal but still folk play (or ritual), and that is hazing.

Risky Behavior

The Scoutmaster of the California troop I studied for my 2001 book, *On My Honor*, gave the young men (ages twelve to sixteen) his "three I's" speech whenever they did something dangerous. "At your age," he would lecture them, "you believe in the '3 I's'—you think you are immune, immortal, and infertile. I won't worry about the third one at Scout camp, but I do worry about the other two." Young men do tend to believe they are immortal, and that feeling usually lasts well into their twenties. This is why old men can send young men to war.

Young men notoriously take physical risks, sometimes exposing their bodies to great danger of harm and death. As in other behavior, other vernacular (folk) practices we observe in boys in groups, both the boy's "nature" (the biological substrate) and his "second nature" (his socialization in the group within larger social and cultural contexts) contribute to the tendency of boys to engage in risky behavior.

Evolutionary psychology gives us some ideas about how risk-taking might be hardwired into the brains of preadolescent and adolescent males. As Sapolsky (1997, 2017) reminds us, human behavior is, in most cases, never purely the result of biology but usually reflects a complex interaction between biology and culture. We see this in the research by evolutionary psychologists on risk-taking in young men.

When evolutionary psychologists examine risk-taking in children, they argue that such "motivated behavior" as seeking high places by climbing trees and structures or seeking the sensation of rapid speed by swinging or sliding serves survival by creating "anti-phobic" effects in the children's consciousness (Sandseter and Kennair 2011). Thus, certain "exhilarating" experiences in the play frame can give the child the experience of mastering the fearful situation in a way that keeps the child in charge of the experience. To me this resembles the argument Wallis and I (2019) make in showing how several genres of male folklore in the combat zone, especially first-person shooter games (FPS), serve as a short-term therapy for PTSD. Rehearsing a fearful experience in the play frame tames the fear and maintains the individual's sense of agency, control, and mastery.

In looking at the biological elements in risk-taking by young men, we look at the brain science and then at the evolutionary, sociobiological explanation. The science tells us that, beginning in puberty, the adolescent brain is very susceptible to peer influences and responds to peer relationships more than do adults (Mounts 2015; Ludden 2020). The brain imaging also tells us that adolescents "are more distressed than adults when excluded by peers," and that the prefrontal cortex (the PFC), the seat of self-regulation, develops slowly in adolescence (Steinberg 2014; Mounts 2015). Mounts reports research by Gardner and Steinberg (2006) in which they found that in a computerized driving task, early "adolescents were more likely to engage in risky driving when friends were present," and "late adolescents were somewhat more risky in their driving when they were with friends" (Mounts 2015). What this means for my inquiry is that the young men are highly susceptible to peer pressure, that they are likely to engage in risky behavior with an audience of peers, and that they lack certain cognitive controls on their risky behavior. And we note that most of this brain research is on male brains, so we will come back to that below.

The slow brain development in male adolescence combined with social and cultural contexts for male adolescence results in what evolutionary psychologists call "the young male syndrome" (Wilson and Daly 1985). The "taste for risk" seems to be "primarily a masculine attribute," and in their survey of research on homicides stemming from "altercations" between men, Wilson and Daly (59) observe that violent male disputes really are about "face," which is to say that even seemingly small slights can lead to male violence. In the view of sociobiologists, young male risk-taking and violence are pieces of the evolutionary strategy to attract females. "We expect a taste for competitive risk taking," write Wilson and Daly (66) "to be an evolved aspect of masculine psychology as a result of sexual selection." They go on: "In a sociable species such as our own, in which there are long-term consequences of success and failure in competition, mediated by rank and reputation, we furthermore expect an evolved inclination toward social display of one's competitive risk-taking skills, and again this should be an especially masculine trait" (66).

This passage from two evolutionary psychologists suggests a lot about what is going on with the risk-taking by young men. The authors recognize that a characteristic trait of American culture is competitive individualism, a trait in large part a consequence of American capitalism. "Success" and "failure" loom large in the consciousness of young men (we get to women below), and the notions of "rank and reputation" are as important in the small male friendship group as they are in the larger society, maybe even more so. The social psychological understanding of young men in groups recognizes that, like the primates studied by Sapolsky (1997), men in groups figure out a hierarchy of status and power. One way to impress one's peers in the male friendship group is to show bravado in risk-taking, to accept dares and other challenges (tests) and to "prove" one's masculinity and one's qualifications to belong to the group. The annual "Darwin Awards" and other semihumorous accounts of stupid, dangerous things young men do testify to the "young male syndrome" as a driver of that behavior. Back to the Scoutmaster's lecture on "the three I's" and "Here, hold my beer and watch this!" Experimental evidence, note Wilson and Daly (1985, 67), shows that "groups generally tend to arrive at riskier decisions than do individuals," which confirms the brain science evidence cited by Mounts (2015).

Risk-taking in the male friendship groups is not just for status in the group. It comes as no surprise that the evolutionary psychologists find lots of evidence that young men take risks as a sexual display strategy to attract women (e.g., Pawlowski, Atwal, and Dunbar 2008; Ronay and von Hippel 2010). "Showing off" for females is an everyday phenomenon in the lives of boys.

Daredevil

A common genre of children's folklore is the "dare." Boys and girls both challenge others in the friendship group (dyads and larger) to engage in some risky or forbidden behavior. Sometimes the dare is simple ("I dare you to lick that"), and sometimes the dare is embedded in a larger game of truth or dare, a game in which young people take turns as "it," the central person who is asked by the other(s) whether she or he wants a challenge to tell the truth about something or take a dare. I shall resist the temptation here to offer a full analysis of the interesting dynamics of truth or dare in a friendship dyad or group, and (of course) the verbal versions of the customs around dares leave no photographic evidence. It is only the action of a physical response to a dare that might be captured in a snapshot, as certainly must be the case in Figure 6.1.

It used to be that folklorists and other scholars who study children's folk cultures would conclude that girls and young women keep to verbal and less risky sorts of dares, whereas boys more often engage in more physically risky behavior in response to the dares from friends. That gender difference has largely disappeared, though in truth we still have little ethnographic evidence

Figure 6.1

of the performance of physical dares in male and female friendship groups. Doubtless many cultural changes and forces over the past half-decade or so have played a part in the observed fact that girls' play has been becoming more and more like boys' play than earlier in American history, but I would point to Title IX of the Education Amendments of 1972 as a crucial moment in giving girls and young women play and game experiences that were pretty much the enclave of boys and men until then. The focus of this book, of course, is boys, so I leave the question of dares in female friendship groups to another ethnographer.

Thinking about boys and dares as tests of masculinity raised in my mind the term "daredevil." This is a term first discovered by etymologists in the late eighteenth and early nineteenth centuries, and the word had both folk uses to describe the fearless risk-taking of boys and men and later in the nineteenth century a popular culture use to describe the thrilling behavior of a performer of dangerous feats for a paying audience. In the mid-twentieth century, 1964, famed Marvel Comics creator Stan Lee introduced a cartoon superhero named Daredevil, who has had a presence in American popular comics, television, and film since then.

The "devil" reference in the term deserves some attention, not least because "devil" is a word often used by adults to describe a boy's behavior ("he's a little devil"), which also signals a folk idea about boys' nature. The "devil" in "daredevil" less symbolizes evil and more symbolizes fate. The fate that awaits us all is death, so the daredevil engages in "death-defying" behavior, taking a dare, passing a risky test, and emerging from the test alive and, ideally, without injury. Evel Knievel (Robert Craig Knievel, 1938–2007) was perhaps the most famous stunt performer of the twentieth century; he earned that nickname with his daredevil motorcycle stunts.

I doubt many of the boys in the snapshots I offer here as evidence of risky behavior think about their own deaths when they take risks with or without the explicit dare (the dare is always present implicitly in the boys' friendship group). Boys believe that they are "immortal," as the Scoutmaster observes in his speech to the boys.

At the same time, boys' thoughts about the possibility of death as a consequence of their risky, daredevil behavior always lurk at the edge of their consciousness. Many boys understand that death can stalk even kids. Urban kids in some neighborhoods might have to deal daily with the knowledge that kids die of gunfire, and sadly many suburban kids now deal daily with the knowledge that active shooters can invade their schools and bring random death to friends. Even without school shootings, suburban children know that disease and accidents can bring death to classmates, friends, and even young family members. Stephen King's novella *The Body* (1982), a story later made into the 1986 film *Stand by Me*, proves that good fiction can be as ethnographic about boys' lives as the work by folklorists, sociologists, and anthropologists who study the friendship groups of boys and young men. Amidst all the details about the folk culture of the friendship group of the four boys in the novel and film, including their risky behavior, is the central quest of following the railroad tracks to view the dead body of another young man, presumably killed by a train walking the same tracks. Finding the dead body of the boy their age turns the shared adventure into a sober moment of reflection on mortality.

Knowing that daredevil behavior risks actual death might dissuade some boys from taking the risk, but the persistent daredevil stunts by boys suggests that even the knowledge of the possibility of death actually heightens the fun, the pleasure of the stunt. Elizabeth Walker Mechling and I (1981) speculate in our analysis of the structures and meanings of two amusement parks in California that the reports of deaths on a roller coaster accident at Great America actually heightens the excitement of taking the ride. The rides would be boring if nobody ever died on the ride, and the rides would

Figure 6.2

be too terrifying if most people died taking the ride. Daredevil stunts by boys, I would say, heighten the fun, intensifying the unconscious pleasure of "beating the devil" and of defying fate, of defying death.

The vernacular photographic record of daredevil behavior by boys documents this form of play, some of it public enough that adults can observe it. Other snapshots capture risky behavior an adult witness would likely bring to an end, which leads me to believe that those snapshots are taken of the boys by a boy.

In my collection of snapshots of boys by boys I see four forms of play that involve some risk of injury and sometimes even risk of death—climbing, swinging, sliding, and hazing. Let me begin with the snapshots of boys climbing. "Deep play" with lethal weapons deserves its own chapter, following this one.

Climbing

Climbing things sticks in my childhood memories of growing up in Miami Beach, Florida. My best friend had a large pepper tree growing along the chain-link fence separating his backyard from the one behind it, and we easily could climb into that tree and spend time there in fantasy play, including viewing the tree as the rigging of an old sailing ship. A neighborhood park had a pyramid-shaped climbing structure (a jungle gym) made of unpainted iron pipes, and my retrospective guess is that its peak was fifteen feet above ground (it loomed much larger to the child, of course). And when a bit older, I would sometimes use a ladder to get onto the barrel-tile roof of my childhood home and view the familiar neighborhood from an unfamiliar vantage point, a vantage point so unfamiliar we might call is "uncanny," *unheimlich*, unhomelike (Jentsch 1906; Freud 2003 [1919]).

Nostalgia aside, we understand at a deep level a combination of fear and elation we felt as children when we climbed something. Children have a natural fear of falling, but they also seem to have a natural drive to climb. Some of the pleasure of climbing must come from the tension between these two impulses. As Bouissac (1976) observes in his semiotic analysis of circus acts, at least two traditional acts (trapeze and high-wire) feature the temporary defeat of gravity, energized by the ever-present understanding in the performer and in the audience that falling is always a possibility. Falling is a feature of the next genre of test—swinging—but for now let us recognize that climbing would not carry the pleasure it does without the fear of falling.

In the previous chapter, we already encountered climbing on a pyramid of human bodies, and while my main point in that discussion of the way that play frame provides a "safe" space for boys to touch each other's bodies and for a boy's understanding his place in the male friendship groups when sorted by size and strength, we should not overlook the gravity-defying element in the human pyramid.

This chapter is about ways boys test each other's masculinity, so everything I have said so far about the *pleasure* of the experience of climbing things leads up to this point: sometimes boys climb things in the company of friends in order to prove the bravery that is an element of the Boy Code. This is why we have snapshots of boys climbing things. Figure 6.2 shows four boys climbing what seem to be the steel beams of a trestle, a dangerous stunt. I have no doubt that it is another boy taking that snapshot, as I cannot imagine that a responsible adult would not put an immediate stop to that climbing. Memorializing that climbing adventure testifies to the boys' courage, a manly quality.

Figure 6.3

Figure 6.4

Having collected many snapshots of Boy Scouts climbing and standing on towers constructed of natural poles and intended to show off the "pioneering" skills of axe work and lashing poles with rope in order to build a large, functional structure, I cannot be sure whether a snapshot was taken by another boy or by an adult. I feel fairly certain that some of these snapshots are of boys by boys. Figure 6.3 seems to me likely to have been taken by one of the boys on the campout.

Swinging

I observed above that children have a natural fear of falling, a fear that seems to emerge in the first seven to nine months of life. Some animals also show a fear of falling, and it is easy enough for the evolutionary psychologists to explain this fear in terms of keeping infants safer from harm. Children's folklorists find a more complicated story, though. Many children's games feature intentional falling, and even in older youths and adults we find games meant to induce dizziness, which leads to falling down. As we saw earlier, *ilinx* is one of the four central principles of games described and analyzed by Caillois (1961), and we humans (and some other mammals) find pleasure in the disorienting feeling of vertigo. Children and youths get some feeling of *ilinx* from simple swings, but usually swings do not pose much risk of injury and would not make a good test of masculinity.

Figures 6.4 and 6.5 are snapshots capturing the more risky versions of falling for fun. Figure 6.4 is one of many I have seen involving tying a rope to a tree branch overhanging water (a river, a pond, a lake) and swinging out over the water on the rope, letting go, and falling some distance into it. Figure 6.5 shows boys perched on the railing of a bridge over water, the camera catching one boy mid-fall. The "No Jumping from Bridge" sign we see so often when crossing a bridge testifies to the danger inherent in that "stunt." In both cases—the rope swing over water and jumping from a bridge—the source of the danger is the unknown depth of the water into which one is jumping. I have seen boys jump from rock ledges, as well.

Sliding

Rope slides and zip lines provide yet another, distinct version of *ilinx* play with ropes. Visual evidence from photographs suggests that young people, especially boys, have constructed rope slides for a long time, especially at beaches. All the players need is a long, fairly thick rope, a high point to tie

Figure 6.5

off one end of the rope, and a low point to anchor the other end. The player starts at the high end, puts over the rope a shirt or piece of canvas or some other material that will slide on the rope, and pushes off for a long slide to the bottom. Gravity takes over. The angle the rope creates with the ground determines the speed of the slide down the rope, and the greater the speed, the more important the soft landing into sand or water.

The rope slide I observed (Mechling 2001) during my fieldwork with a California Boy Scout troop at their annual summer encampment high in the Sierra Nevada serves as a perfect example of the rope slide as a folk-play construction. Figure 6.6 is actually a snapshot I took, but boys were taking snapshots of the rope slide over the years I studied the troop, so I offer this snapshot as a sample of what I would find if I had access to all those snapshots taken by the boys at camp.

The rope slide is the first activity in an afternoon full of Scout games on an island in the middle of the lake. The Scouts used two logs (each about six inches in diameter), lashed them together into an "X," and mounted that construction on a rocky bluff overlooking the part of the lake near the camp

Figure 6.6

(the teen boys called the structure "the Grand Erection"). A heavy rope was attached to the "X" and the anchor end was tied to a tree stump in the water, a soft landing place. Actually, it would have been dangerous to ride all the way down to the stump, so the boys released their hold on the pulley sliding down the rope some distance above the water for a soft landing. Each boy in turn climbed up to the top of the slide, grabbed a short rope attached to the pulley, and pushed off to ride down the slide, probably forty feet. As I note, the occasional new camper is frightened about riding the slide, but a combination of coaxing and reassuring finally gets him to push off, and the thrill of the experience is worth it.

These examples of risky climbing, falling, swinging, and sliding are all examples of the everyday tests of masculinity peers pose for each other in the adolescent male friendship group. The boys frame all of these tests as play. I close this chapter with a folk practice closer to ritual than to play, though the play frame and the ritual frame have many similarities (Handelman 1977). I turn to folk hazing in the male group.

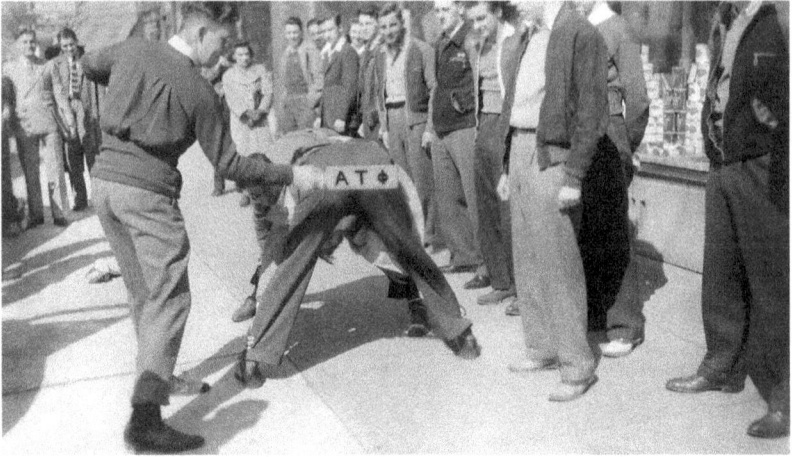

Figure 6.7

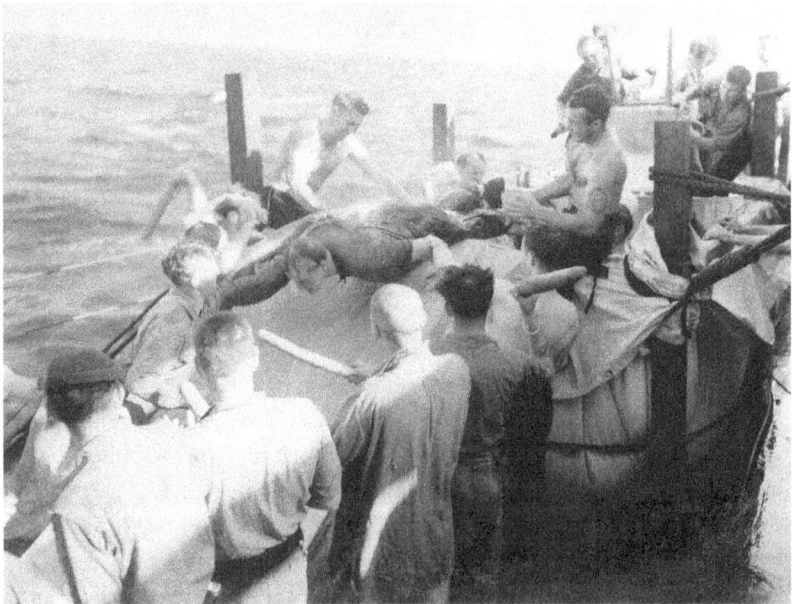

Figure 6.8

Hazing

Anthropologists and historians have documented male initiation practices and rituals across much of human space and time. The rites aim to give heavy symbolic significance to the boy's transition into manhood. The rites often follow a formula identified by van Gennep (1960), with three distinct stages: separation from the group, a liminal stage "betwixt and between" categories (as Victor Turner [1970] would put it), and then a stage when the initiate is reincorporated into the group (van Gennep 1960, 11). Cultures desire order; we might even say that a key function of culture is to provide order to our ordinary and extraordinary experiences. Cultures abhor disorder, and when presented with an anomalous phenomenon, literally an "a-nomic" (out-of-order), disorderly phenomenon, cultures devise strategies for bringing order to experience (Babcock-Abrahams 1975). Things that do not fit easily into a culture's categories exist in a liminal space (a limen is the threshold of a door, the space between inside and outside); thus, those liminal things pose a threat to the cultural order, and the liminal object must be placed in a safe category. Male puberty creates a disorderly thing, a male who is neither boy nor man. The formulaic male puberty rite carries the boy swiftly through the liminal status between categories and places him in the new, familiar category—adult male member of the group.

What we call hazing is a common element of the middle, liminal stage in the move from boy to man. Most often the hazing takes the form of a test of manhood, and there are many well-known examples of the sorts of tests of manhood the adult male members of a group impose upon the initiates, the neophytes.

More industrialized, bureaucratic societies have created formal fraternal organizations, some in schools and some for adult males. These fraternal organizations have devised tests to see if the male wishing to join the organization is worthy of membership. British boys' schools invented hazing rituals, and those rituals moved quickly to male schools in the US. The military has always had a good deal of hazing traditions, and navies in Europe and the US have had hazing traditions connected with crossing the equator (Bronner 2006). In the US we find hazing traditions in all male settings, including school fraternities, sports teams, summer camps, and the military. Increasingly, girls and women in groups also haze potential new members as a test toward initiation, but my focus here is on boys.

Figures 6.7 and 6.8 are snapshots capturing moments in the hazing of young men, in Figure 6.7 it is a fraternity public paddling, and in Figure 6.8 it is a moment in the lengthy and elaborate naval Crossing the Line ritual. In these formal organizations, the group establishes traditional forms of tests, which often involve discomfort, true pain, and humiliation. I have argued elsewhere (Mechling 2008c, 2009) that the hazing usually takes place in the play frame, so the initiates "know" that the humiliation is "not real." The discomfort, pain, and humiliation are temporary.

Some snapshots of hazing are set in private spaces, usually fraternity houses or remote sites, away from the public eye and the eyes of authorities (e.g., school authorities and officers of the law). Aside from the desired secrecy of the event, many practices in hazing are against the law (in forty-four states) or institutional rules, such as underage drinking and physical assault (e.g., paddling and, in extreme cases, anal penetration with objects). Also, many male hazing events involve nudity.

Other snapshots of hazing are set in public places, as in Figure 6.7. Humiliation is one of the practices common in hazing, so snapshots can document the public humiliation (paddling, leading the pledges on a rope, tying pledges to a tree or lamppost, making pledges wear embarrassing signs). A member's or even bystander's photographing the public hazing adds to the humiliation.

Given the goal here, we should ask whether the snapshots of hazing tell us anything the oral and written accounts of hazing do not. The snapshots document lots we know about the hazing customs, but the remarkable thing is how many of the young men being hazed are smiling for the snapshots.

When we see people smile, we assume that they are enjoying something, having fun. Hazing is in the play frame (Mechling 2009), and the paradox of play is that messages and actions in the play frame do not mean what they would mean outside the play frame. The humiliation experienced in the play frame is not "real," as would be humiliation in other settings and frames. So the humiliation in the play frame of hazing is "stylized" humiliation, just as play fighting in the play frame is "stylized" aggression. Moreover, because the humiliation in the hazing is part of a test and initiation process, the pledge understands that the temporary stylized humiliation paradoxically is a sign of male bonding in the group. The paradox of play provides a valuable, safe, even pleasurable space and time for signaling male friendship by subordinating the self to the more dominant male. In some cases even pain at the hands of the dominant male can be pleasurable for the initiate, though that issue would take us into psychological theorizing beyond the goal of this essay (Mechling 2016a).

The Crossing the Line (equator) ceremonies on board merchant and military ships (Bronner 2006) are among the best-documented male hazing events in the universe of snapshots, and because the "pollywogs" being hazed by the experienced "shellbacks" tend to be young and at the top range of my definition of "boy," I include those events here, though not for an extended analysis. Let us just note that the pollywogs in most of the snapshots I have seen are smiling, clearly enjoying the hazing (see chapter 11 in Mechling 2021).

Certainly in the case of equator ceremonies but also in a few other hazing snapshots, we see young men dressing as women. In the case of the maritime ceremony, it is the shellbacks who crossplay in ways resembling the theatricals in the all-male military (see chapter 9, "Cross-Dressing," in Mechling 2021 and chapter 5 herein). In fraternity and sports team hazing, though, it is the pledges who are made to dress in female clothing or in diapers, signaling in both cases the infantilization of the pledge, in both cases because women are often infantilized by men in the patriarchal society (Dundes and Dundes 2002).

Formal organizations, however, are not the only site for hazing. While fraternities and the navy have fairly continuous traditions in their hazing practices, informal male groups also haze prospective new members. For example, Delfino and I (2017) cite several reports of hazing in wrestling teams, and there is anecdotal evidence that other informal male groups haze. Raphael (1988, 17) argues that most male initiation rituals in the US are "casual," far less structured than traditional cultural rituals passing the boy into manhood, and for his book he collected many firsthand stories from men about such informal rituals, including examples in a chapter he titles "freestyle variations" (Raphael 1988, 49–66). While hunters practice certain well-known forms of initiating newcomers on their first kill, even those informal groups vary the traditions (Raphael 1988, 52; Bronner 2008).

Raphael's discussion of "freestyle variations" raises a form of male testing I have not mentioned yet, namely, the self-imposed challenge (1988, 54–58). Sometimes a young man needs to "prove" his masculinity to himself, so he might take on a challenge, such as swimming solo the one mile under the San Francisco Golden Gate bridge (where tides are formidable) or taking a challenging hike solo. One of Raphael's informants invented his own, personal "triathalon" (1988, 57). And in other testimony Raphael hears rock climbers explain the feeling of power and accomplishment in taking on a difficult climb solo (1988, 61–63). The climbers used language that reminds us of Csikszentmihalyi's (1975) discussion of "flow" experienced by climbers.

I have no snapshots of these freestyle variations on initiation rituals by young men, and for obvious reasons. They test themselves alone, solo, an example of what I have called "solo folklore" (Mechling 2006). The peer group of male friends does not witness the test and its successful passing, so there are not other males there to photograph the test. They might hear the story after the fact.

Even without the snapshots of the solo initiation rituals, I include the examples here as evidence of the power of cultural rituals about masculinity as a guide to the individual's behavior. Men test themselves—their strength and courage and persistence—both alone and in the company of others; which tells us how successfully young men internalize the cultural norms and expectations about the Boy Code and the Guy Code. When the test is posed by the group, the question is "Can you take it like a man?" When the boy creates his own test, the question becomes "Can I take it like a man?"

Many of the tests I have discussed here, along with some photographic evidence, involve not just potential danger but actual discomfort and even pain. The psychological puzzle here is why young men experience their shared discomfort and pain as pleasurable. I wondered about this paradox of pleasure in pain while writing "The Erotics of Adolescent Male Altruism" (Mechling 2016a), and while writing about traditional male hazing (Mechling 2008c, 2009), but the drive to solve the puzzle of pleasure in shared pain peaked when my coauthor for the PTSD book (Wallis and Mechling 2019), a marine with two tours in Iraq, told me that when he and his marine buddies get together, they tell stories remembering the instances where they experienced pain together. Young men sometimes bond in pain, it seems, and when I presented and analyzed the "soldier snapshots" in my book of that title (Mechling 2021), I turned to psychoanalytic ideas about what Theodore Reik, a student of Freud's, calls "moral masochism," not masochism of the sexual sort, but an everyday sort of taking pleasure in pain, which can include a subordination of the self to the interests of the group, as well as a "test" of masculinity (Reik 1962 [1941]). Male initiation rites have been a favorite topic for psychoanalytic analysis for some time (e.g., Reik 1962 [1941]; Bettelheim 1954). I shall not repeat here the details of my analysis offered in *Soldier Snapshots* (2021). The simple point I want to make here in relation to "tests of masculinity" is that risk of injury, discomfort, and pain are not mere side effects of male tests. The pain often is a crucial ingredient in the male bonding.

Never Enough

Beneke (1997) and others who write about "tests" of manhood to "prove" one's masculinity observe that the tests never accomplish the goal. As in the film *Groundhog Day* (1993), the boy and man are trapped in a never-ending series of tests, causing boys and men some anxiety. It is best to keep in mind Raphael's point, though, that boys and men rarely fail the test. The male group usually is not looking to exclude the initiate from the status of fratriarchal manhood. Not the outcome but the *process* of the testing is the aim of the group test. The testing process is a strong male bonding experience, and one dimension of the bonding is that those administering the test actually feel as much anxiety as do those being tested.

This last point provides a different view on why men in groups haze prospective members. The common wisdom is that (for example) fraternity members haze initiates as a sort of revenge for having been hazed themselves, that the hazing is an exercise in sadism. I offer here a different view. The members are as anxious about proving their own masculinity as are the initiates. Witnessing the pain experienced by the initiates and seeing that they emerge from the experience, "passing" the test, serves as a vicarious experience of success. The male bonding between the hazer and the hazed taps strong feelings of social masochism, not sadism.

Chapter Seven

Deep Play

Chapter 6 uses boys' snapshots to show a variety of ways boys prove their masculinity by "taking it like a man," by accepting risky dares, and by enduring happily the physical and mental tests of male hazing. The present chapter looks at instances where boys push the risk-taking into even more dangerous territory.

The symbolic anthropologist Clifford Geertz (1973a) borrows the phrase "deep play" from the British utilitarian philosopher Jeremy Bentham, to make sense of the Balinese cockfighting Geertz observed in his ethnographic fieldwork. Deep play describes play in which the stakes are so high that it is irrational to play, and yet the players continue. When Sutton-Smith and Kelly-Byrne (1984) solicited examples of deep play from their students, most of the examples involved risky play, such as riding a motorcycle at high speeds at night with the headlamp off or unprotected sex with strangers. Clearly, for the young university students, risk-taking, thrill seeking, was an important motive for and element of the play.

In previous chapters we have seen rough-and-tumble play fighting and, in chapter 3, the knife as one of the "things" boys like to own and play with. In this chapter we return to look at snapshots of boys with knives, but in this case the boys are not harmlessly carving a stick but are play fighting with knives and, in a few cases, axes or hatchets. Older young men in the military have captured in snapshots their play fighting with sharp objects and real guns (Mechling 2021, 156–61, 185–89). Outside the play frame, the warriors use those weapons to kill other humans. Play with sharp objects and guns carries considerable risk of injury, which is why I characterize such play as "deep play," with stakes so high that it seems foolish to engage in the play. The snapshots of the youngest boys also feature real guns (most often hunting rifles), but many snapshots capture boys' play with toy guns.

Figure 7.1

Boys' play fighting with knives, axes, and guns, even toy guns, surely would stir adult caretakers to make the boys stop the play, so we can be reasonably sure that the snapshots I examine in this chapter are photographs of boys taken by boys away from adult surveillance. First I present a few examples of snapshots with sharp objects and then a few with real and toy guns. Then I move on to the interesting question of what sort of pleasure this deep play brings to boys.

Deep Play with Sharp Objects

In chapter three I examine some snapshots of boys playing with knives, mainly whittling sticks. That activity is dangerous enough, but here I am interested in the snapshots of boys playing more dangerously with knives and other sharp objects, engaging in rough-and-tumble play fighting.

Figure 7.1 features four young men, perhaps in late adolescence, two of them play fighting with knives, seeming to pause in the act of stabbing the boy in the middle (we can barely see the fourth boy behind the three). The

setting may be a summer camp. The snapshot in Figure 7.2 catches two boys
grappling in R&T play fighting, one holding a knife. In Figure 7.3 a boy is
threatening a boy with a pickaxe at Boy Scout camp.

Deep play with potentially lethal weapons begs for a thick description,
and for that reason I muster insights from depth psychologies to speculate
about unconscious motives and meanings, as I do in chapter 6 in my analysis
of male hazing. Again, depth psychology unpacks some of the unconscious
meanings and pleasures of the male play.

Play fighting with knives almost always requires the players to grapple
in some form of rough-and-tumble play fighting, and as such it delivers
the same pleasures of touch with a friend in the play frame. Unlike other
R&T play fighting, though, play fighting with knives has a more aggressive,
competitive edge, turning mere grappling into a competition of strength
and attempts at dominating the other boy. The added risk of knives and the
chance that a miscalculation will lead to a real injury simply magnifies the
excitement of the play.

Grossman (2009), working from a military perspective and attempting
to analyze the experience of learning to kill in combat, describes killing at
different ranges. In the snapshots here we are watching boys *pretend* to kill,
which is not actual killing, but what Lt. Col. Grossman has to say about
actual killing another human in combat is not irrelevant to *the experience
of pretending to kill.*

Grossman devotes separate chapters to "Killing at Maximum and Long
Range," "Killing at Close Range," "Killing at Edged-Weapons Range," "Killing
at Hand-to-Hand Combat Range," and "Killing at Sexual Range," the most
close and intimate range of all (Grossman 2009, 134–37). R&T play fighting
with knives, which adult soldiers also do (Mechling 2021), resembles the
closer of the ranges of killing and as pretend play "stands for" actual killing.
Grossman uses the testimony of warriors and veterans to see fighting with
knives as an experience resembling having sex, involving close grappling
with another man and "the piercing of the enemy's body" with a knife as a
symbolic sexual act (2009, 121). The soldiers Grossman interviews and writes
about are only a bit older than most of the boys pictured in this book and
taking the pictures, but they are well in the range of late adolescence (ages
eighteen to twenty-six) I count as "boys" here.

Delfino and I borrow wisdom from Gregory Bateson on the play frame
in order to analyze the experience of male scholastic wrestling. Our central
argument is that we understand the experience of male wrestling best when
we recognize that wrestling both is and is not fighting, and that wrestling
both is and is not sex (Delfino and Mechling 2017). The play frame permits

Figure 7.2

Figure 7.3

and even masks unconscious desires satisfied by aggressive, competitive, close grappling of a boy with his close friend. They would not consciously describe the R&T play fighting with knives as resembling sex. Indeed, it is likely that most of these boys have never experienced real sex, so the erotic nature of the play fighting invokes not real memories but fantasies of sex with another boy.

All of this symbolic equivalence of play fighting, real fighting, and sex is mostly unconscious. The point is to understand how the boy experiences the R&T play fighting with knives and how that play give him pleasure, how it is "fun."

While in the analytical mode about motives and experiences, I can set aside the instances where boys who would identify themselves as gay or bisexual, young men who might consciously or unconsciously engage in play fighting for the pleasure of grappling with another boy, using the play frame to "mask" motives not necessarily suspected by the other boy or boys (Sutton-Smith and Kelly-Byrne 1984). Let us assume that the two boys R&T play fighting with knives align themselves with normative heterosexual identity. That does not change the erotic nature of the experience, but to understand this we need to turn to yet another idea from psychoanalytic theory and practice, namely, ideas about social masochism, as described in chapter 6 and in Mechling (2021).

My analysis of R&T play fighting with knives pretty much follows my analysis of the pleasure of social masochism boys feel when they experience pain with and for other boys. In hazing the pain and humiliation are real, though also stylized and in the play frame (e.g., the humiliation in hazing is not real, as it is when humiliated in everyday life). In the deep play version of R&T play fighting with knives, the pain of the physical grappling is real enough, but there is an edge to this fighting, a dangerous edge. If Grossman is right, the close hand-to-hand combat strongly resembles sex, and in real combat the piercing of the enemy body with the knife or bayonet resembles the penis entering the enemy's body.

The dynamics and meanings of the R&T play fighting with knives reminds me of a male folk custom I have analyzed elsewhere (Mechling 2008c), the use of a wooden paddle in male hazing. In paddling, the initiate "takes it like a man" in order to bond with the fraternity brother or teammate delivering the hits. The pain of the paddling bonds them. Moreover, I see the paddle as representing the fraternity brothers' or teammates' penises, threatening to feminize the initiate. It is important that the paddle does not actually penetrate the anus of the initiate—penetration would literalize the meaning of the paddle and destroy its symbolic meaning and usefulness as a coded symbol of the paradoxical male bonding experienced in the paddling.

In the case of R&T play fighting with knives, the mock threat is for one boy to pierce the other with a knife. It does not happen, unless there is an accident, but the possibility is always there. It makes the R&T play fighting a bit more exciting. Moreover, returning to the idea of social masochism between men and the pleasure of sharing pain, the R&T play fighting with knives adds the element of the symbolic penis to the contest, which is about "putting down" the opponent (Dundes 1979, 1987, 1997), that is, putting the opponent in the passive "female" position in sex. All symbolic of course and not conscious. Young men occasionally do get erections while R&T play fighting, according to some wrestlers (Pronger 1990, 184–85; Delfino and Mechling 2017), but an erection destroys the value of the play frame by literalizing and making conscious an unconscious meaning of the physical grappling. The play frame is that fragile.

Deep Play with Guns

Elsewhere I have written at length on play with guns (Mechling 2008b), though that article was not accompanied by any of the many snapshots I have. My article "Picturing Hunting" (Mechling 2004) does have an array of boys, girls, men, and women with guns. Here, then, I am returning to some of the themes I explored in the "Gun Play" article, only now adding the snapshots of boys and their guns by boys as additional "texts" to interpret.

The most common reason a boy will own a rifle is for hunting, and while adults taking the boy hunting in most cases educate the boy in how to use firearms safely, in less supervised settings, boys play with those same guns. Real guns and toy guns carry the same meaning, actually, the one having the potential for real harm, and the other causing stylized harm, symbolically standing in for the real weapon and the real violence. The boys in Figure 7.4 display an array of types of toy guns, each held by one of six boys, each pointing the gun at his own head in mock suicide. Surely this tableau would alarm adults.

That boys take so many snapshots of their playing with real and toy guns should alert us to the fact that guns are important "things" they own. Guns are tools for exercising power at a distance, and as members of society and of groups (family, school) boys feel like they lack power, agency. So boys "play with power" (Jones 2002), turning to guns as tools for access to power.

One of the powers guns bring is the ability to kill a living animal, including humans. Hunting is one experience of killing with a real gun, but young men also seem drawn to pretend killing and pretend dying. Wallis and I see

Figure 7.4

this in the first-person shooter (FPS) games he and his fellow marines played during down time in Iraq (Wallis and Mechling 2019). The FPS video games play with death and resurrection, as players die and regenerate. The same is true of live playing with toy guns, as when boys play war. Pretending to kill and pretending to die and then not dying obviously has its pleasures, pleasures we need to analyze.

Real guns and toy guns force upon the user some level of consciousness about the meaning of death. Boys who hunt and boys who live in urban areas with high murder rates know close up that guns bring death. Boys who don't hunt or boys who live in places where you do not hear gunfire at night and do not hear the next morning about a boy your age who was shot and killed—those boys understand the death guns bring, but that understanding is through the mass media, from films and television shows to FPS video games.

While most boys do not think often about death in the course of their everyday lives, except perhaps when a family member or beloved pet dies, they do think about death in the play frame. The value of the play frame, as we have seen, is that actions and messages in that frame do not mean what they would mean outside the play frame. Pretend killing and pretend dying and pretend resurrection make it possible for boys to think about death without thinking about death. That means there must be some value in our thinking about death, especially contemplating our own deaths.

Julie Beck's 2015 *Atlantic* article "What Good Is Thinking About Death?" describes the current thinking of some philosophers and psychologists about the benefits of imagining our own deaths. In some respects this is a revival of the idea put forth by the classic Stoic philosophers that, paradoxically, we can achieve happiness by thinking about the bad things that might happen to us, an idea that reemerges in social psychology as "terror-management theory," which describes the strategies people use to "quell their fear of death" (Beck 2015; Solomon, Greenberg, and Pyszczynski 2015).

Boys' playing with guns, pretending to kill friends and pretending to die at the hands of friends, might be one of those unconscious strategies people use to quell their fear of death. If guns are a form of "playing with power," they are also a form of "playing with death."

The Pleasure of Deep Play

As I discussed in earlier chapters, adolescent boys take risks. The control areas of their brains are not yet fully developed, so their impulses for the excitement experienced in risky behavior, excitement caused by the pleasurable hormones triggered by the "flight or fight" scenario, are free from the control of ego and superego. Deep play resembles the risky play we see in chapter 6 in terms of the pleasures the experience brings—beginning with the pleasure hormones in the brain and then the pleasure of doing things with close friends. Deep play ups the stakes of the risky play and, unlike swinging and jumping, often entails the close grappling of the boys, the pleasure of the play fight but with the added risk of real, possibly fatal, harm.

Play and Fantasy

Nancy Chodorow, in her masterful drawing-upon both her expertise in sociology and in psychoanalysis, sees the psychic process of *transference* as the key concept for understanding the ways our experiences create meaning in our lives. She writes,

> Projection (sometimes called externalization) and introjection (sometimes called internalization), as these express unconscious fantasy, are the major modes of transference. In projection and projective identification, we put feelings, beliefs, or parts of our self into an other, whether another person . . . an internal object . . . or an idea, symbol or any other meaning or entity. . . . All projection and introjection express unconscious fantasy, an affect-laden image or account, often nonlinguistic, nonverbal, and simply sensed, of what the nature of the object is, what the object's intentions are, how the self can or should react or is liable to be affected by the object, what effect of the self-object interchange might be on both and so forth. (Chodorow 1999, 15)

That is a long passage, I know, but for the points I want to make about boys' play and fantasies, we need to understand why fantasy "embodies" (one might say) both the projection of the boy's psyche into the external world and the introjection of the external world into the boy's psyche. My question is how these boy fantasies might show up in the snapshots, as they are bound to show up in the male friendship group.

Chodorow puts "the power of feelings" at the center of her argument that the dual processes of projection and introjection in transference create "personal meaning, our unconscious reality" (Chodorow 1999, 13). I had made a similar argument in an essay aimed at folklorists, "Folklore and the Emotional Brain" (Mechling 2019b), my extension of the argument made by Sutton-Smith (2017) that the evolutionary and deep psychological function of many games is to regulate our emotions. I had not discovered Chodorow's 1999 book when I wrote that 2019 essay, though I wish I had. I argued there that perhaps all folk practices aim at one thing—making our feelings available to ourselves and to others. In fact, argues Chodorow, "transference is psychologically necessary: without transference, our inner life, our relations with others, even our experiences of the physical world, would be empty and devitalized" (1999, 23).

In the concept of transference, which originated with Freud, Chodorow provides the process for the link between folk practices and personal meanings, adding an important point about fantasies. "'Feelings' here encompass feeling-based stories or protostories—unconscious fantasies—that constitute our unconscious inner life and motivate our attempts to change that inner life to reduce anxiety and other uncomfortable or frightening affects or to put such uncomfortable affects outside the self" (Chodorow 1999, 13). Fantasies are expressed in "stories or protostories."

We find the external versions of such fantasies in two visible, observable frames—in the folklore practices, notably play, within the boy's friendship group, and in the popular culture, mass-mediated images and narratives, the boys consume, from comic books to movies to television shows to video games. *I think I can construct the triangle of meanings—internal fantasies, fantasies enacted in the folk practices of the friendship group, and fantasies enacted in the popular culture aimed at boys.* I think I see that triangle of public and private meaning in the snapshots boys take of boys.

It should be apparent from the foregoing chapters that Bateson's frame theory of play informs my analysis of the meanings of much of the boy behavior captured by the snapshots. I often reread the essay "A Theory of Play and Fantasy," which originally was published in 1955 and then reprinted in *Steps to an Ecology of Mind* (Bateson 1972). I see something new on each reading. My focus usually is on the theory of play, but the title, after all, is "A Theory of Play and Fantasy," and fantasy deserves as much attention as does play in understanding the everyday friendship cultures of boys.

While I have not described here in detail the theory of logical types Bateson borrows from Whitehead and Russell's *Principia Mathematica* (1910), it is that theory that led Bateson to understand how the metamessage "This is play" governs the players' understanding of the messages, especially the paradox that the messages in the play frame do not mean what they would mean outside the frame, such as the ritual frame or the frame of "everyday life." We saw how this paradox works in several instances of boy play in the snapshots.

What is not so evident in reading "A Theory of Play and Fantasy" is Bateson's embrace of psychoanalytic theory, though it should not surprise the reader, because Bateson and Margaret Mead and others in his circle put psychoanalytic theory at the center of their approach to the field of culture-and-personality in anthropology and social psychology. Bateson notes that in play, "primary process" (unconscious thinking) and "secondary process" (conscious thinking, mainly the ego) combine; both are present in the play frame.

Delfino and I (2017) used this paradox of primary and secondary process in play to write that wrestling both is and is not fighting and that wrestling both is and is not sex. Wallis and I (2015, 2019a) employed the same point in seeing R&T play fighting, a folk version of wrestling, as involving the same paradox. Relevant to the point I want to make in this excursus is the fact that Bateson uses examples from Hollywood films to demonstrate the coded "pseudosexual fantasy" and its relation to the paradox of play, especially the combination of primary process and secondary process. My analysis of the pleasure of hazing, both here and in my book *Soldier Snapshots* (2021), also uses the paradox of play in male hazing to explain the repressed fantasies underlying the social masochism experienced by the young men being hazed.

Taking Chodorow's point that our fantasies are the gateway between our individual, personal realties and the social worlds we inhabit, we can speculate on the sources of the fantasies that might provide the "scripts" for the boys' play in the snapshots, and the likeliest place to look is American popular culture.

On the Relation Between Folklore and Popular Culture

Scholars who study American culture routinely refer to three "levels," or realms, of culture—elite, popular, and folk (Mechling 1989; Bronner 2022). Elite culture is created by well-educated, middle-to-upper-class writers, musicians, and artists, and their products (novels, plays, art, architecture, music, dance) are aimed at and produced by an audience that resembles the creators in social class and education. In the world of elite culture, authorship matters greatly. We study the products of elite culture because the texts give us a window into understanding American culture through the eyes and ears of extremely bright and talented writers and artists.

Both popular culture (mass-mediated culture) and folk culture tend to be highly formulaic, a feature that distinguishes them from elite culture, which abhors familiar, predictable formulas and values originality. Authorship in popular culture often is and may as well be anonymous. We study popular culture largely because large numbers of people pay money to consume the texts, so we assume that the details of the stories and images appeal to some core ideas and values held by the average person.

American popular culture first appeared in print form, words and images, but by the late nineteenth century, the mechanical mass production of printed materials and, eventually, radio, film, television, and digital culture created a truly "mass-mediated" culture. Holding a special place in this constellation of mass-mediated texts are commercial films (movies).

Some stories told and retold in a group rise to the level of *mythologies*, large stories that address such issues as the meaning of life (see Slotkin 1992 on American mythologies in film). Whereas anthropologists and folklorists find a culture's mythologies in oral stories, in American studies we look to popular culture for the mythologies that many Americans know and internalize, providing meaning to the ordinary and extraordinary events in everyday life.

The critical literature on American films and television shows is vast, but I am interested in the ways popular culture stories and images consumed by boys and young men interact with the folk cultures (oral, customary, and material) of the boys. That, after all, is what Chodorow has in mind when she sees the system of projection and introjection in connecting private, individual meanings to shared, public meanings.

Actually, those folklorists and other ethnographers who study the cultures children and youth create in their friendship groups often discover the ways children appropriate characters and storylines from popular culture (television, film, comic books, video games) into their play. Children are far from the passive consumers portrayed in the adult moral panics about the dangers of popular culture for children, or the calmer worry that popular culture is killing creativity and imagination in today's children. The panic and worries are simply adult projections onto children and have little connection to the actual process by which children incorporate the images and stories in popular culture into their everyday lives. Only the study of children in their "natural settings," study such as the fieldwork-based, ethnographic study of children's cultures conducted by folklorists and by some other social scientists, clarifies the power and agency children exercise when appropriating popular culture into their folk cultures (for examples, see Mechling 1994). I describe in *On My Honor* (2001) how the Boy Scouts I studied themed a day of contests on an island in the lake around current popular culture texts, including television's *Gilligan's Island* and the films *Star Wars* and *Austin Powers*. The ethnographic evidence is clear. Far from possibly losing their folk culture, the children take control of the popular culture narratives and images and appropriate those for their own motives and uses.

The realization of this pattern of boys' appropriation of popular-culture narratives for their own framed interactions at play turns our attention back to the snapshots in previous chapters, raising the question: What are the sources of the fantasy in these examples of play by boys, fantasies they "act out" in their play and games and rituals?

In some cases in my interpretation of a snapshot or category of snapshots, I already have pointed to some popular-culture sources, especially for such constructed playthings as rafts and forts. But the lingering question is whether these play fantasies show up in the boys' group cultures even when the boys have not been exposed to related popular-culture texts, like Huck Finn or Tarzan films or the *Our Gang* comedies. A version of this question is whether the popular-culture images and narratives shape the boys' fantasies and play, or whether the fantasies already existed in the minds of the authors, artists, filmmakers, television writers, directors, and creators of comics and video games, most of whom were boys once themselves.

The most likely answer to that question is that there is a dialectical relationship between the popular culture versions of what Kidd (2004) calls "the feral tale" in folklore and mythology about the "wildness of boys" and elements in the boy's nature (biology and evolutionary psychology) that suggest impulses toward "feral" behavior, as evidenced in the examples of escapism, male exclusiveness, and play in the snapshots I have examined here. The wild boy, the feral child, shows up in the narratives created by the adults, but those adults (at least the men) were boys themselves and consumed their own generation's popular culture versions of the tale. The formula tale about boys' wildness, however, would not carry much weight if people did not observe that boys are, in fact, sometimes wild and animal-like.

Boys actually know this reputation and are capable of relishing performing their wildness, their uncivilized, feral state for others. In *On My Honor* (2001), I had to sort through the puzzle of the fact that the older young men and alumni of the troop behaved in such gross ways at the "after campfire campfire" at the end of camp, when girlfriends and wives joined the campfire circle and witnessed their boyfriends and husbands telling the sorts of raunchy jokes males usually reserve for their exclusively male settings, like locker rooms and hunting camps or even the adult staff campfire at the camp. When I expressed my puzzlement to the Scoutmaster, he replied that "boys know that girls think they are gross," so the boys respond to that judgment from girls their age, but also from teachers and other adult females, by ratcheting up the gross behavior. "You think that's gross? Watch this!"

What Pete, the Scoutmaster, observed is the phenomenon Bateson calls "schismogenesis" (Bateson 1972). The point behind that term (drawn from the Greek and meaning "the creation of division") is simple to grasp. When we interact with others, we are enmeshed in a system in which the communication consists of both messages (verbal, paralinguistic, and nonverbal) and metamessages, messages about the messages in the interaction. Metamessages communicate the rules about how the messages should be interpreted—hence the paradox of play that in the play frame messages do not mean what they would mean outside the frame. Metamessages also communicate information about the *relationship* between the participants in the system, a point made by both Bateson and his colleagues Watzlawick, Beavin, and Jackson (1967, 121). As I mentioned earlier, boys communicate the dimensions and depths of their friendships, including their private feelings, doing things side by side and without verbalizing the contours and importance of that friendship. Doing things side by side is precisely what the boys' snapshots capture on film and document for shared memories.

In the system of communication between two or more boys, each boy is engaged in a constant process of interpreting the behavior of the other(s), and he usually modifies his own behavior as he understands (or *thinks* he understands) the behavior of the other(s). This process of the feedback in information circuits and the modification of behavior in light of the feedback is fundamental to the cybernetic revolution in thinking about human behavior (Wiener 1948; Heims 1991; Pias, ed. 2016), a revolution that Bateson embraced.

What this means for my inquiry is that the boys in these snapshots are enmeshed in a "web of significance" (Weber in Keyes 2002) they create themselves in their friendship group. The group is a system, and the communications between the boys signal their relationships and signal their moods, their feelings. In a sense each boy is "performing" his identity for both himself and the others, perhaps still unsure of his niche in the group. And if Chodorow is right, the boys are cooperating ("conspiring," even "breathing together" as that phrase wonderfully puts it) in enacting their fantasies, their personal fantasies as well as their collective fantasies and whatever fantasies they have internalized consuming the popular culture aimed at them.

Kidd (2004) does a thorough job of showing how the elements of the idea of the "wild boy" appeared and changed across time in the adult discourses, both fiction and nonfiction, both verbal and visual, about American boys. With those elements in mind, my task here shifts from an examination of the adult discourses about wild boys to an examination of how those ideas affected the cultures of the boys' friendship group. The hunch I am pursuing here is that the snapshots will reflect the dynamic system of interaction between the boys' psyches, the features of their friendship groups, and the popular culture stories and images familiar to them.

As I list and explore these elements, remember that they are fantasy and that they appear both as projections from the individual boy into his social world and as introjections from the social world (including the mass-mediated world of popular culture) into the boy's psyche. Doubtless this list is partial, incomplete, but it touches on several themes I see in the boys' snapshots.

Escape

Most of the social science literature on boys' running away from home focuses on boys who have good reasons to run away, fleeing terrible, dangerous family life, including alcohol- or drug-addicted parents and physical or sexual abuse. While this social problem is worthy of attention, what I have in mind here is the frequent, everyday running away from home, often for perceived slights or "unfair" rules and decisions by parents. One of my mother's favorite stories to tell others was how when I was very young, preschool age, in a huff about some unfair treatment, I packed a small suitcase with a stuffed animal and a few toys and books and headed out the door to "run away" from home. I took a slow walk around our residential block and eventually ended up at home. My mother asked why I came home. "Because I'm not allowed to cross the street." Which was true. So back into my bedroom to sulk a bit more (I was an only child).

I cannot find any statistics on this everyday phenomenon of "running away from home," but I feel safe in saying that it is common and that probably most boys "run away" from home at some age, often as young as I did. Of course, the teen runaways are a more at-risk group in need of help, but even in teenagers the drives and motives might not differ much from the younger boy's. Running away, as far as I can tell, does not leave a snapshot record of that escape from home, though there are a few documentary photographers, such as Mary Ellen Mark (1988), Jim Goldberg (1995), and Manny Fernandez (1998), who have recorded the lives of homeless teenagers on the streets. Instead, we must infer from the snapshots we do have the motives, emotions, and meanings of snapshots that seem to portray boys' escaping adult surveillance and control. That is most clear in the snapshots of rafts on water, but any snapshot portraying movement (e.g., bicycles and cars) also suggests escape, as do the snapshots of the clubhouses and treehouses and other "places where boys hide" from view.

Recall van Gennep's (1960) description of the classic structure of male initiation rituals, which begins with "separation" of the initiate from the adult group of men, sometimes a solitary separation or sometimes a group separation. And recall, too, Raphael's (1988) point that American adolescents lack the formal initiation rituals anthropologists find in other cultures across space and time, so in the American case the boys themselves must "invent" new traditions for their folk rituals of initiation into the male friendship group. No wonder, then, that the boy in early-to-mid-adolescence seeks escape from adult surveillance.

Secrecy

Some, perhaps many, of the snapshots analyzed here record secret places and secret activities boys engage in when not under adult surveillance. The desire for autonomy and agency in adolescent boys naturally emerges in the boy's construction of his identity. The perspective I am borrowing from Chodorow, however, impels me to understand the dynamic of transference, projection and introjection, in relation to secrecy.

American culture has a long history of secret fraternal organizations, some borrowed from Europe and some homegrown (Parfrey and Heimbichner 2012). Several scholars writing about the social construction, maintenance, and repair of masculinity in American culture observe that in many ways the US is a fratriarchy, more than a patriarchy. Without rehearsing that socio-historical argument here, we can observe briefly that the US was founded by a "band of brothers" who symbolically "killed" the father, King George. American distrust of authority is a result of this transfer of identity from the father to the brother.

American culture is not unique across time and space in establishing exclusive male societies, which often have elaborate secret customs. But secret fraternities, from the Freemasons to modern-day college fraternities, are a common feature of life for many American males (Moisey 2018; Robbins 2019).

My earlier chapter on hazing, as well as my discussion of hazing in *Soldier Snapshots* (2021), explores how "fraternities," organizations for men, invent secret rites of passage to test and then initiate new members. Here I want to explore why men like secrets, which amounts to understanding the ways internal drives interact with cultural norms in the group and in mass media. The initial snapshot in this book demonstrates the fascination of boys with magic, and (one supposes) with the element of magic that is "secret."

In the next section of this excursus, I discuss power, but in analyzing the male attraction to secrets we should not miss the element of power in magical experiences and in having and sharing secrets selectively. There might be a gender difference in the ways children and youth use secrets to manage their social relationships, though we do not have enough ethnographic evidence to be confident in any generalization along those lines. My hunch from some of the ethnographic evidence collected by folklorists who study children's small group culture is that girls are much more transactional than are boys in their strategic use of telling and withholding secrets in the female friendship group, while boys are more likely to use secrets (secret places to escape, for example) as a group to shield them from surveillance by others, including girls their age and adults.

Boys and young men seem to like taking snapshots documenting hazing events, despite the increasing illegality of hazing in state law. Some snapshots in my collection are of hazing events in public places, and I have just a few taken in the secret places, where male nudity is a common feature of the photographs. Film-based snapshots of the practices of fraternities as they haze prospective members are rare, and the photographs taken by Moisey (2018) for his book on fraternity rituals do not really count as snapshots of boys by boys. If we look at digital snapshots, however, we see male hazing, including nudity, in abundance (see Ward 2015).

Bruno Bettelheim (1962) tackles the issue of children's secrets in his 1954 book *Symbolic Wounds: Puberty Rites and the Envious Male*, revised in 1962, which offers a psychoanalytic inquiry into the psychological functions of circumcision and other genital mutilation in male groups. You don't have to accept his analysis attributing circumcision to male envy of the reproductive role of women (signaled by menstruation), and I know that Bettelheim's reputation has suffered from revelations about how he treated children in therapy (Raines 2002), but I still find value in his psychoanalytic insights into the lives of children. His chapter "The Secret of Men" (122–32) in *Symbolic Wounds* draws upon both his clinical observations of a group of pubescent children in residential treatment and his reading anthropological accounts of male initiation rites in many cultures. His curiosity about circumcision in male initiation rites originated in his observing that a handful of pubescent boys at the residential treatment center "invented" a "secret" society involving cutting their fingers. Bettelheim sees four major aspects of their "spontaneous efforts at 'group formation'": "These were (1) the secrecy of the rite, (2) the boys' cutting themselves monthly in a secret part of their bodies, (3) the loss of blood by the boys and its use in parallel with menstrual blood, and (4) the conviction that this ritual would assure sexual pleasure and success in the adult world" (Bettelheim 1962, 43). Bettelheim observes that boys perceive that girls have "secrets" involving menstrual blood, sex, and reproduction. In his view the boys invent their secret blood-brother rituals to parallel the secrets the girls have.

I witnessed similar behavior in early adolescent boys during my fieldwork for *On My Honor* (2001). I overheard one evening, after the boys bedded down (open air in sleeping bags) and continued chatting in the dark, a conversation about which girls in their school classes were having their "periods." These boys, ages twelve to fourteen, were very aware of the changes in their own bodies in the transition from puberty to early adolescence, but it was the changes in the girls' bodies that seemed, from the conversation, to simultaneously fascinate and scare the boys, who realized the girls were sexually maturing faster than they were. Just as the pubescent boys observed by Bettelheim "invented" a ritual to assert male control over their bodies and to make a clear distinction between male and female, so the Boy Scouts I observed "invented" a game of Poison Pit to enact symbolically and unconsciously their fascination about and dread of menstrual blood (Mechling 2001, 83–84). And as for secrets, I have no doubt that the boys would be very reluctant to play that game in the presence of girls their ages.

Magic

The first snapshot in this book, the one of two boys "goofing" in a mirror with a camera, continues to draw me back to gaze at it and to speculate on both the pleasure that snapshot captured at the moment and its value sufficient for one or both boys to save it as a reminder of that moment of pure fun. Back in the introduction, I mentioned briefly some of the elements of that snapshot, notably the fact that boys taking snapshots of themselves in mirrors is a form of self-portrait, a genre of art which has a long history of documenting ideas about the individual self across history. I also mentioned briefly the long history of ideas from developmental psychologists about the role of mirrors in the child's growing understanding of a self apart from others.

Claiming that boys are attracted to "magic" and that they sometimes incorporate "magic" into their young male folk culture raises some complicated issues, not least because "magic" can mean a number of things, some quite different from the others. For example, developmental psychologists note the prevalence of "magical thinking" in children up to age five or so, defining magical thinking as "the belief that events or the behavior of others can be influenced by one's thoughts, wishes, or rituals" (American

Psychological Association nd; Phelps and Woolley 1994). The psychologists
have a nasty tendency to see "magical thinking" past childhood as a sign of
mental illness, such as "magical ideation," an obsessive-compulsive disorder
(OCD). This attitude toward magical thinking past the age of ten or so rightfully annoys the anthropologists, sociologists, and scholars of religion, who
see "magical thinking" as both an everyday and sometimes a special ritual
aspect to the lives of people they study.

Another version of "magic" has to do with illusions. Barker and Rice
(2019) wrote an interesting book on the ways children and adolescents play
with "folk illusions," and the authors catalog seventy-some variants of the
illusions. Children's fascination with folk illusions is akin to some children's
and adolescents' interest in "magic tricks" resembling those by professional
magicians. I remember ads in comic books in the 1950s for "magic sets" of
tricks, and I even asked for and received such a set one Christmas when I
was nine or ten.

Again, the point of this excursus is to link children's play to fantasies
portrayed in the mass-mediated culture consumed by children and adolescents, and we do not have to look far to find this brand of magic in popular
books, films, and video games. Two words: Harry Potter. But that is just the
latest and most famous version of magic, as television shows aimed at young
people are filled with characters with magical powers.

I would include the game of Magic, The Gathering and its precursors in
the fascination adolescent boys have with magic. The game started as a card
game like Dungeons & Dragons (Fine 1983) and moved to digital versions.
The documentary film *Hell House* (2003), about the Halloween "haunted"
houses some evangelical churches were setting up to scare teens and warn
them away from drugs, violence, abortions, and suicide, claims that Magic,
The Gathering attracts young people to Satanism.

Still another version of the "magic" that might attract some boys is conjuring. The form of play with magic that leaps to mind is the Ouija board, a
toy or game with a long history stretching back into the nineteenth-century
American fascination with spiritualism and necromancy (Macknik and
Martinez-Conde 2010, 188–90; McRobbie 2013). I recall as a preteen playing a few times with a Ouija board with a female friend, but my impression
talking with other children's folklorists is that the Ouija board was and is a
form of play mainly among girls.

Another conjuring game is well known among American children and
adolescents—the ritual of Bloody Mary. Dundes (1998) presents about a dozen
typical descriptions of the Bloody Mary ritual game, drawing on examples collected by students and deposited in the Folklore Archives at the University of

California, Berkeley, and on examples collected by the Knapps (1976), Bronner (1988), and others. The following is typical, collected by a twenty-year-old Berkeley student as a memory from when she was somewhere between ages ten and twelve: "A bunch of us girls went into the bathroom to call Bloody Mary. We turned off the lights, turned around 5 times, chanting 'Bloody Mary' over and over, then stopped quickly and looked in the mirror. We were supposed to look for a headless female in a white gown with a bloody knife in one hand and her head in another" (Dundes 2002, 81).

Details vary in the accounts, but the constant elements seem to be the female players, their ages (pubescence or early adolescence), and blood. Those elements lead Dundes, perhaps the most famous psychoanalytic folklorist, to understand the Bloody Mary ritual as a folk solution to young girls' anxieties about menstruation.

What of the boys at the same age? Friends who also study children's folklore tell me they know of a few boys who either have joined girls in the ritual or may have even themselves performed Bloody Mary without girls present. Boys at that age (puberty, early adolescence) are as confused and anxious about the changes in their bodies as the girls, which leads some of us scholars who write about the folk play and rituals of children and youth to turn to depth psychology, as does Dundes, to analyze the motives and meanings underlying the visible practices.

While I am certain that boys are attracted to magic in its many forms and that magic is one of those play and ritual forms well represented in popular culture stories and protostories, grist for the internalization into the boy's inner life, that attraction is not the sort of thing that boys are likely to capture in snapshots.

The exception, and one warranting the inclusion of magic in a book about the snapshots boys take of boys, is the presence of magic in the rituals boys create as part of their adolescent male culture. The history of secret fraternal organizations in the United States is filled with mystical and magical references. I have written elsewhere (Mechling 1980a) about "the magic of the Boy Scout campfire," and I have snapshots of Scouts gathered around a campfire.

Horror Stories

I raise here another interesting genre of story that demonstrates the interaction of popular culture and boys' folk culture but, like some other themes and genres, appears rarely if at all in snapshots. Just as girls like to be scared in the conjuring game of Bloody Mary, boys like to tell and hear scary stories, especially on campouts around the fire. The campfire (the magic of the campfire) certainly is conducive to scary stories, with the friends huddled around the light and warmth of the fire, knowing that just a few feet away the world turns dark, unknown, and full of "things that go bump in the night." Adolescents have their own repertoire of urban legends meant to frighten people (e.g., "The Hooked Hand"), but I have in mind here the genre of horror story told at summer camps and in less formal gatherings of boys around the campfire (Ellis 1982). In my experience with Boy Scout campfires, a horror story always has a local angle, a local monster or a named insane person who escaped the hospital and lives in the woods. Counselors (late teens themselves) usually tell these stories, and the scholarly consensus is that the counselors tell these stories to warn younger kids against wandering away from camp, a story functioning much like "La Llorona" stories told by Mexican and Mexican American parents to scare their kids away from rivers and other dangerous bodies of water or even dry riverbeds subject to flash floods. The message to young campers is the same: stay in your tents or cabins, and don't stray into the forest around us.

Even though there seem to be no snapshots taken to document campfire scary stories, I do want to note that the physiological and emotional response by the pubescent and adolescent male audience resembles the physiological and emotional experience created by many of the practices that are recorded by the snapshots in this book, which is to say that the boys take pleasure in fear. In my chapters on hazing here and in *Soldier Snapshots* (2021), I posed and attempted to answer the question of why young men take pleasure in pain administered by friends or shared with friends. Here I ask a similar question: Why do young men take pleasure in fear, especially when the fear is experienced in and by the male friendship group?

In his nonfiction collection of essays *Danse Macabre* (1981), Stephen King speculates that horror stories (and his book surveys the genre, in which he is "the king") tap the deep, old part of our brain, our mammalian "memory" of when we were the prey rather than the predator. The neuroscientists have filled in the details. Fear starts in the amygdala, as King suspected, but the same chemicals (hormones) that fear triggers in the "fight or flight" (or "freeze") response are similar to the hormones that stimulate pleasant emotions (Javanbakht and Saab 2017). Young children are frightened more by scary stories around the campfire because the parts of their brains responsible for distinguishing real from unreal threats (the hippocampus and the prefrontal cortex) are still developing, and their experiences with real and imagined threats are still rare.

The brains of adolescent males are not much more developed than the brains of younger children, but in the adolescent male we add hormones as a new factor in the learning curve for dealing with fear. Taking risks (and dares) and hearing scary stories provide the same mixture of hormones that triggers the paradoxical combination of fear and pleasure in the adolescent brain.

Beyond the neurological pleasures of sharing scary stories around the campfire, we easily see the social functions. First, some storytellers are better than others, so the storytelling event helps boys find their talent and niche. More important, though, is shared fantasy. Boys in that setting often experience a strong male bonding feeling.

Psychoanalytic analysis suggests still another source of pleasure in telling and hearing scary stories around the campfire. Many adolescent urban legends and campfire stories feature assaults on the body. Boys are hyperaware of what is going on in their bodies, and, as seen in chapter 5, the boys use their bodies in the male friendship group to manage their interpersonal relationships.

Folklorists' analysis of many adolescent urban legends, such as "The Hooked Hand," find a sexual theme in the story, and we easily see the sexual themes in the genre of films dramatizing the urban legends. If we turn to the campfire stories of wild beasts in the woods, escapees from insane asylums, demented hermits living in the woods, and other threatening figures out in the dark beyond the lighted safety of the campfire, we have to mention the fantasy threat of bodily mutilation and ask why that fantasy is "fun."

First, as in PTSD (Wallis and Mechling 2019), there is some value in experiencing the heightened neurochemical stimulation of the reaction to fear and then not being harmed. The campfire story pushes all the fear buttons, and then the real threat never arrives. The boys around the campfire are not mutilated, they are not killed.

Second, we cannot ignore the significance of the "pubertal wound" in the psychology of the boy. Anthropologists describe the various ways in which the pubescent boy's body is "mutilated," most notably as circumcision but in some cases other scarification of the boy's body, marking his transition from boy to man. The "pubertal wound" seems to carry significant symbolic weight in folklore and mythology.

In short, the horror story is one of those genres that moves back and forth between folk performances and mass-mediated, popular culture texts, a near-perfect example of the dynamic of projection and introjection in the fantasies of boys.

Power

Those who study children's cultures, but especially boys' group cultures, note the role of power in their fantasy play, play stoked by and modeled in the popular culture they consume (Jones 2002). Children live perpetually in a low power niche. Those who study children's folklore have found that girls' play with power and boys' play with power have changed over the past four decades, with the girls' play with power becoming more and more like the boys' play, due (I would argue) to Title IX Amendments to the Education Act of 1972.

By "power" I mean the ability to influence others. Adolescent boys' interest in exercising power shows up in the snapshots in many forms. A large part of the fantasy life of boys consists of stories in which boys and men exercise power, usually physical power. Among my snapshots are many of boys and young men assuming the classic pose of flexing the biceps, a common pose in the military snapshots as well (Mechling 2021). Physical strength, as evidenced by muscles, is one of the forms of power boys understand, and the pubescent boy is eager for the hormones in his body to give him the muscles he can show off. Popular culture aimed at boys feeds the fantasy of power through muscles.

Boys who do not develop strong, muscular bodies explore other ways to take power in the friendship group, relying more on their personalities and verbal skills to influence other boys. Popular culture aimed at boys has plenty of examples of the funny, wise-cracking kid who fills that niche in the friendship group. (Again, Stephen King's novella *The Body* nicely shows us four boys and each boy's niche in that friendship group.) Some boys make up for a less-muscular body by demonstrating the courage to take risks, as we saw in previous examples of boys' proving their masculinity by accepting a dare. Both the risk-taking and the ability to withstand pain can elevate the reputation of a boy in his friendship group.

The popular culture created for and marketed to boys and young men is filled with fantasies about power (Jones 2002). Keep in mind that my goal is to understand how the individual boy's private fantasy meets in public both the collective enactment of a fantasy in the folk practices of the boys in the group and the public manifestations of a fantasy in mass-mediated, popular culture consumed by boys. The two previous sections have explored that system of transference (projection and introjection) for fantasies about escape and secrets, and the next section, on Lost Boys, does the same. Here my attention is on power.

Boys' fantasies of power, stirred by narratives and images in comic books, manga, television, films, video games, and some song lyrics, raise adult concerns about the violence in the popular culture consumed daily by so many boys. Historians call this adult reaction a "moral panic," and these panics are as old as adults' fears in the late nineteenth and early twentieth centuries about the effects of the violence in dime novels on the boys caught reading them. The moral panic in the 1950s over comic books even prompted Congress to hold hearings on this "menace" to boyhood innocence, and subsequent moral panics have targeted song lyrics and video games (Wright 2001). The underlying fear is that violent narratives and images in the mass media stimulate boys to act out the violence they are seeing and hearing in the media.

I shall not plunge into the whole issue of moral panics about boys and the violence in the popular culture products they consume, but relevant for my purposes is the view that, far from harmful to boys, the fantasies boys appropriate from mass-mediated culture are actually beneficial to them. Boys are not the passive consumers of images and narratives of power but actually appropriate the images and stories for their own purposes. Jones (2002) nicely makes the important point (which I have made often in my own scholarship [e.g., Mechling 2008b]) that boys *need* the stories and protostories about power, that most boys are perfectly capable of distinguishing between real and fantasy violence, and that *stylized violence* between boys, violence in the play frame, is a valuable element in their managing their relationships in the boys' friendship group. We saw that in the earlier chapter on play fighting (also in Wallis and Mechling 2019 and in Mechling 2021). Boys engaged in some form of play fighting are communicating many things in the group, including their relationships and their feelings.

The boy's need to play with power comes from strong instinctual forces of identity and belonging, forces that take the shape of fantasies. When the boy projects that need into the external world, his private fantasies encounter the traditional folk practices of the boy's friendship group, practices that enact fantasies of power, and he encounters mass-mediated stories, protostories, and images that provide additional fantasies of power, fantasies based in cultural mythologies.

So, yes, boys "play with power," and that is a good thing, and the boys apparently agree because they so often record their play with power in the snapshots they take of each other.

Lost Boys

My wife, Elizabeth Walker Mechling, herself a rhetorical critic, recalls playing "lost children" with playmates in their primary school years, a play scenario made possible by their living on the edge of the Florida Everglades, where their suburban homes bumped up against wilderness. Some play memoirs recount similar play among boys, in which the play group is somehow separated from the everyday world dominated by adults. The "lost boys" motif is not difficult to find in popular culture, from J. M. Barries's 1904 play *Peter Pan; or, The Boy Who Wouldn't Grow Up*, to the 1987 horror movie *The Lost Boys* (dir. Joel Schumacher). William Golding's well-known novel *Lord of the Flies* (1954), and two films (1963 and 1990) made of that novel, belongs to that genre, and the fact that the novel has been required reading in the high school English curriculum for decades suggests its impact on both young men and young women (though we really need a reader-response study of the different ways boys and girls read that novel).

The themes of "escape" and "secrets" clearly imply a "lost boys" scenario, so some of the snapshots we already examined can be read as involving that particular fantasy. Note that there are two elements in the "lost boys" fantasy. The first is a separation from the adult world of surveillance and control. The second asks what sort of social structure and relationships the boys construct when on their own. *Lord of the Flies* (1954) asks and offers one answer to that latter question.

The psychoanalytic perspective on transference casts some light on the fantasy of the lost boys. The fantasy features freedom from adult surveillance and, accordingly, freedom to do what the boys want to do. So the fantasy and acting it out in the wilderness provide a strong sense of independent agency. That much can be conscious. There is more to the fantasy, though, an unconscious dimension.

The lost boys (captured in so many of the snapshots here) are free of super-ego, of society's rules about how boys are to behave. The absence of society's judgment could mean that the adolescent boy's id could run free. But the adventure in the wilderness (even if it's just a backyard) sets free the boy's ego to invent ways to contain the id and the libido. Many of the folk practices in the adolescent male friendship group, including those in the snapshots, are "invented" by the boys precisely to keep the id under the control of the group. In the fratriarchy, as opposed to the patriarchy, it is the "band of brothers" who control behavior and channel adolescent libidinal energies.

Sutton-Smith and his team of graduate student researchers describe an instructive example of boys' uses of play to manage the libidinal energies in the male friendship group, libidinal energies that, if not controlled, would threaten the cohesion of the group (Sutton-Smith, Gerstmyer, and Meckley 1988). The team was observing children at play at a preschool in Philadelphia, and at that time the television show *Power Rangers* was very popular. The boys were playing Power Rangers, which could get quite physical. One boy seemed a bit too aggressive, playing a bit more roughly than he should, so the boy "directing" the game assigned the problematic boy a "role" in the story they were enacting, a role that would tame the boy's aggression. They used the formal structure of the fantasy play to control the libidinal excesses of one of their own.

Sex

Thinking about pubescent and adolescent boy fantasies, we cannot ignore boys' sexual fantasies. With the onset of puberty in the boy (sometime between the ages of eight and fourteen, most often around twelve), the hormonal and physical changes in his body are very often on his mind. Some boys actually have sex with another person. The CDC (Center for Disease Control and Prevention) surveyed over five thousand male and female adolescents (ages fifteen to nineteen) and found that 44 percent of the boys had had sex by age eighteen. Scholars and journalists continue to chronicle the sexual attitudes and behavior of American teenagers (e.g., Savin-Williams 2017; Orenstein 2020).

My decision to limit this inquiry to film-based snapshots and not plunge into the world of digital photography means that boy sex—or, more precisely, boys' fantasies about sex—is not represented in any snapshots offered here for analysis. With the advent of digital photography and the fact that now every smartphone is also a camera, the snapshots taken by boys completely bypass any chances for an adult to censor the images, which has given rise to "sexting"—sending photographic images of genitals and other body parts— among children and youth, some as young as eight, and by age thirteen a quarter of teens report receiving and sending such images (Genovese 2019).

I raise sex as the subject of boys' fantasies because these fantasies certainly demonstrate transference, as the boy's internal feelings, emotions, and drives become externalized in the male friendship group and they also encounter fantasies of sexual behavior in mass-mediated, popular culture. The boy internalizes (introjects) the images of sexualized bodies and acts, providing details for his imagination and possibly ideas for when he actually has sex. This combination of projection and introjection, after all, is what caused the moral panic in parents, teachers, and other adults.

Where do we look in the snapshots I present here for evidence of sexual fantasies in the boys in the snapshots and taking the snapshots? I see at least two categories of boys' snapshots that suggest sexual fantasies, albeit indirectly.

Look back at my examples and discussion of crossplay in the boys' friendship group. Look also at my chapter on crossplay in *Soldier Snapshots* (Mechling 2021, 130–50), and keep in mind that the examples of military snapshots often record the crossplay of men under age twenty-four. In my discussion in chapter 5 here, I make mention of the crossplay I witnessed in the "theatricals" at the Boy Scout camp I studied (Mechling 2001).

The projected fantasy in the crossplay in public has a few dimensions as an adolescent fantasy about sex. For the teen boy dressing as a girl in a skit at Boy Scout camp or for the slightly older military man dressing as a woman in a play frame with his buddies, the fantasy is stepping into the role of the female as object of the male sexual gaze. Let me speculate first on the pleasure that a crossplaying boy enjoys, and then turn to the pleasure experienced by his audience.

In speculating about what gives the fifteen-year-old Boy Scout pleasure in dressing like a girl for the group's theatricals, I acknowledge but set aside the strong wishes by some boys to *be* a girl. We know that many boys realize early in life that they are in "the wrong body," that they "feel" like a girl. If the boy is lucky, he has parents and other adults around him who understand that feeling, sometimes even assisting the young man's transition from male to female (Brill and Pepper 2008; Brill and Kenney 2016; Singal 2018).

In far more cases, however, the crossplaying boy identifies as a male but understands that in the play frame he is "pretending" he is a girl, stepping into the subjunctive "what if?" brief time and place of the play frame, all for fun. Pubescent and adolescent boys feel that girls have a great deal of power over them, being the object of the boys' heterosexual desires. One possible pleasure in crossplaying, therefore, is playing with that power, and I saw the boys who dressed as girls in the Boy Scout skits aggressively flirt with the boys.

That sexual flirtation by the crossplaying boy in the play frame possibly signals another sort of sexual fantasy, the fantasy I discussed when I drew on Reik's (1962 [1941]) theory of moral masochism in explaining the possible pleasure in the pain experienced in hazing. The crossplaying boy can briefly and usually unconsciously fantasize about having sex with one of the boys. At many points in my analysis, I have acknowledged the very difficult task facing boys in the friendship group, where they must understand their very strong attachments to some other boys in the group as "normal" male bonding and not homosexual desire. The informal and formal play (e.g., games and rituals) that dominate so much of the boys' lives together, play well documented in the snapshots, largely serves to maintain the definition of their strong emotions in friendship as nonsexual.

But as in many instances, such as crossplay, the paradox of play serves to let the boys experience in the brief time and space of the play frame fantasies of sexual experiences with their close friends. These fantasies are largely unconscious, though in some adolescent boys the fantasies are more conscious. Pubescent and adolescent boys sometimes "experiment" with sexual play with male friends.

The Primacy of Fantasy

I had not anticipated writing such a long excursus on play and fantasy, but it makes sense that I did. *Fantasy* is the key to passing from inner reality to outer reality and back to inner reality. The snapshots in this book show us many things about boys' bonding with friends, the centrality of their bodies as they "embody" their relationships, their love of risk, their flirtations with imagining their own deaths, and more. The snapshots are full of the fantasy of escape from the world of adults and even of girls their own age. They author their own fantasies, borrow fantasies from popular culture, and sometimes even create unique fantasies modifying the popular culture fantasies to suit their needs and desires. In a world they only occasionally control, they have full control over their fantasies. And, like all forms of play, fantasies create a "what if?" subjunctive frame of mental and social life. What if we were a society of adolescent boys (*Lord of the Flies*)? What if we built a raft and sailed down the river (*Huckleberry Finn*)? What if?

Chapter Eight

Hitler Youth and Fantasies of the Adolescent Tribe

In planning this book, I very early embraced the idea that I should write a final chapter on German Boy Scouts and the Hitler Youth (the Hitlerjugend). Quite by accident over the years I have accumulated a substantial collection of snapshots taken of German boys (many doubtless taken by boys) in the 1930s. While collecting snapshots of Boy Scouts on eBay, I bid on and purchased several snapshots that I thought were of Boy Scouts in the US, but upon receiving the snapshots and finding German names and writing in distinctive German script on the backs of the photographs, I realized that I had been fooled by the Hitler Youth uniform and the snapshots of boys hiking and camping, which resemble so strongly the snapshots I have of American Boy Scouts.

Except for a few esoteric clues, the snapshots of American Boy Scouts and of German Hitler Youth are indistinguishable. That resemblance seemed to me an interesting pattern to explore as a comparative gesture in this book. American studies scholarship benefits greatly from comparative work across cultures (past and present), especially distinguishing what is distinctly, uniquely American from what is characteristically American but not unique.

Lord Robert Baden-Powell's (1857–1941) creation of the Boy Scouts in England in 1908 led rapidly to the creation of Boy Scout movements in other countries, including the United States in 1910 and Germany in 1909 (Honeck 2018). As in the US, in Germany the various forces of modernization and urbanization led to the creation of youth movements in the last half of the nineteenth century, including the Wandervogel, a youth revitalization movement founded by Karl Fischer (1881–1941) in 1901 and dedicated to improving the health and character of young men through outdoor recreation, such as hiking and camping (Stachura 1981; Wiliams 2007; Kupers 2008). By 1934–35, however, other youth organizations closed down as the Hitler Youth became the primary state-approved youth movement for both girls and boys.

Along with the recognition that outdoor recreation for boys (dubbed "muscular Christianity" by historians) was the key to drawing boys away from the corrupting influences of the modernization of consciousness that accompanied urbanization and industrialization, the adults fashioning youth movements on both continents recognized the drawing power of the uniform and ritual to adolescent males. Growing anxiety in the US and in Europe about juvenile delinquency in the late nineteenth century and into the twentieth led youth workers to hope to substitute the wholesome Boy Scout patrol (eight boys) for the streetcorner boys' gang, and that notion of the natural boys' "gang" received strong support from psychologists like Hall (1904).

My interpretive pathway seemed clear as I examined the German snapshots. I would present and interpret the German photographs much as I did the American snapshots, using some social and historical contextual information to see if one could "read" cultural differences into the snapshots, which seem identical in most ways. I would look for patterns in the boy photographer's selection of activities to document with a snapshot, and I would look for any clues to the feelings of the boys as they play with their chums.

And then history intervened. In mid-May of 2017 young white nationalists descended on Charlottesville, Virginia, to protest the city's decision to take down a prominent statue of Confederate General Robert E. Lee, a symbol of the Confederacy in the American Civil War and a constant reminder of the racist history of the United States (Spencer 2018). On Saturday night, May 13, a mob of white nationalists, largely young men, staged a torchlight march, chanting "You will not replace us" (a reference to the white supremacist "white replacement theory") and "blood and soil," a Nazi slogan (Bromwich 2017; M. Wagner 2017). Then, three months later in Charlottesville, another white supremacist demonstration, under the banner of "Unite the Right," turned violent and resulted in a death.

The violent insurrection at the national Capitol on January 6, 2021, bore a strong resemblance to the Charlottesville white supremacist riots, including Nazi symbols and Confederate flags. And while the insurrectionist mob included both men and women and ranged in age, many Americans questioned what leads young Americans to engage in such violent mob behavior. Some commentators see in the events of January 6 echoes of Kristallnacht, "the Night of Broken Glass," the name referring to Nazi mob violence against Jewish and other scapegoated groups across Germany on November 9–10,

1938, violence unanswered by the German authorities, but others caution against comparisons between Germany in the 1930s and the United States in the years after the presidential election of 2016. Alan Steinweis's (2009) book *Kristallnacht 1938* lends some support to drawing the resemblance between the grievances felt by the individuals in the mob and the failure of the government to stop the rioting,

I begin with these resemblances not because I wish to revisit the violent clashes in Charlottesville or the insurrection of January 6, but because the puzzle in both instances is this: what leads to the "radicalization" (on the extreme left or right of the political spectrum) of men in their late adolescence and twenties? What is it about the nature and second nature of males in that age cohort that makes it possible for leaders to create a mob mentality?

The issues and events I have already raised in this chapter deserve a book or books of their own, but I do not want to be distracted from the main goal of this book, namely, to read the snapshots taken by boys of boys in order to understand how their collective behavior in their friendship groups, away from adult surveillance, gives us valuable information in understanding the dynamic relationship between boys' nature and their socialized second nature, between their internal experiences and the external realties of their group culture and society.

I begin with the German snapshots themselves. The reader can judge whether my impression is true, whether the snapshots of American boys (filling this book) are pretty much indistinguishable from the snapshots of German boys in the 1930s. The resemblance I see tells me that boys' nature remains a constant to be fashioned in detail by a group culture.

I carry into this chapter the perspectives provided by Chodorow (1999 and 2020) and by Erikson (1963 [1950], 1968, 1980 [1959]), a trove of psychoanalytic ideas that might help me see subtle differences between the German boys and the American boys on display in the snapshots. I am very much aware that I am comparing German boys in the 1930s with American boys across a longer period of time; the comparison would be "neater" (i.e., more scientific) if I simply compared two sets of snapshots from the 1930s, which would require information and a sample I do not have.

The title of this chapter hints at the key idea unlocking a deep meaning linking the snapshots across time and cultures—a shared fantasy. Recall that Chodorow points to our shared stories and protostories as narratives connecting our internal realities with the external realities of life in social groups. After examining the German snapshots, I propose a shared fantasy of the "adolescent male primitive tribe" linking them to the American snapshots of boys by boys.

Figure 8.1

The Hitler Youth Snapshots

The snapshot in Figure 8.1 attracted my attention while searching for Boy Scout snapshots because of the friendly horseplay in the photo. The boys are all laughing at the joke, and the joke clearly is that one boy is reaching between another boy's legs and sticking out his finger as if that were the penis of the other boy. The boys are in uniforms, and at first I thought this was a snapshot of Boy Scouts in the US. But soon I noticed the swastika on the armband of the boy on our far right, and then I realized that I was gazing not at a group of Boy Scouts in the US but at a group of boys in the Hitler Youth organization. In fact, this happened to me many times as I was searching for snapshots of Boy Scouts. I would find a snapshot that interested me, and then I realized it was not of American Boy Scouts but of boys in that dreaded, despised Nazi organization for young people. Sometimes there were no clues in the image itself, as in Figure 8.2, which easily could be American Boy Scouts on an outing, but once the snapshot arrived in the mail, I could read on the back the names of the boys and the date: 1935. What does it mean that I so easily mistook snapshots of boys in the Hitler Youth for snapshots of Boy Scouts in the USA?

Dr. Alexander Lion translated Baden-Powell's *Scouting for Boys* (1908) into German in 1909, creating a new word, *Pfadfinder* ("path finder"), for a term equivalent to Scout (Schaefer 2007). After WWI there were several youth organizations in Germany, including both the Boy Scouts and the Catholic youth organization Christian Jungschar, that Metelmann (2004, 73)

Figure 8.2

writes about in his autobiography of his time in the Hitler Youth. Scouting in Germany flourished until 1934–35, when such organizations were closed and the members forced to join the Hitler Youth. Organized when Hitler came to power in 1933, the Hitler Youth had more than two million members by the end of that year, and by 1939 some 90 percent of German youth were members of the organization (Blakemore 2018). The Hitler Youth served two main goals of the Nazis—the socialization of young people away from the family, and the larger project of Nazi propaganda extolling the master race and its historical destiny.

Here are two of the snapshots I have of Hitler Youth boys in hikes and campouts to make my point that the snapshots of American Boy Scouts, many of boys by boys, strongly resemble the snapshots from Germany in the 1930s.

The value of the German snapshots is that they are not products of the sophisticated and substantial propaganda efforts by the Nazi regime to use images of German youth as symbols of Germany's future (e.g., Von Halasz, ed. 2008; Seidler 2013). As with so many of the snapshots of boys and young men from the US in this book, I cannot be sure in every case that the photograph was taken by a fellow boy, rather than by an adult accompanying the boys on the hike or campout. I can say that the horseplay and casual poses of the boys in the German snapshots suggest, at least to my reading of them, a far less disciplined version of the German boy than the Nazi propagandists wished to portray.

Figure 8.3

Figure 8.4

Consider a few examples of German snapshots of boys (likely) by boys from the 1930s, snapshot vignettes familiar from the American examples. On their campouts the Hitler Youth boys often engaged in R&T play fighting, providing a safe frame for their close bodily contact as a reinforcement of their emotional bonding, much like the American boys. The two snapshots in

Figure 8.5

Figure 8.5 are from the same campout at Berlin's Tempelhof airfield, a common site for large-scale Hitler Youth campouts (what Americans would call a "camporee") in the 1930s. Also familiar among the Hitler Youth snapshots are images (Figure 8.6) of boys in a "fort" dug into the sand and boys standing on logs reminiscent of rafts, and other snapshots showing the German boys "goofing" (Figure 8.7).

Figure 8.6

I have only one snapshot of older German boys playing naked in the water and on the beach (Figure 8.8), and I know this is a Hitler Youth campout because I bought it in a set including other Hitler Youth camp snapshots.

As is the case with snapshots in chapter 5 and many in *Soldier Snapshots* (2021), the photographs show the naked male body from behind. I already have discussed the informal "skinny dipping" we know took place in the US

Figure 8.7

Figure 8.8

Figure 8.9

and the custom of nude swimming in many high schools and universities until the 1970s, a custom not uncommon beyond the borders of the United States. We should be even less surprised to see the German boys swimming nude on campouts and at formal camps, because the Nazi regime actually endorsed nudism as part of the celebration of German physical culture (Krüger, Krüger, and Treptau 2002; Ross 2005; Williams 2007).

Although outdoor nudism did not take on the state-sponsored ideology it did under the Nazis, the United States had its own cultural revitalization movement to return urban youth to the wilderness in summer camps, and boys regularly swam naked at those camps. In 1919, barely a decade after the creation of the Boy Scouts of America, Samuel Scoville published a novel, *Boy Scouts in the Wilderness*, in which the "two main characters of the novel prove their worth to the Scouting movement when they go naked into the wilderness to live off the land for an entire month" (Scoville 1919). As in Germany, American nudists touted the value of wilderness nudism in the 1930s (Hoffman 2015, 51). I had to include Figure 8.9 in this discussion because it is so reminiscent of the imagery in Stephen King's novella *The Body* (1982) and the 1986 film adaptation, *Stand by Me*.

The comparison of the American boy snapshots and the Hitler Youth snapshots from the 1930s suggests that some of the dynamics of puberty and adolescence in boys are common across at least these two cultures and, possibly, across the youth cultures of modern, industrialized societies, for the Scouting movement is international. The folk practices in the adolescent male friendship group in American and German snapshots are remarkably similar, including the ways the boys use their bodies to negotiate their bonds of friendship and to construct, maintain, and repair (if necessary) their performance of normative masculinity. The snapshots of Boy Scouts in the US and of Hitler Youth in uniforms remind us of a truth those who work with youth movements understand well; namely, that adolescents embrace wearing uniforms as bodily signs of belonging to a group larger than the self.

Observing the similarities in the American and German snapshots could be enough to be satisfied with these observations that in many respects the adolescent male friendship group works the same across some cultures (even across species, the primatologists would say). My commitment to the research goals Chodorow outlines for us—showing how the transference between personal, individual, inner reality and the social, cultural, historical, and material reality outside the self operates through projection and introjection—impels me to seek a "thick description" of the similarities and differences between the German and the American boys. That is what I attempt in the next section.

The American Fantasy

If we follow Chodorow's lead on the role of stories and protostories in connecting internal realities with external realties, then we should look for similarities between the fantasies we believe give structure and meaning to the boys' activities together. We must infer these stories and protostories, but our guesses can be reasonable when we find cultural stories that seem to be enacted in the snapshots.

In previous chapters I have suggested that some of the activities captured in the boys' snapshots enact the desire by boys to escape from the world of adult surveillance and control into a world populated only by the band of brothers. Snapshots of hiking, of rafting, of clubhouses, of bikes and cars, and of skinny-dipping all reflect a make-believe world of male friendship and autonomy. In the mass-mediated popular culture consumed by boys, from nineteenth-century dime novels through the era of juvenile boys' adventure fiction, through comic books and into the age of video games, in those fantasy worlds we find the narratives that real boys enact in their play and rituals with other boys.

Literary critic Leslie Fiedler long ago described a narrative formula he finds in much of American literature. The typical male protagonist in American literature, he writes, "has been a man on the run, harried into the forest and out to sea, down the river or into combat—anywhere to avoid 'civilization,' which is to say, the confrontation of a man and woman which leads to the fall to sex, marriage, and responsibility. One of the factors that determine theme and form in our great books is this strategy of evasion, this retreat to nature and childhood which makes our literature (and life!) so charmingly and infuriatingly 'boyish'" (Fiedler 1960, xx–xxi).

Fiedler is describing what Dan Kiley later (1983) called the "Peter Pan Syndrome" in adult men who never "grow up." Of course, the Peter Pan story has a different cathexis for the adolescent boy, who anticipates the feeling of being trapped in adult roles. The formula narrative Fiedler describes in American novels crosses genres into films and television. It would be a rare adolescent American boy whose conscious and unconscious is not soaked in the messages of that formula.

Beyond Huck Finn and Tom Sawyer, the stories and protostories of masculine escape known to adolescent boys in the US would include Stevenson's *Treasure Island* (1882) and Golding's *Lord of the Flies* (1954), which is still required reading in some high schools. Two of the key founders of the Boy Scouts of America understood well the formula narrative Fiedler describes, and they created romantic narratives of primitive boys' life in the wilderness; Ernest Thompson Seton (1860–1946) created his Woodcraft Indians organization based on American Indian lore, and Daniel Carter Beard (1850–1941) based his youth movement, Sons of Daniel Boone (1905), on the white frontiersman.

The authors (including Seton) who contributed to successive editions of the Boy Scout *Handbook for Boys* directly invoked the fantasy of the tribe of boys in the wilderness. Take my own 1956 edition of the 1948 *Handbook* as an example. Born in 1945, I was a Cub Scout from age eight to age ten (1953–55), and on reaching my eleventh birthday in the summer of 1956, I was eligible to join a Boy Scout troop. The night I brought home my first *Handbook*, I stayed up late reading it in my bedroom. The painting on the cover of that *Handbook* offered an iconic image of three Scouts in uniform, sitting around a campfire, and in the grey smoke was the image of an American Indian, bare-chested and in a full feather headdress, holding his arms in a gesture of solemn prayer. The opening passage of the *Handbook* hooked me immediately:

Have you ever dreamed of hiking the wilderness trails that were worn down under moccasin feet hundreds of years ago? Do you hear in your imagination the almost noiseless dip-dip of Indian canoe paddles in that stream where you fish today?. . . .

Wherever you live, you are not too far from the woods and prairie, the desert or mountain—the country where once the Indians roamed and where the great Scouts of yesterday did their part in making America. There is some place where you can go camping and feel you are in company with men. . . . (Boy Scouts of America 1948, 1–2)

Mind you, I was reading these words in my bedroom in Miami Beach, Florida, not exactly wilderness, though the Everglades lay a mere twenty miles or so to the west. That introductory passage and more made me eager to join the promised outdoor "fun and adventure in Scouting," and in the company of other boys.

Not every adolescent American boy was a Boy Scout in the years represented in the snapshots in this book, but many thousands were, and the boys who were not Scouts still encountered in novels and films similar versions of the seductive myth of an independent life in a tribe of adolescent boys in the wilderness, escaping the everyday world dominated by adults and their rules. And away from girls and the ways they disrupt male friendship groups. The boys carry those stories into their play with the chums.

The German Fantasy

It turns out that German culture offered adolescent boys similar stories of escape into the wilderness. In the closing decades of the nineteenth century, several youth organizations coalesced around the *Wandervogel* ("Wandering Bird") movement, which (as in America) was founded on the idea that adolescent males could be revitalized in body, mind, and character by taking them out of the city and into the wilderness. Karl Fischer (1881–1941) and a small group of men founded the first formal group in 1901, and over time up to eighty thousand young men and women joined the movement. The German Boy Scout organization embraced the same set of ideas about outdoor recreation for boys. In 1933 the Nazis banned the *Wandervogel*, the Boy Scouts, and other youth organizations other than the Catholic youth program. In 1936 the Hitler Youth was the only permitted youth organization.

The Hitler Youth understood the psychology and sociology of male adolescence, so it encouraged the boys to engage in the hiking and camping that were a central feature of Boy Scouting. In his 2004 book on his experience as a young man in the H-J, Metelmann describes games and outdoor activities indistinguishable from a boys' summer camp in the US. Metelmann loved summer camp and the ritual trappings of flags, songs, drumming, and drilling.

The H-J also understood the power of mythologies in the imaginations of boys as they trekked into nature. The American sociologist Howard P. Becker (not to be confused with sociologist Howard S. Becker) spent years studying German society on research trips there and from afar, and in 1946 he published a book, *German Youth: Bond or Free*, based on his own research and that of his graduate assistants. Becker acquired such a deep and extensive understanding of German culture that he was recruited to the Office of Strategic Services (the OSS, precursor to the Central Intelligence Agency) during the war.

World War II and the discovery of the scale of Nazi atrocities in 1945 prompted social scientists such as Becker to focus their theories of culture and personality in order to understand German national character. Understandings gleaned from the scholars would assist the Allied war of propaganda, but even after the war, scholars searched for patterns that could account for the behavior of "good Germans" who embraced Nazi ideology and actions. It was puzzling enough that adult men and women contributed to the horrors of the Nazi regime. That German children and teenagers also embraced the imagery and narratives of the Nazis was doubly puzzling, and troubling. Questions about the interaction of human nature and socialization needed answers.

Anthropologists who were working on ideas connecting culture and personality in the 1930s, all committed to a psychoanalytic approach to those connections, joined the war effort in the early 1940s. The Allies relied on the anthropologists to "explain" the "national character" of the Germans and of the Japanese for uses in war propaganda efforts but also for guidance on how to occupy Pacific islands, and eventually both Japan and Germany themselves. Ruth Benedict's work (1934) leading up to the publication of *The Chrysanthemum and the Sword* (1946) delved into the contradictions of Japanese national character, and both Margaret Mead and Gregory Bateson offered their expertise in Pacific island cultures to the military occupation of Pacific islands taken back from the Japanese. The story of the work by anthropologists in WWII is told in detail elsewhere (e.g., Price 2008), but of immediate interest to me is the fact that both Erik Erikson and Gregory Bateson applied their psychoanalytic skills to German national character. In the wake of the war, social scientists sought to understand "the totalitarian personality" (Adorno, Frenkel-Brunswik, Levinson, and Sanford 1950), especially the German personality as the horrors of the Holocaust became widely known.

Becker wrote *German Youth* (1946) at the end of the war to offer his thoughts on "what should be done" with German youth, especially boys, as the US and its allies occupied Germany and sought to steer the country away from its destructive history. Becker begins the book with the simple declarative sentence, "Man lives by myth" (1), recognizing how mythologies shape reality. "No one can understand the rise of the German youth movement, its unhappy fate and its uncertain future," he writes, "unless he succeeds in projecting himself, however imperfectly, into the myth-inspired minds of the boys and girls, men and women, who strove to realize what they held to be an ideal Germany" (1). That mythology was forged in the Romantic period of German thought and literature, and it was the mythology moving Karl Fischer and others to create the *Wandervogel* movement.

During the war, Erik Erikson had worked on various projects studying German national character and German war prisoners (Friedman 1999, 163–76). Erikson identified himself as a Danish Jew raised in Germany, and he understood in Hitler's rise in 1933 that Hitler appealed to the "wayward, delinquent quality" in Austrian and German young men (166). Erikson's first formulation of the appeal of Hitler to German boys appeared in 1942 in *Psychiatry*, and he incorporated into his analysis his interviews with German prisoners of war in Canada (167–68).

Erikson's chapter in *Childhood and Society* (1963 [1950]), "The Legend of Hitler's Youth," drew on his wartime work and offered an understanding of the appeal of Hitler as a gang leader of "delinquent youths." For many psychoanalysts, the key to unlocking the puzzles of adolescent behavior lies in the family dynamics. Erikson's analysis of what we know of Hitler's family life and his relations with his mother and father explains a great deal about that man.

Bateson, who was well-acquainted with Erikson and his wartime work on German character, and Hitler's character in particular, came to his own analysis of the Nazi propaganda film *Hitlerjunge Quex* (1933), building on Erikson's conclusions about German character. Bateson's lengthy, extremely detailed analysis of the film, first written in 1945 and then published in Margaret Mead's edited volume gathering anthropologists who developed ways to "study culture at a distance" (Mead and Métraux 1953) and then published again in *Studies in Visual Communication* in 1980, also saw family dynamics as the set of relationships driving the action of the fictional story about Heine, the young man torn between allegiance to his father (linked to communism) and his mother (linked to Nazism and Hitler Youth).

There are details in the analyses by Erikson and Bateson worth reading but not very useful for my examination of the snapshots. Their analyses are tied closely to German history and society in 1933, especially family dynamics and patterns of child-rearing, which makes sense since Erikson made the point at every opportunity to show how interior, individual psychic reality is projected into an external world of small group cultures and larger social and historical forces that shape the projections and fold back into the individual's interior reality.

What I do see of value in their analysis for my interpretation of the snapshots are their comments on the *stories and protostories* (recall Chodorow's point) that carry the feelings experienced by the boys as their personal, individual realities interact with group cultures and larger systems (technology, history, society). Erikson links German family dynamics with the mythology the Nazis created for adolescents, primarily males. He describes a "breakdown of the cultural institution which had taken care of the adolescent conflict in its traditional—and regional—forms," and in particular the tradition of *Wanderschaft* was lost, the tradition of the boy's leaving home to learn as an "apprentice in foreign lands," a tradition Hitler ended (Erikson 1963 [1950], 324). Instead, alternative narratives provide stories for boys' dealing with adolescent conflict, including the "Wanderbirds," a movement in which adolescent boys "would indulge in a romantic unity with nature," a movement that excluded fathers and identified nature as a "superimage" of a "pure mother" (325). Erikson notes that we can find this motif in the German Romantic fairy tale (329) and "ancient rites" of passage, including magic and mysticism, both embraced by the Nazi mythology (336, 343). The Nazis created rites resembling the primitive adolescent rites, rites that bonded the adolescent boys as "emancipated equals" free of the bad father (332).

Bateson, as an anthropologist, is as attuned as Erikson to the power of mythologies in making sense of experience. Bateson (1953) sees in the propaganda film he analyzes several symbols with deep psychological meanings, including knives and holes, the latter representing female protection, as does the clubhouse for the Nazi youth (30, 37), and a persistent linking of food and sex (30). Like Erikson, Bateson sees adolescent male sexual anxiety as a motivating force in the traditions of the male friendship group. The film has two separate sequences of death and resurrection for Heine, and Bateson also sees the resemblances between Nazi rites and traditional male initiation rituals (28).

Both Erikson and Bateson provide me with a link between the ideas in their analyses and the snapshots of both American boys and boys in Hitler Youth. What they share is attraction to a romantic mythology about the restorative power of experiences in "mother nature," but also about collective hikes in nature with other adolescent boys. Bateson contrasts the images of the "ragged disorderly Communists" as those boys hike in nature with the "neat, disciplined Nazi hikers" (30).

Chodorow would have us consider the fantasies represented by the snapshots of German and American boys hiking in nature, and I would argue that *the shared fantasy of living a primitive life in the wilderness, away from civilization and the surveillance by adults, is embodied in the snapshots.* I also want to argue that it is the Native American (the American Indian) that attracts the fantasies of both German and American boys through much of the twentieth century. Their *shared fantasy* is to lead the lives of American Indians in the wilderness, away from civilization, its technologies, and its repression of the powerful instincts and emotions adolescent boys experience in their own bodies.

Erikson, it turns out, had a long history of romanticizing the American Indian. His biographer notes that "as a youngster, Erik had read the immensely popular novels by the German writer Karl May idealizing the Plains Indians for their noble and adventurous qualities" (Friedman 1999, 133–34). May's books sold seventy million copies by the 1980s, and Hitler was a fan of May's stories (Penny 2013, 3). Penny notes that both the Socialists (Communists) and the Nazis admired May's books and their themes of "nobility, masculinity, modernity, and tragedy" (8).

Penny's analysis of the attraction of American Indian images and stories for a German audience sees what he calls the "tribal polycentrism" of German culture as the key (Penny 2013, 15–16). By the 1930s the long-standing (back to Tacitus and the Roman occupation) sense Germans had of being an oppressed tribal people made the stories of American Indian tribal histories and experiences a familiar one (31–32). The virtues Germans saw in American Indian cultures "included heroism, a martial bearing, a diminished fear of death, the mythification of war, a willingness to engage in brutal physical violence, an aggressive chauvinistic masculinity grounded in a joy of adventure, faith in one's own mental and physical strength, honesty, and truthfulness" (166). As in the American case, the youth workers in Germany from the end of the nineteenth century on into the twentieth saw themselves as fashioning a "revitalization movement" that would rescue masculinity in German boys, and in both countries the youth leaders counted on *tribal* experiences in the wilderness.

May's novels seem to have left Erikson with a lifelong fascination with American Indian cultures. *Childhood and Society* (1950), in addition to the chapter on Hitler's childhood, has two chapters on American Indian tribes, both based on his actual visits to those communities. As told in his chapter "Hunters Across the Prairie," Erikson accompanied Scudder Mekeel, a field representative of the commissioner of Indian Affairs, to South Dakota to spend time with the Oglala subtribe of the Sioux nation. In another chapter of *Childhood and Society*, also based on a fieldwork visit and meant "for comparison and counterpoint" to the Sioux, Erikson analyzes the Yurok tribe in the Pacific Northwest coast. As one might expect from a psychoanalyst pursuing the connections between the cultures and personalities in these two groups, Erikson stresses the patterns of child training that he sees connected to adult personality traits, such as customs he characterizes as "holding and letting go" in the Sioux (134–35) and Yurok customs he associates with a compulsive interest in ritual hoarding and anal compulsiveness, both traits Erikson traces to Yurok toilet training (172).

More important for my thinking about the snapshots are Erikson's observations about the mythologies and rituals (especially male adolescent testing and initiation) he finds in both societies. Magic, rituals, initiations, play and games that mimic adult themes—all these customs in the American Indian communities show up in the adolescent male youth movements in both the United States and Germany. The snapshots capture the enactments of the boys' play and rituals and often convey the feelings experienced by the participants.

The genius of the Boy Scout movement in the US and of the German youth movements was the realization that adolescent boys were drawn to rituals and magic. As I noted earlier, the youth movement created by Canadian naturalist and author Ernest Thompson Seton (1860–1946), Seton's Woodcraft Indians (1901), influenced the Boy Scouts at the founding in 1910, as Seton was one of the founders. Seton's novel *Two Little Savages: Being the Adventures of Two Boys Who Lived as Indians and What They Learned* (1903) was read by thousands of boys (likely by some girls as well), and in 1920 Samuel Scoville's popular novel *Boy Scouts in the Wilderness*, which features two Boy Scouts who are challenged to spend a month naked in the winter wilderness for the prize of a cabin for the boys' troop, provided yet another fantasy. One of those boys is half Athabascan Indian, and he teaches the white boy all sorts of American Indian ways of surviving in the wilderness. Seton made sure that "Indian Lore" had a strong presence in the first *Handbook for Boys* (1911), an element that established the Boy Scouts of America as distinct from the Boy Scouts founded by Baden-Powell in England in 1908. In 1915 Philadelphia Scout field executive, E. Urner Goodman (1891–1980), founded the honor society, The Order of the Arrow, within the Boy Scouts, building that group within the BSA around American Indian lore. These developments took place within a larger history of "playing Indian" in American culture (Mechling 1980b; Deloria 1998; Huhndorf 2001; Barbour 2016), a history resembling the culture of American Indian "hobbyists" in Germany from the end of the nineteenth century to the present (Penny 2013).

Comparing the American snapshots and the German ones, the analyst can be fairly certain that the similarities across the snapshots stem from the interaction of the dynamics of male adolescence and the strategies adopted by the adults as they created organizations for the revitalization of masculinity in adolescent boys. In the culture of the male adolescent friendship group, the boys can fantasize about going into the wilderness to lead a primitive, tribal life away from adult surveillance, using their folk play and rituals to cement their bonds of friendship.

I believe that the similarity of the snapshots of boys by boys from two cultures demonstrates how the dynamics of projection and introjection can result in similar patterns across cultures. The biology and evolutionary psychology of adolescent boys raised in two modern, Western cultures provide a behavior substrate, including the ways feelings link to physiological emotions, and the similarity in family structures between the US and Germany provide similar primary socialization. The secondary socialization, which builds upon primary socialization in the family, takes shape in both informal institutions (e.g., the adolescent male friendship group) and formal institutions (e.g., the Boy Scouts and Hitler Youth). Those secondary institutions, in turn, are partially shaped by larger cultural patterns, including mass-mediated popular culture. The American and German identification with Native Americans, as enacted through "playing Indian" imaginatively and actually, provides stories and protostories linking for the individual boy his internal, experienced reality and the external world of special relations. As Chodorow says, our "emotions are not raw, psychobiological affects but *feelings with stories*—about our self, our body, the other and the other's body, about self with other, and so forth" (Chodorow 2020, 252; emphasis in original).

Admittedly such an interpretation of the snapshots involves speculation, ideally principled inference. A snapshot of Boy Scouts dressed in Native American costumes requires less speculation than "reading" American Indian fantasies of primitive adolescent male tribal life on a hike or campout, but I think it is highly likely that the primitive story lurks behind the pleasure of hiking, camping, and rafting we see in the snapshots.

Young American Nazis

I said earlier that the stakes for this inquiry into the similarity between the snapshots American boys take of each other and the sample of snapshots I have of German boys in Hitler Youth, many of them of boys by boys, changed from merely interesting from an American studies point of view to deadly serious in light of the white supremacist, fascist demonstrations by young men in Charlottesville in May and August of 2017. What lesson about the interaction of male adolescent biology and psychology on the one hand and larger cultural patterns on the other can we draw from this comparison and from the evidence that young men will march in favor of white supremacy, chanting Nazi slogans such a "blood and soil"?

We do know that in the social and economic turmoil of the Great Depression, totalitarian movements from both the extreme Left and extreme Right vied in the public sphere to offer solutions to the crisis. Among the famous American sympathizers with the rise of the Nazis in Germany was American hero Charles A. Lindbergh, and Philip Roth's counterfactual novel *The Plot Against America* (2004) imagines that Lindbergh runs for president in 1940 and defeats FDR. Father Coughlin famously offered an anti-Semitic, Catholic-based fascist alternative in the 1930s, but of most relevance to the rise of white power in the US in 2021 is the creation of the German American Bund (*Amerikadeutscher Volksbund*) in 1936. The Bund created a number of summer camps for young Americans across New York, New Jersey, and Pennsylvania, and one in Wisconsin (Miller 1983). Judging from the ample photographic record of these camps, there were a great many young American men who attended the camps (Taylor 2017). In my own collection, I have several press photos from Camp Siegfried in Yaphank, New York.

Knowing this history of American young men attracted to fascist organizations in the twentieth century, it is not difficult to understand the events in Charlottesville. The nature of adolescent males seems to incline many of them to be attracted to fraternal organizations and to the elements of play and ritual in those male groups. Those who worked with adolescent youths as a project "rescuing" young men from the ill effects of social change from the late nineteenth into the twentieth century discovered that by recognizing the attraction of the adolescent boy's gang and the deep psychological and evolutionary energy behind that attraction, youth workers could reproduce the attractive elements and build them into the youth programs they created. Rather than the recapitulation theory favored by the Darwinists, the youth workers figured out what evolutionary psychologists in this century gleaned from primatology.

Starting with boys' nature, the youth workers designed organizations and experiences toward building a "second nature" of habits and customs that would harness the primary nature of the boy and turn the energy toward positive behavior, customs, and goals. In 1910 the founders of the Boy Scouts of America explicitly thought of themselves as creating the Boy Scout troop of eight boys as the parallel to the boys' gang on the streets.

Recreating the structures of the male friendship group, however, would not be enough to sustain the positive version of the adolescent male gang. The formal organization needed to tap the power of the mythologies consumed by boys in mass-mediated popular culture, stories and protostories, especially the stories that featured adolescent male escape into the wilderness with a primitive "tribe" of other adolescent boys. The BSA founders turned to American frontier mythologies of the iconic frontiersmen and the Native American. The German founder of the *Wandervogel* and, then of the Hitler Youth turned to mythologies based in German Romanticism.

Becker's 1946 assessment of German youth moves toward the present question of whether German youth will remain under the thrall of Nazi ideology even into the postwar occupation. He speculates on how the "United Nations" (the allied forces occupying Germany) might steer the energies of the young people "into socially acceptable channels" (Becker 1946, 219). Becker suggests that perhaps the international youth movements relying on wilderness experiences to steer youthful energies into positive outcomes would do the trick (Becker 1946, 225). Becker is not optimistic, but he sees no satisfactory alternative to trying.

This book is not the place to propose with confidence a solution to the problem of the appeal of authoritarian, white supremacist narratives, images, and rituals for American young men. I fear, for example, that there are as many of these young men in the Boy Scouts as in the right-wing extremist groups like the Proud Boys and the Boogaloo Boys. For all I know, the Proud Boys count in their number some Eagle Scouts.

Boys Will Be Boys; or, *Jungs Sind Nun Mal So*

Here is the final paragraph of my 2001 book, *On My Honor*, a passage written in 2000 as I was finishing the revision of the manuscript for publication: "Based on my experience . . . I would say that the Boy Scouts is neither the Hitler Youth of its worst detractors nor the virtuous community of its stalwart defenders. The Boy Scout experience is plural. It creates many different kinds of men capable of performing a broad range of masculinity. Whether recent developments will narrow that range remains to be seen. I remain optimistic because I know that the messiness of culture, the disorderliness of play, and the always fresh creativity of adolescents are almost certain to carry the day against the forces of orderly sameness" (Mechling 2001, 283). The "recent developments" I refer to in that paragraph are the Supreme Court victory by the Boy Scouts in the Dale case, affirming the right of the BSA to exclude gay boys and men from membership (a policy later changed). Writing today, the "recent developments" are the ones in Charlottesville and then in DC on January 6, 2021.

The comparison of the American boy snapshots and the German boy snapshots (at least the Hitler Youth snapshots of the 1930s) carries a few lessons. The snapshots capture remarkably similar folk practices on hikes and campouts, a similarity easily explained with references to the shared developmental forces in the boys during puberty and adolescence, no matter what society the boy belongs to. It is clear that in both the US and Germany, the adults fashioned in the late nineteenth and early twentieth centuries formal youth organizations meant to "revitalize" boys. It is also clear that boys in both cultures consumed popular culture stories and images feeding a rich fantasy of the tribe of "lost boys" in the wilderness, away from adult surveillance and left to their own invention of play and games.

I cannot say that the formal "education" in the Boy Scouts of America and in the Hitler Youth were far different then (the 1930s) or even now. Scouting teaches loyalty to friends, patriotism, service to others, duty before self, obedience to authority, bravery, and cleanliness of body and mind. That list sounds a lot like the one followed by the Hitler Youth.

It is difficult to look at the Hitler Youth snapshots and not know where those young men are headed in life (Seidler 2013). It is difficult to look at the young, innocent German boys playing and goofing with each other on hikes and campouts without wondering what made "good Germans" embrace such evil as the Third Reich perpetrated.

All this amounts to a lesson in humility. It can happen here. It does happen here.

Boys' Snapshots as Melancholy Souvenirs

I never had any friends later on like the ones I had when I was twelve.
Jesus, did you?
—STEPHEN KING, *THE BODY* (1982)

A word we borrow from the French, *souvenir*, nicely captures our use of an object to help us remember an experience, to conjure feelings that somehow resemble the feelings that accompanied the original experience. Snapshots are souvenirs of experiences and at best remind us of the feelings of the experience. Most snapshots do this, especially for families. The boys taking snapshots of other boys serve that same purpose. Like some other snapshots, though, the snapshots I have examined here likely evince mixed feelings of pleasure and melancholy. That is why I call them melancholy souvenirs. They remind the viewer of something lost. This coda asks and tries to answer the question, what is lost? What do the boys mourn?

This coda will return to the analytical tool I first introduced in the introduction—psychoanalytic theory, especially as modified by feminist scholars. Again, if the reader has a deep aversion to or objection to psychoanalytic theory for the analysis of culture and personality, then perhaps the reader will want to stop reading the book now. But, as I have said before, to skip the psychoanalytic insights is to prefer a thin description of the meanings of the snapshots, as opposed to a thick description of their meanings.

Both Ibson and I find useful for our analysis of snapshots of boys and men Niobe Way's (2011) discussion of the grief felt when an adolescent boy

loses a close, deep friendship for an array of reasons, usually in late adolescence. Way's interviews with adolescent boys helped me realize that the
soldier snapshots I have (Mechling 2021) were actually displaying what would
become nostalgia for the close male bonding represented in them. Ibson puts
Way's point about the grief of losing those friendships at the center of his
book *The Mourning After: Loss and Longing among Midcentury American
Men* (2018), in that book focusing more on the literature of the 1950s and
1960s, fiction and memoirs that reinforce the evidence of separation and
loss Ibson finds in the snapshots after WWII. And "mourning" is a perfectly
accurate word for describing the grief of loss of close male bonds.

I titled this coda in a way meant to draw attention away from familiar, conscious grief and mourning in order to open the door to explore
mourning's unconscious cousin, melancholia. Ibson and I agree on much,
but we part ways on the necessity of mobilizing depth psychology in order
to understand the unconscious meanings of both the practices captured by
the snapshots and the snapshots themselves.

Freud wrote *Mourning and Melancholia* in 1915 and published the essay in
1917, during the Great War, distinguishing between *mourning* loss (such as the
death of a friend or family member in war), which we certainly experience
at the conscious level, and *melancholia*, a response to loss that lies mainly in
the unconscious and persists. Freud's attention to clinical melancholia (what
we would call depression) and the subsequent interest in melancholia in the
psychoanalytic community (Fiorini, Bokanowski, and Lewkowicz, eds. 2019)
had and still has a therapeutic intention. Mourning is conscious and natural,
possibly needing a therapeutic intervention but not seriously threatening
the health of the mourner. In contrast, melancholia seriously threatens the
mental and physical health of the individual and requires intense therapeutic intervention. As Freud explains, melancholia "is mentally characterized
by a profoundly painful depression, a loss of interest in the outside world,
the loss of the ability to love, the inhibition of any kind of performance
and a reduction in the sense of self, expressed in self-recrimination and
well-directed insults, intensifying into the delusory expectation of punishment" (1917, 204). We recognize these symptoms in clinical depression, still
a challenge to therapy.

My appropriation of the term "melancholy" to describe the snapshots
in this book is not at all meant to suggest the pathological, clinical meanings of that term. As an American studies scholar, I am interested in how
a personality trait once classified by the medical profession as a disorder
comes to seem far more pervasive in the general population. Karen Horney
accomplished this move in her 1937 book *The Neurotic Personality of Our*

Time, and Theodore Reik distinguished a nonsexual, nonpathological sort of everyday social masochism in his 1941 book *Masochism in Modern Man.* Reik's formulation of social masochism was the piece of the puzzle I needed in order to understand how men take pleasure in their own shared pain in the male friendship group, and I made extensive use of that idea in *Soldier Snapshots* (2021) and in my discussion of hazing in this book. The psychohistorian Christopher Lasch shows in *The Culture of Narcissism* (1979) how the personality traits and behavior previously attached to the clinical definitions of narcissism can be found in a great many people considered "normal."

Those scholars, all trained in psychoanalysis, provide what I take to be a warrant to poach the traditional, clinical definition of melancholia and apply the term to a more widespread, "normal," everyday set of symptoms experienced by many American young men. I understand well the challenge I face. Freud and subsequent psychoanalysts writing about melancholia want to understand the syndrome toward a therapeutic treatment of the individual patient. In contrast I am attempting to apply the concept of melancholy to the ongoing, unconscious experiences of many young men when they lose close male friends, internal experiences that are real but that do not cross the threshold into the sort of melancholia the psychiatrist believes is interfering with the normal, happy everyday life of the patient.

I realize, as well, that in this exploration of the internal states of the young man I am switching my attention from the evidence of the customs of play and ritual in the male friendship in the snapshots to speculation about the internal state of the young man and then the older adult man who saves these snapshots and gazes upon them over time. I cannot point to visual evidence in the snapshots to support my speculations about long-term, persistent, low-level melancholia in young men as they look longingly at their melancholic souvenirs months and years after the events and experiences captured in the snapshots.

The "social melancholy" (let's call it, suggested by Reik's "social masochism") feels to the young men a lot like simple mourning, but what remains inexpressible by the men are the unconscious sources of the pain of loss. My analytical challenge is to make some reasonable inferences about the unconscious emotions of loss, emotions the snapshots likely evoke.

Freud's thinking through melancholia and narcissism at about the same time (he published *On Narcissism: An Introduction* in 1914) provides an important clue to the deep loss. Recall that in the long passage quoted above defining melancholia and distinguishing it from mere mourning, Freud lists "a reduction in the sense of self," a phrase that seems as likely to show up in "social melancholia" as in the clinical versions. A useful analogy comes from research on Alzheimer's disease, a form of dementia. Writers and documentary filmmakers looking at Alzheimer's often mention the special pain felt by friends and family when the patient no longer recognizes them. More than we realize, our own sense of self relies upon our interactions with those who know us well. When the loved one or close friend no longer remembers us, that strikes a blow to our "sense of self." The social melancholia we experience cannot be expressed.

Although some of the leading psychoanalytic thinkers and analysts (Fiorini, Bokanowski, and Lewkowicz 2018 [2007]) extend and elaborate Freud's ideas about melancholia still aiming the elaborations at analytic practices with patients, a few argue that in *Mourning and Melancholia* Freud was developing an object-relations theory along the lines of the psychoanalytic theories of Melanie Klein. Such a theory opens the door to thinking about normal, nonpathological attachments to objects and people. This view of Freud's changing mind about the internal structure of the psyche is controversial, but it suits well my intention of formulating a theory of "social melancholia." Accordingly I draw here on three essays—Priscilla Roth's "Melancholia, Mourning, and the Countertransference," Thomas H. Ogden's "A New Reading of the Origins of Object Relations Theory," and Vamik D. Volkan's "Not Letting Go: From Individual Perennial Mourners to Societies with Entitlement Ideologies"—all contributions to the Fiorini, Bokanowski, and Lewkowicz 2018 [2007] volume, for a conception of "social melancholia" that I believe is an unconscious response when a man gazes at the sort of snapshots from his youth we see in this book.

Freud's theory, not surprisingly, starts with the libidinal energy attached to an object, usually sexual libidinal energy but not always. The loss of a love object usually results in some grief and mourning over the loss, but for simple mourning the individual usually can find a new love object to which to direct the libidinal energy and desire. In melancholia, though, the free libido was not "displaced on to another object, but instead drawn back into the ego. But it did not find any application there, serving instead to produce an identification of the ego with the abandoned object. In this way the shadow of the object fell upon the ego, which now could be condemned by a particular agency as an object, as the abandoned object. Thus the loss of object had been transformed into a loss of ego." (Freud 1917, 209).

More than one psychoanalyst reading the "Mourning and Melancholia" essay falls in love with the passage "the shadow of the object fell upon the ego," and, of course, the "particular agency" that condemns the ego-become-narcissistic-object is the superego, the conscience, society's judgment about right and wrong.

Keep in mind that Freud and the subsequent commentators on melancholia have a therapeutic goal in mind, aiming to relieve the patient of the symptoms of depression and even of mania, which the depression sometimes becomes (Freud 1917, 213–14). Even so, those commentators who see Freud moving here to adopt something akin to Melanie Klein's theory of object relations suggest to me that there is a "social melancholia" common among many men, but unconscious.

For example, Priscilla Roth (2018 [2007]) reads the Freud essay as a profound move toward a focus on "internalized love objects all relating to each other in complex ways" (37). The essay, she writes, "introduced the idea that the quality of these relations between parts of our self and our internalized love objects is what defines our moods, our sense of well-being, and, indeed, our character" (37). Thomas Ogden (2018 [2007]) makes as strong a case as Roth for reading Freud on melancholia as a "theory of unconscious internal object relations" (128). For Ogden, an important aspect of Freud's ideas in that essay is the realization that the individual has "ambivalent feelings for the loved object" (129), an idea I return to below as I think about the snapshots. Moreover, as a psychoanalyst Ogden finds significance in the fact that the melancholic patient "preserves" the abandoned love object through identification with the object, which solves the pain of the loss of the object: "the object is me and I am the object" (131). I also find support for a notion of "social melancholia" in Volkan's (2018 [2007]) ideas that some individuals become "perennial mourners," never lapsing into depression, and that there are some societies that actually enhance perennial mourning (90).

This discussion of the swirl of ideas around Freud's distinction between mourning and melancholia might seem too much ado about nothing when "mourning" seems an apt and adequate term to describe the feelings of loss Way sees in the young men she counsels and Ibson sees in the photographs and novels and memoirs he analyzes in the years after WWII. I think more lies beneath the surface. Ogden thinks that "Freud's expansion of the concept of ambivalence . . . represents the most important contribution . . . to the development of his object relations theory" (139). The snapshots in this book capture joyful moments of intense male bonding in the friendship group. The snapshots might not capture all the ambivalence in adolescent male friendship, but certainly we can speculate on the ambivalent feelings as the boy and then the man gazes at the saved snapshots.

Consider the ambivalence in adolescent male friendship. We observed earlier that humans resemble other primates in their tendency to create hierarches in the friendship group, sorting themselves on a range of talents, including physical strength, verbal ability, humor, and cunning, The hierarchy is not necessarily static, and just as high school band members or college rowers can "challenge" another member for a seat with more prestige, so a male friendship group might experience some power challenges. In older adolescents, the competition might be for female attention (a form of power and prestige), and very close male friendships can be destroyed in competition for a girl. Thus, one sort of ambivalence in the male friendship group arises from the conflict between cooperation and competition.

The ambivalence toward a lost love object most likely to induce social melancholia is the love for a male friend. In both *Soldier Snapshots* (2021) and this book I have argued that a major challenge for young males in the situations we see in the snapshots is to distinguish between the strong feelings of bonding with male friends and the similar feelings of sexual desire. The boys and young men in the snapshots often are figuring out their own sexual orientation and desire, and many experience confusion and ambivalence in adolescence. At the same time, whatever the leaning of their sexual desire, the boys and young men know that the society prefers normative male heterosexuality. The feelings of intense male bonding we see in the snapshots must be "managed" in such a way as to distinguish those feelings from homosexual desire. As I have said, the boys and men in these snapshots use their bodies to manage the distinction, and it is especially true that the frequent nudity in the male friendship group serves to strengthen the message that "we can be naked in front of each other because we do not see each other as objects of sexual desire."

In my use of Reik's notion of "social masochism" to explain why men often find pleasure in experiencing pain with close friends, as in hazing, I followed Reik by asking and answering two questions that stem from the understanding that social masochism "names the drive to find pleasure in pain. The person's 'need for punishment,' a reaction to the 'forbidden wishes of the ego'" (Reik 1962 [1941], 10—quoted in Mechling 2021, 174–75). Those two questions are "What is feared? "What is longed for?" With hazing rituals in mind, here is my answer:

> The young male initiate represses three thoughts and their related feelings. First, the initiate represses aggression and anger toward his tormenters. . . .
> The second thought necessarily repressed in the initiate is identification with the female. . . .
> The third thought necessarily repressed in hazing, and related to the second, is of incest, the unconscious desire for sexual relations with the brother.. (Mechling 2021, 177)

The male ego represses these thoughts and then takes pleasure in punishment (pain) for the repressed thoughts.

As I think about male melancholia as a persistent feature of men's loss of the close bonds of adolescent friendship, I turn back to my work with John Paul Wallis (2019a) on post-traumatic stress disorder and wonder anew how many of the symptoms associated with PTSD are also associated with persistent social melancholia.

Back to the snapshots. Even though many of the boys pictured in the snapshots are still in the early stages of adolescence and might not yet have experienced the loss and grief Way writes about in her analysis of male friendship, the fact that the boys saved the snapshots into later life tells me that they eventually did come to see the snapshots as souvenirs of that stage in their lives before the loss of special, close friendships. Their feelings gazing at the snapshots later could be called mourning.

The snapshots are "small" and personal, but there are also American cultural stories and protostories to give impersonal meaning to the feelings evoked by the snapshots.

Fiedler's famous analysis of Twain's *Huckleberry Finn* in the last chapter, "*Huckleberry Finn*: Faust in the Eden of Childhood" (1960, 553–91), discusses grief and loss in the mythological American formula without calling the feelings mourning or melancholia; but the meanings are clear, and in his preface Fiedler acknowledges his debt to Freud and Jung (xii–xiii).

Fiedler sees Twain as the primary mythologist of American boyhood. Twain, he writes, "creates a myth of childhood, rural, sexless, yet blessed in its natural Eden by the promise of innocent love, and troubled by the shadow of bloody death. . . . but it is also one in which a pure love between males, colored and white, triumphs over witches and ghosts and death itself" (561). The love between boys in the "natural Eden" is not sexual, and, in fact, according to Fiedler, the friendship of boys is a safe haven away from the possibility of sex with girls. "In all three Tom Sawyer stories," notes Fiedler, "Huck is Tom's Noble Savage, a sentimentalized id-figure (and in this respect Jim is his double), representing the Good Bad Boy's dream of how bully life would be without parents, clothing, or school" (567–68). The river, the raft, and the island in the river play an important role in the mythology Twain weaves in the novels, though in *Tom Sawyer* the myth is pleasant, the island a "boy's paradise," while in Huckleberry Finn the island is but a "temporary asylum . . . from pursuit, enslavements, and death" (568–69). The two books, says Fiedler, "are the same dream dreamed twice over, the second time as nightmare" (568). "By and large, it is possible to say that *Tom Sawyer* is a fable of lost boyhood written by Tom, while *Huckleberry Finn* is that same fable transcribed by Huck" (573). And here is Fiedler's final paragraph: "If *Huckleberry Finn* is, finally, the greatest of all books about childhood, this is because it renders with a child's tough-mindedness and a child's desperate hilarity a double truth fumbled by most other books in the subject: how truly wonderful it is to remember our childhood; and yet how we cannot recall it without revealing to ourselves the roots of the very terror, which in adulthood has driven us nostalgically to evoke that past" (591).

If Fiedler is right about the novel's being "the greatest of all books about childhood" (and I think he is, having read a great many of those other books that "fumbled" the job), then perhaps I should let Fiedler have the last word about the inchoate melancholia we men often experience when we gaze at these snapshots of boys by boys.

References

Aamodt, Sandra, and Sam Yang. 2012. *Welcome to Your Child's Brain: How the Mind Grows from Conception to College*. London: Bloomsbury.

Abrahams, Roger D. 1962. "Playing the Dozens." *Journal of American Folklore* 75: 209–20.

Adorno, Theodor W., Else Frenkel-Brunswik, Daniel Levinson, and Nevitt Sanford. 1950. *The Authoritarian Personality*. New York: Harper & Bros.

Agar, Michael. 1996. *The Professional Stranger: An Informal Introduction to Ethnography*. 2nd ed. New York: Academic Press.

Agee, James, and Walker Evans. 1960 [1941]. *Let Us Now Praise Famous Men*. 2nd ed. Boston: Houghton Mifflin.

American Psychological Association. nd. "Magical Thinking." *APA Dictionary of Psychology*. https://dictionary.apa.org/magical-thinking.

Arluke, Arnold, and Lauren Rolfe. 2013. *The Photographed Cat: Picturing Human–Feline Ties, 1890–1940*. Syracuse, NY: Syracuse University Press.

Armstrong, Robert Plant. 1971. *The Affecting Presence: An Essay in Humanistic Anthropology*. Urbana: University of Illinois Press.

Ayoub, Millicent R., and Stephen A. Barnett. 1965. "Ritualized Verbal Insult in White High School Culture." *Journal of American Folklore* 78: 337–44.

Babcock-Abrahams, Barbara. 1975. "Why Frogs Are Good to Think and Dirt Is Good to Reflect On." *Soundings* 58: 167–81.

Ballen, Roger. 1979. *Boyhood*. Broomall, PA: Chelsea House.

Barbour, Chad A. 2016. *From Daniel Boone to Captain America: Playing Indian in American Popular Culture*. Jackson: University Press of Mississippi.

Barker, K. Brandon, and Claiborne Rice. 2019. *Folk Illusions: Children, Folklore, and Sciences of Perception*. Bloomington: Indiana University Press.

Barthes, Roland. 1980. *Camera Lucida: Reflections on Photography*. New York: Hill and Wang.

Bateson, Gregory. 1953. "An Analysis of the Nazi Film *Hitlerjunge Quex*." In *The Study of Culture at a Distance*, ed. Margaret Mead and Rhoda Métraux, 331–47. Chicago: University of Chicago Press. Reprinted in *Studies in Visual Communication* 6 (3): 20–55.

Bateson, Gregory. 1972 [1955]. "A Theory of Play and Fantasy." In *Steps to an Ecology of Mind*, 177–93. New York: Ballantine.

Bateson, Gregory. 1979. *Mind and Nature: A Necessary Unity*. New York: Dutton.

Beck, Julie. 2015. "What Good Is Thinking About Death?" *The Atlantic*, May 28. https://www.theatlantic.com/health/archive/2015/05/what-good-is-thinking-about-death/394151/.

Becker, Howard. 1946. *German Youth: Bond or Free*. London: Kegan Paul, Trench, Trubner & Co.

Becker, Howard S. 1995. "Visual Sociology, Documentary Photography, and Photojournalism: It's (Almost) All a Matter of Context." *Visual Sociology* 10 (1–2): 5–14.

Behar, Ruth, and Deborah A. Gordon, eds. 1995. *Women Writing Culture*. Berkeley: University of California Press.

Benedict, Ruth. 1934. *Patterns of Culture*. Boston: Houghton Mifflin.

Benedict, Ruth. 1946. *The Chrysanthemum and the Sword: Patterns of Japanese Culture*. Boston: Houghton Mifflin.

Beneke, Timothy. 1997. *Proving Manhood: Reflections on Sex and Sexism*. Berkeley: University of California Press.

Bennett, Roger, and Jules Shell. 2008. *Camp Camp: Where Fantasy Island Meets Lord of the Flies*. New York: Crown.

Beresin, Anna R. 2010. *Recess Battles: Playing, Fighting, and Storytelling*. Jackson: University Press of Mississippi.

Berger, Peter L., Brigitte Berger, and Hansfried Kellner. 1973. *The Homeless Mind: Modernization and Consciousness*. New York: Random House.

Berger, Peter L., and Thomas Luckmann. 1966. *The Social Construction of Reality: A Treatise in the Sociology of Knowledge*. Garden City, NY: Anchor Books.

Best, Joel. 1993. *Threatened Children: Rhetoric and Concern about Child-Victims*. Chicago: University of Chicago Press.

Bettelheim, Bruno. 1954. *Symbolic Wounds: Puberty Rites and the Envious Male*. New York: Collier Books.

Blakemore, Erin. 2018. "How the Hitler Youth Turned a Generation of Kids into Nazis." History, August. https://www.history.com/news/how-the-hitler-youth-turned-a -generation-of-kids-into-nazis.

Bordo, Susan. 1999. *The Male Body: A New Look at Men in Public and Private*. New York: Farrar, Straus and Giroux.

Bouissac, Paul. 1976. *Circus and Culture: A Semiotic Approach*. Bloomington: Indiana University Press.

Boy Scouts of America. 1911. *Handbook for Boys*. New York: Boy Scouts of America.

Boy Scouts of America. 1926. *Photography: Merit Badge Series*. New York: Boy Scouts of America.

Boy Scouts of America. 1948. *Handbook for Boys*. New Brunswick, NJ: Boy Scouts of America.

Brill, Stephanie, and Lisa Kenney. 2016. *The Transgender Teen: A Handbook for Parents and Professionals Supporting Transgender and Nonbinary Teens*. Jersey City, NJ: Cleis Press.

Brill, Stephanie, and Rachel Pepper. 2008. *The Transgender Child: A Handbook for Families and Professionals*. Jersey City, NJ: Cleis Press.

Bromwich, Jonah Engel. 2017. "White Nationalists Wield Torches at Confederate Statue Rally." *New York Times*, May 14. https://www.nytimes.com/2017/05/14/us/confederate -statue-protests-virginia.html.

Bronner, Simon J. 1985. *Chain Carvers: Old Men Crafting Meaning*. Lexington: University Press of Kentucky.

Bronner, Simon J. 1986. "Folk Objects." In *Folk Groups and Folklore Genres: An Introduction*, ed. Elliott Oring, 199–223. Logan: Utah State University Press.

Bronner, Simon J. 1988. *American Children's Folklore*, annotated edition. Little Rock, AR: August House.

Bronner, Simon J. 1995. "Material Folk Culture of Children. In *Children's Folklore: A Source Book*, ed. Brian Sutton-Smith, Jay Mechling, Thomas W. Johnson, and Felicia R. McMahon, 251–71. New York: Garland.

Bronner, Simon J. 2006. *Crossing the Line: Violence, Play, and Drama in Naval Equator Traditions*. Amsterdam: Amsterdam University Press.

Bronner, Simon J. 2008. *Killing Tradition: Inside Hunting and Animal Rights Controversies*. Lexington: University Press of Kentucky.

Bronner, Simon J. 2012. *Campus Traditions: Folklore from the Old-Time College to the Modern Mega-University*. Jackson: University Press of Mississippi.

Bronner, Simon J. 2014. *Strongmen in History and Culture*. An Online Exhibition. https://sites.psu.edu/strongman/.

Bronner, Simon J. 2019. *The Practice of Folklore: Essays Towards a Theory of Tradition*. Jackson: University Press of Mississippi.

Bronner, Simon J. 2022. *Americanness: Inquiries into the Thought and Culture of the United States*. New York: Routledge.

Brook, P., dir. 1962. *Lord of the Flies* [film]. Hodgdon Productions and Two Arts.

Brummett, Barry. 1991. *Rhetorical Dimensions of Popular Culture*. Tuscaloosa: University of Alabama Press.

Brummett, Barry. 2004. *Rhetorical Homologies: Form, Culture, Experience*. Tuscaloosa: University of Alabama Press.

Burghardt, Gordon M. 2005. *The Genesis of Animal Play: Testing the Limits*. Cambridge, MA: MIT Press.

Burke, Kenneth. 1969 [1945]. *A Grammar of Motives*. Berkeley: University of California Press.

Butler, Judith. 1990. *Gender Trouble: Feminism and the Subversion of Identity*. New York: Routledge.

Caillois, Roger. 2001 [1961]. *Man, Play, and Games*. Translated by Meyer Barash. New York: Free Press.

Carlin, George. 1981. "A Place for My Stuff." On *A Place for My Stuff* [album]. Atlantic.

Caughey, John L. 1982. "The Ethnography of Everyday Life: Theories and Methods for American Culture Studies." *American Quarterly* 34 (3): 222–43.

Cavna, Michael. 2020. "'Calvin and Hobbes' Said Goodbye 25 Years Ago. Here's Why Bill Watterson's Masterwork Enchants Us Still." *Washington Post*, December 31. https://www.washingtonpost.com/arts-entertainment/2020/12/31/calvin-hobbes-bill-watterson/.

Chalfen, Richard. 1987. *Snapshot Versions of Life*. Bowling Green, OH: Bowling Green State University Popular Press.

Chodorow, Nancy J. 1978. *The Reproduction of Mothering: Psychoanalysis and the Sociology of Gender*. Berkeley: University of California Press.

Chodorow, Nancy J. 1994. *Femininities, Masculinities, and Sexualities: Freud and Beyond*. Lexington: University Press of Kentucky.

Chodorow, Nancy J. 1999. *The Power of Feelings: Personal Meaning in Psychoanalysis, Gender, and Culture*. New Haven: Yale University Press.

Chodorow, Nancy J. 2020. *The Psychoanalytic Ear and the Sociological Eye: Toward an American Independent Tradition*. New York: Routledge.

Clark, Cindy Dell. 1999. "The Autodriven Interview: A Photographic Viewfinder into Children's Experience." *Visual Studies* 14: 39–50.

Clark, Cindy Dell. 2011. *In a Younger Voice: Doing Child-Centered Qualitative Research*. New York: Oxford University Press.

Clark, Larry. 1971. *Tulsa*. New York: Rapoport.

Clark, Larry. 1987. *Teenage Lust*. New York: L. Clark.

Clark, Larry. 1993. *The Perfect Childhood*. London: LCB.

Clifford, James, and George E. Marcus, eds. 1986. *Writing Culture: The Poetics and Politics of Ethnography*. Berkeley: University of California Press.

Cochran, Thomas C. 1964. *The Inner Revolution*. New York: Harper & Row.

Cole, Sarah. 2003. *Modernism, Male Friendship, and the First World War*. Cambridge: Cambridge University Press.

Coles, Robert. 1977. *Privileged Ones: The Well-Off and the Rich in America*. Boston: Little, Brown.

Collier, John Jr., and Malcolm Collier. 1967. *Visual Anthropology: Photography as a Research Method*. New York: Holt, Rinehart.

Cross, Gary. 1997. *Kids' Stuff: Toys and the Changing World of American Childhood*. Cambridge: Harvard University Press.

Csikszentmihalyi, Mihaly. 1975. *Beyond Boredom and Anxiety: Experiencing Flow in Work and Play*. New York: Jossey-Bass.

Csikszentmihalyi, Mihaly, and Eugene Rochberg-Halton. 1981. *The Meaning of Things: Domestic Symbols and the Self*. London: Cambridge University Press.

Cumming, Laura. 2009. *A Face to the World: On Self-Portraits*. New York: HarperCollins.

Damasio, Antonio. 1999. *The Feeling of What Happens: Body and Emotion in the Making of Consciousness*. New York: Harcourt.

Deetz, James. 1977. *In Small Things Forgotten: An Archaeology of Early American Life*. New York: Anchor Books.

Deitcher, David. 2001. *Dear Friends: American Photographs of Men Together, 1840–1918*. New York: Harry N. Abrams.

Delfino, Andrew, and Jay Mechling. 2017. "Wrestling with Masculinity." *Children's Folklore Review* 38: 57–77.

Deloria, Philip J. 1998. *Playing Indian*. New Haven: Yale University Press.

Denworth, Lydia. 2020. *Friendship: The Evolution, Biology, and Extraordinary Power of Life's Fundamental Bond*. New York: W. W. Norton.

Denzin, Norman K. 2014. *Interpretive Autoethnography*. 2nd ed.; Los Angeles: SAGE.

Dewey, John. 1934. *Art as Experience*. New York: Minton, Balch.

Dinnerstein, Dorothy. 1976. *The Mermaid and the Minotaur*. New York: HarperCollins.

Douglas, Mary. 1966. *Purity and Danger: An Analysis of Concepts of Pollution and Taboo*. London: Routledge and Kegan Paul.

Dundes, Alan. 1971. "Folk Ideas as Units of Worldview." *Journal of American Folklore* 84: 93–103.

Dundes, Alan. 1979. "Into the Endzone for a Touchdown: A Psychoanalytic Consideration of American Football." *Western Folklore* 37 (2): 75–88.

Dundes, Alan. 1987. "The American Game of 'Smear the Queer' and the Homosexual Component of Male Competitive Sport and Warfare." In Dundes, *Parsing Through Customs: Essays by a Freudian Folklorist*, 178–94. Madison: University of Wisconsin Press.

Dundes, Alan. 1997. "Traditional Male Combat." In Dundes, *From Game to War, and Other Psychoanalytic Essays on Folklore*, 25–45. Lexington: University Press of Kentucky.

Dundes, Alan. 1998. "Bloody Mary in the Mirror: A Ritual Reflection of Pre-Pubescent Anxiety." *Western Folklore* 57: 119–35.

Dundes, Alan, and Lauren Dundes. 2002. "The Elephant Walk and Other Amazing Hazing: Male Fraternity Initiation through Infantilization and Feminization." In *Bloody Mary in the Mirror: Essays in Psychoanalytic Folkloristics*, by Alan Dundes, 92–121. Jackson: University Press of Mississippi.

Ellis, Bill. 1982. "'Ralph and Rudy': The Audience's Role in Re-creating a Camp Legend." *Western Folklore* 41: 169–91.

Erikson, Erik H. 1963 [1950]. *Childhood and Society*. New York: Penguin Books.

Erikson, Erik H. 1968. *Identity: Youth and Crisis*. New York: W. W. Norton.

Erikson, Erik H. 1980 [1959]. *Identity and the Life Cycle*. New York: W. W. Norton.

Ewald, Wendy, et al. 2000. *Secret Games: Collaborative Works with Children, 1969–1999*. Zurich: Scalo Verlag.

Fernandez, Manny. 1998. "Nobody's Child: A Lost Nation of Runaways in The Haight." *San Francisco Chronicle*, November 17. https://www.sfgate.com/news/article/NOBODY-S -CHILD-A-lost-nation-of-runaways-in-the-3312155.php.

Fiedler, Leslie A. 1960. *Love and Death in the American Novel*. New York: Criterion Books.

Fine, Gary Alan. 1983. *Shared Fantasy: Role Playing Games as Social Worlds*. Chicago: University of Chicago Press.

Fine, Gary Alan. 1987. *With the Boys: Little League Baseball and Preadolescent Culture*. Chicago: University of Chicago Press.

Fiorini, Leticia Glocer, Thierry Bokanowski, and Sergio Lewkowicz, eds. 2019. *On Freud's Mourning and Melancholia*. London: Routledge.

Foley, Douglas E. 1990. *Learning Capitalist Culture: Deep in the Heart of Tejas*. Philadelphia: University of Pennsylvania Press.

Forbush, William Byron. 1902. *The Boy Problem: A Study in Social Pedagogy*. Chicago: The Pilgrim Press.

Francisco, Jason. 2007. "Teaching Photography as Art: A Short Critical History." *Smithsonian American Art Journal* 21 (3): 19–24.

Friedman, Lawrence J. 1999. *Identity's Architect: A Biography of Erik H. Erikson*. Cambridge: Harvard University Press.

Freud, Sigmund. 1914. "On Narcissism: An Introduction." In *The Standard Edition of the Complete Psychological Works of Sigmund Freud*, trans. J. Strachey, vol. 14. London: Hogarth Press.

Freud, Sigmund. 2003 [1919]. *The Uncanny*. New York: Penguin Books.

Freud, Sigmund. 2005 [1917]. *On Murder, Mourning and Melancholia*. Trans. Shaun Whiteside. London: Penguin Books.

Frosh, Stephen. 1994. *Sexual Difference: Masculinity and Psychoanalysis*. London: Routledge.

Galván, Adriana. 2017. *The Neuroscience of Adolescence*. New York: Cambridge University Press.

Garber, Marjorie. 1992. *Vested Interests: Cross-Dressing and Cultural Anxiety*. New York: Routledge.

Gardner, Margo, and Laurence Steinberg. 2006. "Peer Influence on Risk Taking: Risk Preference and Risky Decision Making in Adolescence and Adulthood: An Experimental Study." *Developmental Psychology* 41: 625–35.

Geertz, Clifford. 1973a. "Deep Play: Notes on the Balinese Cockfight." In *The Interpretation of Cultures*, 412–53. New York: Basic Books.

Geertz, Clifford. 1973b. "Thick Description: Toward an Interpretive Theory of Culture." In *The Interpretation of Cultures*, 3–40. New York: Basic Books.

Gelwicks, Jesse. 2002. "Redwood Grove: Youth Culture Within a Group Home." *Children's Folklore Review* 24 (1/2): 65–83.

Genovese, Daniella. 2019. "Sexting Study Shows Kids Starting Before They Even Turn 13." *Fox Business*, December 18. https://www.foxbusiness.com/lifestyle/sexting-children-study.

Gibson, Henry W. 1922. *Boyology; or, Boy Analysis*. New York: Association Press.

Gillespie, Angus K., and Jay Mechling, eds. 1987. *American Wildlife in Symbol and Story*. Knoxville: University of Tennessee Press.

Goffman, Erving. 1959. *The Presentation of Self in Everyday Life*. New York: Doubleday.

Goffman, Erving. 1961. *Asylums: Essays on the Condition of the Social Situation of Mental Patients and Other Inmates*. New York: Vintage Books.

Goffman, Erving. 1979. *Gender Advertisements*. New York: Harper & Row.

Goldberg, Jim. 1995. *Raised by Wolves*. New York: Distributed Art.

Golding, William. 1954. *Lord of the Flies*. London: Faber and Faber.

Goodwin, Marjorie Harness. 1991. *He-Said-She-Said: Talk as Social Organization Among Black Children*. Bloomington: Indiana University Press.

Goodwin, Marjorie Harness. 2006. *The Hidden Life of Girls: Games of Stance, Status, and Exclusion*. New York: Wiley-Blackwell.

Goranin, Näkki. 2008. *American Photobooth*. New York: W. W. Norton.

Goyton, Rurik. 1998. "'Pissing Out the Fire': Reasserting Masculine Identity in a Closure Ritual." Prized Writing, University of California, Davis, Writing Center. https://prizedwriting.ucdavis.edu/sites/g/files/dgvnsk15806/files/media/documents/1997%E2%80%931998%20GOYTON.pdf.

Grady, John, and Jay Mechling. 2003. "Editors' Introduction: Putting Animals in the Picture." Special section of *Visual Studies* 18 (2): 92–95.

Greenfield, Lauren. 1997. *Fast Forward: Growing Up in the Shadow of Hollywood*. New York: Knopf.

Greenfield, Lauren. 2002. *Girl Culture*. San Francisco: Chronicle Books.

Greer, Germaine. 2003. *The Beautiful Boy*. New York: Rizzoli.

Grier, Katherine C. 2006. *Pets in America: A History*. Chapel Hill: University of North Carolina Press.

Grossman, Dave. 2009. *On Killing: The Psychological Cost of Learning to Kill in War and Society*. New York: Back Bay Books.

Grossman, Dave, and Loren W. Christensen. 2008. *On Combat: The Psychology and Physiology of Deadly Conflict in War and Peace*. Millstadt, IL: Warrior Science.

Hall, G. Stanley. 1904. *Adolescence*. 2 vols. New York: D. Appleton.

Hall, James. 2016. *The Self-Portrait: A Cultural History*. London: Thames and Hudson.

Handelman, Don. 1977. "Play and Ritual: Complementary Frames of Meta-Communication." In *It's a Funny Thing, Humour*, edited by Antony J. Chapman and Hugh Foot, 185–92. Pergamon.

Harper, Douglas. 2012. *Visual Sociology*. New York: Routledge.

Heims, Steve J. 1991. *Constructing a Social Science for Postwar America: The Cybernetics Group, 1946–1953*. Cambridge, MA: MIT Press.

Hetherington, Tim. 2010. *Infidel*. London: Chris Boot.

Hoffman, Brian. 2015. *Naked: A Cultural History of American Nudism*. New York: New York University Press.

Holland, Patricia. 2004. *Picturing Childhood: The Myth of the Child in Popular Imagery*. New York: I. B. Tauris.

Holland, Taylor Mallory. 2018. "Facts About Touch: How Human Contact Affects Your Health and Relationships." DignityHealth, April 28. https://www.dignityhealth.org/articles/facts-about-touch-how-human-contact-affects-your-health-and-relationships.

Honeck, Mischa. 2018. *Our Frontier Is the World: The Boy Scouts in the Age of American Ascendancy*. Ithaca: Cornell University Press.

Hook, Harry, dir. 1990. *Lord of the Flies* [film]. Columbia Pictures.

Horan, Robert. 1988. "The Semiotics of Play Fighting at a Residential Treatment Center." In *Adolescent Psychiatry*, vol. 15, ed. Sherman C. Feinstein, 367–84. Chicago: University of Chicago Press.

Horney, Karen. 1937. *The Neurotic Personality of Our Time*. New York: W. W. Norton.

Huhndorf, Shari M. 2001. *Going Native: Indians in the American Cultural Imagination*. Ithaca: Cornell University Press.

Hunt, Lindsey. 2018. "Biking for Your Brain: The Neurology of Cycling." *Duvine* (blog), May 16. https://www.duvine.com/blog/brain-biking-the-neurology-of-cycling/.

Huyghe, Pierre, and Douglas Coupland. 2003. *School Spirit*. Paris: Dis Voir.

Iacoboni, Marco. 2009. *Mirroring People: The Science of Empathy and How We Connect with Others*. New York: Farrar, Straus and Giroux.

Ibson, John. 2002. *Picturing Men: A Century of Male Relationships in Everyday American Photography*. Chicago: University of Chicago Press.

Ibson, John. 2007. "Picturing Boys: Found Photographs and the Transformation of Boyhood in 1950s America." *THYMOS: Journal of Boyhood Studies* 1 (1): 68–83.

Ibson, John. 2018. *The Mourning After: Loss and Longing Among Midcentury Men*. Chicago: University of Chicago Press.

James, William. 1890. *The Principles of Psychology*. 2 vols. New York: Henry Holt.

Jarvis, Christina S. 2010. *The Male Body at War: American Masculinity During World War II*. DeKalb: Northern Illinois University Press.

Javanbakht, Arash, and Linda Saab. 2017. "What Happens in the Brain When We Feel Fear." *Smithsonian Magazine*, October 27. https://www.smithsonianmag.com/science-nature/what-happens-brain-feel-fear-180966992/.

Jeffords, Susan. 1993. *Hard Bodies: Hollywood Masculinity in the Reagan Era*. New Brunswick, NJ: Rutgers University Press.

Jentsch, Ernst. 1906. "On the Psychology of the Uncanny" [Zur Psychologie des Umheimlichen]. *Psychiatrisch-neurologische Wochenschrift* nos. 22 and 23.

Jones, Gerard. 2002. *Killing Monsters: Why Children Need Fantasy, Super Heroes, and Make-Believe Violence*. New York: Basic Books.

Junger, Sebastian. 2010. *War*. New York: Twelve.

Kahn, Shamus Rahman. 2012. *Privilege: The Making of an Adolescent Elite at St. Paul's School*. Princeton: Princeton University Press.

Kasson, John F. 2001. *Houdini, Tarzan, and the Perfect Man: The White Male Body and the Challenge of Modernity in America*. New York: Hill and Wang.

Kelleher, Kathleen. 1997. "Why Men Just Have to Monkey Around." *Los Angeles Times*, June 30. https://www.latimes.com/archives/la-xpm-1997-jul-24-ls-15813-story.html.

Keyes, Charles F. 2002. "Weber and Anthropology." *Annual Review of Anthropology* 31: 233–55.

Kidd, Kenneth B. 2004. *Making American Boys: Boyology and the Feral Tale*. Minneapolis: University of Minnesota Press.

Kiley, Dan. 1983. *The Peter Pan Syndrome: Men Who Have Never Grown Up*. New York: Dodd Mead.

Kimmel. Michael. 2008. *Guyland: The Perilous World Where Boys Become Men*. New York: Harper.

King, Graham. 1964. *Say "Cheese": Looking at Snapshots in a New Way*. New York: Dodd, Mead.

King, Stephen. 1981. *Danse Macabre*. New York: Penguin.

King, Stephen. 1982. "The Body." In *Different Seasons*, 335–503. New York: Scribner.

Klein, Melanie. 1952. *Envy and Gratitude and Other Works 1946–1963*. New York: Free Press.

Kline, Stephen. 1993. *Out of the Garden: Toys and Children's Culture in the Age of TV Marketing*. London: Verso.

Knapp, Mary, and Herbert Knapp. 1976. *One Potato, Two Potato: The Secret Education of American Children*. New York: W. W. Norton.

Krüger, Arnd, Fabian Krüger, and Sophie Treptau. 2002. "Nudism in Nazi Germany: Indecent Behavior or Physical Culture for the Well-Being of the Nation." *International Journal of the History of Sport* 19 (4): 33–54.

Kuhn, Thomas. 1970. *The Structure of Scientific Revolutions*. 2nd ed. Chicago: University of Chicago Press.

Kupers, Kenny. 2008. "Governing Through Nature: Camps and Youth Movements in Interwar Germany and the United States." *Cultural Geographies* 15 (2): 173–205.

Lacan, Jacques. 2006 [1949]. *Écrits: The First Complete Edition in English*. Trans. Bruce Fink. New York: Norton.

Laqueur, Thomas W. 2003. *Solitary Sex: A Cultural History of Masturbation*. New York: Zone Books.

Lasch, Christoper. 1979. *The Culture of Narcissism: American Life in an Age of Diminishing Expectations*. New York: W. W. Norton.

Leddick, David. 1998. *The Male Nude*. London: Taschen.

Lee, Julia. 2015. *Our Gang: A Racial History of the Little Rascals.* Minneapolis: University of Minnesota Press.

Levin, Jack. 1998. *Sociological Snapshots: Seeing Social Structure and Change in Everyday Life.* Thousand Oaks, CA: Pine Forge Press.

Lévi-Strauss, Claude. 1968 [1962]. *The Savage Mind.* Chicago: University of Chicago Press.

Ludden, David. 2020. "Why Do Young Men Engage in Risky Behaviors?" *Psychology Today,* March 23. https://www.psychologytoday.com/us/blog/talking-apes/202003/why-do -young-men-engage-in-risky-behaviors.

Lyons, Linda. 2004. "One in 10 Teens Thinks Often About Own Death." Gallup, June 29. https://news.gallup.com/poll/12169/one-teens-thinks-often-about-own-death.aspx.

Macknik, Stephen L., and Susana Martinez-Conde, with Sandra Blakeslee. 2010. *Sleights of Mind: What the Neuroscience of Magic Reveals About Our Everyday Deceptions.* New York: Henry Holt.

Mansfield, Alina. 2018. "Slumber Parties as Rites of Passage." *Children's Folklore Review* 39: 1–21.

Mark, Mary Ellen. 1988. *Streetwise.* Philadelphia: University of Pennsylvania Press.

McRobbie, Linda Rodriguez. 2013. "The Strange and Mysterious History of the Ouija Board." *Smithsonian Magazine,* October 27. https://www.smithsonianmag.com/history/ the-strange-and-mysterious-history-of-the-ouija-board-5860627/.

Mead, Margaret, and Rhoda Métraux. 1953. *The Study of Culture at a Distance.* Chicago: University of Chicago Press,

Mechling, Elizabeth Walker, and Jay Mechling. 1981. "The Sale of Two Cities: A Semiotic Comparison of Disneyland with Marriott's Great America." *Journal of Popular Culture* 15: 166–79.

Mechling, Jay. 1975. "Advice to Historians on Advice to Mothers." *Journal of Social History* 9: 44–63.

Mechling, Jay. 1980a. "The Magic of the Boy Scout Campfire." *Journal of American Folklore* 93: 35–56.

Mechling, Jay. 1980b. "'Playing Indian' and the Search for Authenticity in Modern White America." In *Prospects 5: An Annual Review of American Cultural Studies,* ed. Jack Salzman, 17–33. New York: Burt Franklin.

Mechling, Jay. 1981. "Male Gender Display at a Boy Scout Camp." In *Children and Their Organizations: Investigations in American Culture,* ed. R. Timothy Sieber and Andrew J. Gordon, 138–60. Boston: G. K. Hall.

Mechling, Jay. 1983. "Mind, Messages, and Madness: Gregory Bateson Makes a Paradigm for American Culture Studies." In *Prospects 8: An Annual of American Studies,* ed. Jack Salzman, 11–30. New York: Cambridge University Press.

Mechling, Jay. 1986. "Children's Folklore." In *Folk Groups and Folklore Genres,* ed. Elliott Oring, 91–120. Logan: Utah State University Press.

Mechling, Jay. 1989. "An American Culture Grid, with Texts." *American Studies International* 27 (1): 2–12.

Mechling, Jay. 1994. "Children and Colors: Children's Folk Cultures and Popular Cultures in the 1990s and Beyond." In *Eye on the Future: Popular Culture Scholarship into the Twenty-First Century,* ed. Marilyn F. Motz, John G. Nachbar, Michael T. Marsden, and Ronald J. Ambrosetti, 73–89. Bowling Green, OH: Bowling Green State University Popular Press.

Mechling, Jay. 1999. "Reading What Robert Coles Thinks About What Children See." *Visual Sociology* 14: 173–76.

Mechling, Jay. 2000. "Don't Play with Your Food." *Children's Folklore Review* 23 (1): 7–24.

Mechling, Jay. 2001. *On My Honor: Boy Scouts and the Making of American Youth*. Chicago: University of Chicago Press.

Mechling, Jay. 2004. "Picturing Hunting." *Western Folklore* 63 (1–2): 51–78.

Mechling, Jay. 2005a. "The Folklore of Mother-Raised Boys and Men." In *Manly Traditions: The Folk Roots of American Masculinities*, ed. Simon J. Bronner, 211–27. Bloomington: University of Indiana Press.

Mechling, Jay. 2005b. "Found Photographs and Children's Folklore." *Children's Folklore Review* 27: 7–31.

Mechling, Jay. 2006. "Solo Folklore." *Western Folklore* 65 (4): 435–53.

Mechling, Jay. 2008a. "Children's Material Culture." In *Material Culture in America: Understanding Everyday Life*, ed. Helen Sheumaker and Shirley Teresa Wadja, 87–90. New York: ABC-CLIO Publishers.

Mechling, Jay. 2008b. "Gun Play." *American Journal of Play* 1 (2): 192–209.

Mechling, Jay. 2008c. "Paddling and the Repression of the Feminine in Male Hazing." *THYMOS: Journal of Boy Studies* 2 (1): 60–75.

Mechling, Jay. 2009. "Is Hazing Play?" In *Transactions at Play*, ed. Cindy Dell Clark, 45–61. Lanham, MD: University Press of America.

Mechling, Jay. 2012. "Soldier Snaps." In *Warrior Ways: Explorations in Modern Military Folklore*, ed. Eric A. Eliason and Tad Tuleja, 222–47. Logan: Utah State University Press.

Mechling, Jay. 2014a. "Boy Scouts, the National Rifle Association, and the Domestication of Rifle Shooting." *American Studies* 53 (1): 5–25.

Mechling, Jay. 2014b. "Pissing and Masculinity." *Culture, Society and Masculinities* 6 (1): 19–34.

Mechling, Jay. 2016a. "The Erotics of Adolescent Male Altruism." *Boyhood Studies* 9 (2): 92–115.

Mechling, Jay. 2016b. "Sandwork." *American Journal of Play* 9 (1): 19–40.

Mechling, Jay. 2019a. "American Folk Ideas, Themes, and Worldview." In *The Oxford Handbook of American Folklore and Folklore Studies*, ed. Simon J. Bronner, 59–74. New York: Oxford University Press.

Mechling, Jay. 2019b. "Folklore and the Emotional Brain." In *Contexts of Folklore: Festschrift for Dan Ben-Amos*, ed. Simon J. Bronner and Wolfgang Mieder, 217–28. New York: Peter Lang.

Mechling, Jay. 2019c. "Total Institutions: Camps, Boarding Schools, Military Bases, Hospitals, and Prisons. In *The Oxford Handbook of American Folklore and Folklore Studies*, ed. Simon J. Bronner, 671–87. New York: Oxford University Press.

Mechling, Jay. 2021. *Soldier Snapshots: Masculinity, Play, and Friendship in the Everyday Photographs of Men in the American Military*. Lawrence: University Press of Kansas.

Mechling, Jay. 2023. "Pulling Together in Tug of War." *Children's Folklore Review* 41: 2–36.

Mechling, Jay. 2024. "Gun Play as Folk Religious Experience." In *Gunlore: Firearms, Folkways, and Communities*, ed. Robert Glenn Howard and Eric Eliason, 238–61. Jackson: University Press of Mississippi.

Mechling, Jay, and Angus Gillespie. 1987. "Introduction." In *American Wildlife in Symbol and Story*, ed. Angus Gillespie and Jay Mechling, 1–14. Knoxville: University of Tennessee Press.

Melchior-Bonnet, Sabine. 2000. *The Mirror: A History*. New York: Routledge.

Mergen, Bernard. 1982. *Play and Playthings: A Reference Guide*. Westport, CT: Greenwood.

Messerschmidt, Donald A. 1981. *Anthropologists at Home in North America: Methods and Issues in the Study of One's Own Society*. New York: Cambridge University Press.

Messner, Michael A. 2002. *Taking the Field: Women, Men, and Sports*. Minneapolis: University of Minnesota Press.

Metelmann, Henry. 2004. *A Hitler Youth: Growing Up in Germany in the 1930s*. Staplehurst, UK: Spellmount.

Metzger, Walter P. 1963. "Generalizations about National Character: An Analytic Essay." In *Generalization in the Writing of History*, ed. Louis Gottschalk, 77–102. Chicago: University of Chicago Press.

Miller, Marvin D. 1983. *Wunderlich's Salute: The Interrelationship of the German-American Bund, Camp Siegfried, Yaphank, Long Island, and the Young Siegfrieds and Their Relationship with American and Nazi Institutions*. Smithtown, NY: Malamud-Rose.

Mintz, Steven. 2004. *Huck's Raft: A History of American Childhood*. Cambridge, MA: Belknap Press.

Mitchell, Jon, and Karis Jade Petty. 2020. "Uncanny Landscapes: An Introduction." *Material Religion* 16: 1–9.

Mitchell, Juliet. 1974. *Psychoanalysis and Feminism: Freud, Reich, Laing and Women*. New York: Knopf Doubleday.

Moisey, Andrew. 2018. *The American Fraternity: An Illustrated Ritual Manual*. Chapel Hill, NC: Daylight Books.

Montagu, Ashley. 1986. *Touching: The Human Significance of Skin*. New York: Perennial Library.

Morgan, Barbara. 1951. *Summer's Children: A Photographic Cycle of Life at Camp*. Scarsdale, NY: Morgan & Morgan.

Mounts, Nina S. 2015. "Why Are Teen Brains Designed for Risk-Taking?" *Psychology Today*, June 9. https://www.psychologytoday.com/us/blog/the-wide-wide-world-psychology/201506/why-are-teen-brains-designed-risk-taking.

Mroz, Jacqueline. 2018. *Girl Talk: What Science Can Tell Us About Female Friendship*. New York: Seal Press.

Nasaw, Daniel. 2012. "When Did the Middle Finger Become Offensive?" *BBC News Magazine*, February 6. https://www.bbc.com/news/magazine-16916263.

Newell, William Wells. 1883. *Games and Songs of American Children*. New York: Harper & Brothers.

Ogden, Thomas H. 2028 [2007]. "A New Reading of the Origins of Object Relations Theory." In *On Freud's "Mourning and Melancholia,"* ed. Leticia Glocer Fiorini, Thierry Bokanowski, and Sergio Lewkowicz, 123–44. London: Routledge.

Olivier, Marc. 2007. "George Eastman's Modern Stone-Age Family: Snapshot Photography and the Brownie." *Technology and Culture* 48 (1): 1–19.

Orenstein, Peggy. 2020. *Boys and Sex*. New York: Harper.

Oring, Elliott. 1984. "Dyadic Traditions." *Journal of Folklore Research* 21(1): 19–28.

Parfrey, Adam, and Craig Heimbichner. 2012. *Ritual America: Secret Brotherhoods and Their Influence on American Society*. Port Townsend, WA: Feral House.

Parr, Martin, and Gerry Badger. 2004. *The Photobook: A History, Vol. 1*. New York: Phaidon Press.

Parr, Martin, and Gerry Badger. 2006. *The Photobook: A History, Vol. 2*. New York: Phaidon Press.

Pascoe, C. J. 2011. *Dude, You're a Fag: Masculinity and Sexuality in High School*. 2nd ed. Berkeley: University of California Press.

Pawłowski, Bogusław, Rajinder Atwal, and Robin I. M. Dunbar. 2008. "Sex Differences in Everyday Risk-Taking Behavior in Humans." *Evolutionary Psychology* 6 (1): 29–42.

Pellegrini, Anthony D. 1988. "Rough-and-Tumble Play and Social Competence." *Developmental Psychology* 24: 802–6.

Pellegrini, Anthony D. 1993. "Boys' Rough-and-Tumble Play and Social Competence, Contemporaneous and Longitudinal Relations." In *The Future of Play Theory*, ed. Anthony D. Pellegrini, 107–26. New York: SUNY Press.

Penny, H. Glenn. 2013. *Kindred by Choice: Germans and American Indians Since 1800*. Chapel Hill: University of North Carolina Press.

Phelps, Katrina E., and Jacqueline D. Woolley. 1994. "The Form and Function of Young People's Magical Beliefs." *Developmental Psychology* 30 (3): 385–94.

Piaget, Jean. 1954. *The Construction of Reality in the Child*. Translated by Margaret Cook. New York: Basic Books.

Pias, Claus, ed. 2016. *Cybernetics: The Macy Conferences 1946–53*. Chicago: University of Chicago Press.

Pierson, George W. 1962. "The M-Factor in American History. *American Quarterly* 14: 275–89.

Pollack, William. 1998. *Real Boys: Rescuing Our Sons from the Myths of Boyhood*. New York: Owl Books.

Price, David H. 2008. *Anthropological Intelligence: The Deployment and Neglect of American Anthropology in the Second World War*. Durham, NC: Duke University Press.

Pronger, Brian. 1990. *The Arena of Masculinity: Sports, Homosexuality, and the Meaning of Sex*. New York: St. Martin's Press.

Putnam, Robert. 2001. *Bowling Alone: The Collapse and Revival of American Community*. New York: Simon and Schuster.

Raines, Theron. 2002. *Rising to the Light: A Portrait of Bruno Bettelheim*. New York: Knopf.

Raphael, Ray. 1988. *The Men from the Boys: Rites of Passage in Male America*. Lincoln: University of Nebraska Press.

Reid, Jason. 2017. *Get Out of My Room! A History of Teen Bedrooms in America*. Chicago: University of Chicago Press.

Reik, Theodore. 1962 [1941]. *Masochism in Modern Man*. New York: Farrar and Rinehart.

Reiner, Rob, dir. 1986. *Stand by Me* [film]. Columbia Pictures.

Robbins, Alexandra. 2019. *Fraternity: An Inside Look at a Year of College Boys Becoming Men*. New York: Dutton.

Robinson, Cicely, ed. 2021. *Henry Scott Tuke*. New Haven: Yale University Press.

Ronay, Richard, and William von Hippel. 2010. "Power, Testosterone, and Risk-Taking." *Journal of Behavioral Decision Making* 23 (5): 473–82.

Ross, Chad. 2005. *Naked Germany: Health, Race and the Nation.* New York: Berg.

Roth, Philip. 2004. *The Plot Against America.* Boston: Houghton Mifflin.

Roth, Priscilla. 2018 [2007]. "Melancholia, Mourning, and the Countertransference." In *On Freud's "Mourning and Melancholia,"* ed. Leticia Glocer Fiorini, Thierry Bokanowski, and Sergio Lewkowicz, 37–55. London: Routledge.

Rubin, Patricia Lee. 2018. *Seen from Behind: Perspectives on the Male Body and Renaissance Art.* New Haven: Yale University Press.

Salinger, Adrienne. 1995. *My Room: Teenagers in Their Bedrooms.* San Francisco: Chronicle Books.

Sandseter, Ellen B. H., and Leif E. O. Kennair. 2011. "Children's Risky Play from an Evolutionary Perspective: The Anti-Phobic Effects of Thrilling Experiences." *Evolutionary Psychology* 9 (2): 257–84.

Sapolsky, Robert M. 1997. *The Trouble with Testosterone and Other Essays on the Biology of the Human Predicament.* New York: Simon & Schuster.

Sapolsky, Robert M. 2017. *Behave: The Biology of Humans at Our Best and Worst.* New York: Penguin Press.

Savin-Williams, Ritch C. 2017. *Mostly Straight: Sexual Fluidity Among Men.* Cambridge: Harvard University Press.

Schachter, Elli P., and Renee V. Galliher. 2018. "Fifty Years Since 'Identity: Youth and Crisis': A Renewed Look at Erikson's Writing on Identity." *Identity: An International Journal of Theory and Research* 18 (4): 247–50.

Schaefer, Louisa. 2007. "Scouting in Germany." *DW (Deutsche Welle).* https://www.dw.com/en/scouting-celebrates-100-years-german-history-is-turbulent/a-2716367.

Scoville, Samuel. 1919. *Boy Scouts in the Wilderness.* New York: Century.

Seidler, Hans. 2013. *Hitler's Boy Soldiers: The Hitler Jugend Story, with Rare Photographs from Wartime Archives.* South Yorkshire, England: Pen & Sword Military.

Senelick, Laurence. 2000. *The Changing Room: Sex, Drag and Theatre.* New York: Routledge.

Seton, Ernest Thompson. 1903. *Two Little Savages: Being the Adventures of Two Boys Who Lived as Indians and What They Learned.* New York: Grosset and Dunlap.

Sex-Lexis. 2016. "Whittling the Stick." https://www.sex-lexis.com/Sex-Dictionary/whittling+the+stick.

Singal, Jesse. 2018. "When Children Say They Are Trans." *The Atlantic,* July/August. https://www.theatlantic.com/magazine/archive/2018/07/when-a-child-says-shes-trans/561749/.

Slotkin, Richard. 1992. *Gunfighter Nation: The Myth of the Frontier in Twentieth-Century America.* New York: Atheneum.

Smith, Henry Nash. 1957. "Can 'American Studies' Develop a Method?" *American Quarterly* (9): 197–208.

Solomon, Sheldon, Jeff Greenberg, and Tom Pyszczynski. 2015. "Thirty Years of Terror Management Theory: From Genesis to Revelation." *Advances in Experimental Social Psychology* 52: 1–70.

Sontag, Susan. 1978. *Illness as Metaphor.* New York: Farrar, Straus and Giroux.

Sontag, Susan. 1984. *On Longing: Narratives of the Miniature, the Gigantic, the Souvenir, the Collection.* Baltimore: Johns Hopkins University Press.

Sontag, Susan. 1986. *AIDS and Its Metaphors*. New York: Farrar, Straus and Giroux.

Spencer, Hawes. 2018. *Summer of Hate: Charlottesville, USA*. Charlottesville: University of Virginia Press.

Stachura, Peter D. 1981. *The German Youth Movement, 1900–1945: An Interpretive and Documentary History*. New York: St. Martin's Press.

Stearns, Carol Zisowitz, and Peter Stearns. 1986. *Anger: The Struggle for Emotional Control in American History*. Chicago: University of Chicago Press.

Steinberg, Laurence. 2014. *Age of Opportunity: Lessons from the New Science of Adolescence*. Boston: Houghton Mifflin Harcourt.

Steinweis, Alan E. 2009. *Kristallnacht 1938*. Cambridge: Harvard University Press.

Stewart, Susan. 1979. *Nonsense: Aspects of Intertextuality in Folklore and Literature*. Baltimore: Johns Hopkins University Press.

Sudnow, David. 1978. *Ways of the Hand: The Organization of Improvised Conduct*. Cambridge: Harvard University Press.

Sutton-Smith, Brian. 1986. *Toys as Culture*. New York: Gardner Press.

Sutton-Smith, Brian. 2017. *Play for Life: Play Theory and Play as Emotional Survival*. Rochester, NY: Strong Museum of Play.

Sutton-Smith, Brian, John Gerstmyer, and Alice Meckley. 1988. "Playfighting as Folkplay Amongst Preschool Children." *Western Folklore* 47: 161–76.

Sutton-Smith, Brian, and Diana Kelly-Byrne. 1984. "The Masks of Play." In *The Masks of Play*, ed. Brian Sutton-Smith and Diana Kelly-Byrne, 184–97. West Point, NY: Leisure Press.

Sutton-Smith, Brian, Jay Mechling, Thomas W. Johnson, and Felicia McMahon, eds. 1995. *Children's Folklore: A Source Book*. New York: Garland.

Sweet, Andy. 2020. *Hello Muddah, Hello Faddah: Andy Sweet's Summer Camp 1977*. Miami Beach, FL: Letter 16 Press.

Tannen, Deborah. 2007. *You Just Don't Understand: Women and Men in Conversation*. New York: William Morrow.

Taylor, Alan. 2017. "American Nazis in the 1930s—the German American Bund." *The Atlantic*, June 5. https://www.theatlantic.com/photo/2017/06/american-nazis-in-the-1930sthe-german-american-bund/529185/.

Thompson, Jenny. 2004. *War Games: Inside the World of Twentieth-Century War Reenactors*. Washington, DC: Smithsonian Institution Press.

Thorne, Barrie. 1993. *Gender Play: Girls and Boys in School*. New Brunswick, NJ: Rutgers University Press.

Tucker, Elizabeth. 2008. *Children's Folklore: A Handbook*. Westport, CT: Greenwood Press.

Tug of War Association, n.d. "History of Tug of War." http://tugofwar.co.uk/3078/index.html.

Turner, Victor/ 1970. "Betwixt and Between: The Liminal Period in Rites de Passage." In *The Forest of Symbols: Aspects of Ndembu Ritual*. Ithaca: Cornell University Press.

Twain, Mark. 1876. *The Adventures of Tom Sawyer*. Hartford, CT: American.

Twain, Mark. 1885. *The Adventures of Huckleberry Finn*. New York: Charles L. Webster.

Twitchell, James B., with photographs by Ken Ross. 2006. *Where Men Hide*. New York: Columbia University Press.

Van Driel, Mels. 2012. *With the Hand: A Cultural History of Masturbation*. London: reaktion Books.

Van Gennep, Arnold. 1960. *The Rites of Passage*. Trans. Monika B. Vizedom and Gabrielle L. Caffee. Chicago: University of Chicago Press

Van Maanen, John. 1988. *Tales From the Field: On Writing Ethnography*. Chicago: University of Chicago Press.

Volkan, Vamik D. 2018 [2007]. "Not Letting Go: From Individual Perennial Mourners to Societies with Entitlement Ideologies." In *On Freud's "Mourning and Melancholia,"* edited by Leticia Glocer Fiorini, Thierry Bokanowski, and Sergio Lewkowicz, 90–109. London: Routledge.

Von Halasz, Joachin, ed. 2008. *Hitler Youth: An Introduction for American and British Readers*. London: Foxley Books Ltd. Originally published in 1936 as *German Youth in a Changing World*.

Wagner, Jon. 1999. "Visual Sociology and Seeing Kid's Worlds." *Visual Studies* 14: 3–6.

Wagner, Meg. 2017. "'Blood and Soil': Protestors Chant Nazi Slogans in Charlottesville." CNN, August 12. https://www.cnn.com/2017/08/12/us/charlottesville-unite-the-right-rally/index.html.

Walker, Barbara M. 2004. "Frames of Self: Capturing Working-Class British Boys' Identities through Photographs." In *Adolescent Boys: Exploring Diverse Cultures of Boyhood*, ed. Niobe Way and Judy Y. Chu, 31–58. New York: New York University Press.

Wallis, John Paul, and Mechling, Jay. 2015. "Devil Dogs and Dog Piles." *Western Folklore* 74: 275–308.

Wallis, John Paul, and Mechling, Jay. 2019a. *PTSD and Folk Therapy: Everyday Practices of American Masculinity in the Combat Zone*. Lanham, MD: Roman/Lexington.

Wallis, John Paul, and Mechling, Jay. 2019b. "Warriors' Bodies as Sites of Microresistance in the American Military." In *Different Drummers: Military Cohesion and Its Discontents*, ed. Tad Tuleja. Logan: Utah State University Press.

Ward, Jane. 2015. *Not Gay: Sex Between Straight White Men*. New York: New York University Press.

Watzlawick, Paul, Janet Helmick Beavin, and Don D. Jackson. 1967. *Pragmatics of Human Communication: A Study of Interactional Patterns, Pathologies, and Paradoxes*. New York: W. W. Norton.

Way, Niobe. 2011. *Deep Secrets: Boys' Friendships and the Crisis of Connection*. Cambridge: Harvard University Press.

Whitehead, Alfred North, and Bertrand Russell. 1910. *Principia Mathematica*. Cambridge: Cambridge University Press.

Wiener, Norbert. 1948. *Cybernetics: Or Control and Communication in the Animal and the Machine*. Cambridge, MA: MIT Press.

Williams, John. 2007. *Turning to Nature in Germany: Hiking, Nudism, and Conservation, 1900–1940*. Palo Alto, CA: Stanford University Press.

Wilson, Frank R. 1998. *The Hand: How It Shapes the Brain*. New York: Pantheon.

Wilson, Margo, and Martin Daly. 1985. "Competitiveness, Risk Taking, and Violence: The Young Male Syndrome." *Ethology and Sociobiology* 6 (1): 59–73.

Winnicott, D. W. 1971. *Playing and Reality*. New York: Routledge.

Worth, Sol, and John Adair. 1972. *Through Navajo Eyes: An Exploration in Film Communication and Anthropology*. Bloomington: Indiana University Press.

Wrangham, Richard, and Dale Peterson. 1996. *Demonic Males: Apes and the Origins of Human Violence*. Boston: Houghton Mifflin.

Wright, Bradford W. 2001. *Comic Book Nation: The Transformation of Youth Culture in America*. Baltimore: Johns Hopkins University Press.

Young, Katherine. 1995. *Bodylore*. Knoxville: University of Tennessee Press.

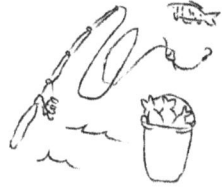

Index

About the Author

Photo courtesy of the author

Jay Mechling is professor emeritus of American Studies at the University of California, Davis. He is a Fellow of the American Folklore Society, and in 2006 he received the Davis Prize, the UC Davis highest honor for excellence in teaching and research.